The Story of
Ain't

The Story of Ain't

America, Its Language, and the Most Controversial Dictionary Ever Published

DAVID SKINNER

HARPER

An Imprint of HarperCollins*Publishers*
www.harpercollins.com

HarperCollins books may be purchased for educational, business, or sales promotional use. For information, please write: Special Markets Department, HarperCollins Publishers, 10 East 53rd Street, New York, NY 10022.

FIRST EDITION

Designed by Lisa Stokes

Library of Congress Cataloging-in-Publication Data has been applied for.

ISBN: 978-0-06-202746-7

12 13 14 15 16   OV/RRD   10 9 8 7 6 5 4 3 2 1

For my wife, Cynthia

controversy, n. Dispute; debate; agitation of contrary opinions. A dispute is commonly oral, and a controversy in writing. Dispute is often or generally a debate of short duration, a temporary debate; a controversy is often oral and sometimes continued in books or in law for months or years.

—*Noah Webster,* An American Dictionary of the English Language, *1828*

CONTENTS

PREFACE

WHEN I STARTED WORKING on this book about *Webster's Third* and what may be the single greatest language controversy in American history, I envisioned using the occasion to offer my own take on what happened. With all the evidence laid out, I would get to say who was right and who was wrong. In the process, I was going to air many, many important thoughts about language and usage, and you, the reader, were going to be very impressed.

While researching this story, however, I became more interested in what brought about this controversy. Put it this way: Why did Americans in 1961 become so exercised—so irate—that several otherwise sane and distinguished persons said a mere dictionary, however imperfect, represented nothing less than the end of the world?

Controversy wasn't what Noah Webster had envisioned when he published his groundbreaking *An American Dictionary of the English Language* in 1828, which he hoped would unite his countrymen culturally and politically. And a century later—long after G. & C. Merriam Company had lost its exclusive right to the Webster name, giving rise to other so-called Webster's dictionaries—when *Webster's Second* was published to general acclaim in 1934, it didn't seem likely that panic and controversy would one day stalk the Merriam-Webster brand.

But a lot changed between 1934 and 1961, obviously. There was the Great Depression, the New Deal, and World War II, all of which left their historical fingerprints on the fast-expanding lexicon. Movies, radio, and television came to the fore, contributing not only new forms of entertainment but new words to describe them. The role of women changed, the baby boom started, the Kinsey reports were published, rock 'n' roll was invented. Cars and roads multiplied. The civil rights movement began.

The idea of America changed. American culture became "popular," and serious culture was popularized. The language of Americans went from being a source of modesty to a source of pride, and mined for literary and scholarly purposes. More Americans became more educated and spoke and wrote like educated people speak and write. Feelings about proper usage changed.

Everywhere you looked there was evidence of progress, but always with a glint of darkness. One war gave way to the next, as science assumed a great and sometimes tragic role in society and world affairs. Its influence could even be felt in the humanities, now a collection of second-place disciplines with seemingly inferior standards of knowledge.

And somehow it all contributed to one of the most delicious bouts of accusation, blame, and name-calling ever to be witnessed outside of reality television and the United States Congress. But why? Well, there were many factors. Pride, ignorance, and the profit motive for starters. And, of course, much of it had to do with how we speak and write and what we think of other people's speech and writing.

LANGUAGE IS the ultimate committee product. The committee is always in session and, for good and bad, every speaker is a member of the committee. But I could not write a book about every speaker of American English in the first half of the twentieth century. So I settled on a discrete cast of characters, whose lives, thoughts, and words not only presaged the controversy over *Webster's Third* but also document, to varying degrees, changing standards in American language and culture.

This parade of individuals—more than any attempt by me to offer the last word on whether it is okay to split an infinitive or to use *ain't* in polite conversation—makes up a large part of this book. The other part of this book describes the making and unmaking of *Webster's Third*: how the editor Philip Gove sought to build a modern, linguistically rigorous dictionary and how his critics—from the *New York Times* to Dwight Macdonald to James Parton and the American Heritage Publishing Company—sought to destroy it.

The Story of Ain't trails from Commencement Weekend at Smith College in 1918, when William Allan Neilson, the editor of *Webster's Second*, was sworn in as the school's new president, accompanied by his mentor, the legendary former Harvard president Charles William Eliot, through the slangy 1920s and Prohibition and the construction of the Chrysler Building in New York City as the young *Fortune* writer Dwight Macdonald watched from a nearby window. Then it proceeds through the Great Depression and the progress of the new linguistics as it sought to examine American English objectively while American writers such as Zora Neale Hurston and John Steinbeck sought to capture the American vulgate on the literary page. Then it marches through World War II, a war of technology and management and astonishing death tolls, all of which make enormous contributions to the standard language, and into the 1950s as literary intellectuals begin to assess what has been wrought in the American language by the increase in education, by the war, by the political turmoil stretching back decades, and by those scholars trusted to know the most about grammar: linguists. All this leads up to the making of *Webster's Third* and the wild, unexpected controversy that came to life.

Throughout, I take particular interest in the efforts of individuals and groups to bring others around to their point of view. The arts of persuasion and polemic must be considered if we are to learn how this

disagreement took shape and then festered, only to blow up on so innocent an occasion as the publication of a new dictionary. And while I
take a close look at the general issue of *communications* (ugh, I know,
it's one of those 1940s words that sound like a piece of machinery, but it
is a major part of *The Story of Ain't*), this tale is, in fact, told historically,
aided especially by documents that show us how the editor of *Webster's
Third* thought about language and what he thought about dictionaries.

The Story of
Ain't

CHAPTER 1

THEY SAY IT IS better to pronounce *aunt* like art. That it's sometimes okay to split your infinitives to, you know, avoid ambiguity. But *okay* is strictly colloquial. *Snide* is always slang, and *alright* is in wide use but not considered polite. Dirty words they never use or acknowledge. And *ain't* they say is dialectal, illiterate.

Who are they? Their names change from one era to the next, but just now they were the Editorial Board of the G. & C. Merriam Company, and they were at the Hotel Kimball in Springfield, Massachusetts, attending a dinner to celebrate the publication of *Webster's New International Dictionary, Second Edition, Unabridged.*

It was June 25, 1934, and Franklin Delano Roosevelt occupied the White House, but few Americans knew their president was bound to a wheelchair. In Hollywood, the actress Mae West was trying to make her film *It Ain't No Sin*, which after the censors were done with it was called *Belle of the Nineties*. A federal court had recently ruled it was legal to sell copies of James Joyce's *Ulysses* in the United States. For more than a dozen years the novel had been banned due to its earthy vernacular and lewd material, beginning with a scene involving *masturbation*, which *Webster's Second* defined with a good whiff of Sunday school as "onanism; self-pollution."

Editor in chief William Allan Neilson, a short, bald man with a white mustache and a neat triangular beard, called the room to order. Standing confidently before an oil portrait of Noah Webster, he held a ceremonial gavel that had just been given to him as a gift from his employer. It was fashioned from applewood grown in West Hartford, Connecticut, Webster's birthplace.

The ballroom had been transformed for supper. It was elegantly strewn with roses and crowded with men in dinner jackets. The menu consisted of consommé vermicelli, breast of chicken with bacon and cream sauce, and then, in the French manner, a salad. History did not record if any libations were served. Prohibition had ended a year earlier, but the very idea of drunkenness was still so vulgar that *Webster's Second* followed polite tradition and denied that Americans even used *drunk* as the past perfect for *drink*.

Neilson was a practiced public speaker and knew what was expected of him. To introduce Merriam's president, Asa Baker, he used the most flattering language possible under the circumstances. President Baker, he said, was a "dictionary man." He was raised in a "dictionary atmosphere" and possessed a "dictionary sense." His solid judgment had affected every aspect of their new unabridged dictionary, even as Baker also bore responsibility for the firm's finances.[1]

Baker then stood, tall, bespectacled, and nervous-looking. He firmly believed that a dictionary should evince a literary quality, and that the writers it quoted should be literary figures, not humble men like himself.[2] He said only a few words, but used one of his favorites to describe *Webster's Second*. It was a "universal" work, he said, meaning it covered all realms of knowledge and provided answers to almost all questions.

If any book could be so described, *Webster's Second* was the one. Weighing seventeen pounds, it contained 600,000 entries, which came to 122,000 more than any other dictionary. It had 12,000 illustrations and 35,000 geographical entries. The cost of its production was staggering: $1.3 million (approximately $21 million in today's dollars). "The greatest single volume ever published," Merriam called it.

Certainly no other American dictionary approached its rigor or reputation. And there was no greater name in American lexicography than Webster. The publishing company told and retold the story of George and Charles Merriam buying the unsold sheets of Noah Webster's 1841 *American Dictionary of the English Language*. The printer-brothers purchased the right to update Webster's dictionary from Webster's family, represented on this night by one of the very few women in attendance, Emily Skeel, Noah's great-granddaughter.

A member of the founding generation, Webster had dedicated his life to the language of the United States. His wildly popular blue-backed spellers taught Americans to be good, mind their books, and remember the virtues of George Washington. In his dictionary he sought to unite the young republic and liberate Americans from their dependence on the British dictionaries of Samuel Johnson and later imitators. "Language is the expression of ideas," wrote Webster in 1828, "and if the people of one country cannot retain an identity of ideas, they cannot retain an identity of language."

Of course, by 1934 there were many languages spoken in the United States. And even the primary language, English, was shot through with breathtaking variety, as linguists had begun to document in the study of American dialectal speech, and as literary critics had come to praise or blame in the experiments of modern fiction and poetry, and as countless readers had begun to notice in the language of journalism. Also, the United States now played a major role in world affairs. Its frame of reference had grown far beyond North America and Western Europe. Since 1890, Webster's big dictionary was called an international dictionary.

Still, the dictionaries bearing Webster's name continued to set the standard for English in the United States, its meanings and its niceties of grammar and usage. Webster's was "the supreme authority on all matters applying to language," as one newspaper put it. From this opinion there was no substantial or credible dissent—and there hadn't been for many years, not since a striking controversy around the time of the Civil War.

For decades in the middle of the nineteenth century (as if there was nothing better to fight over), feuding partisans at Harvard and Yale and among certain newspapers aligned behind competing dictionaries, Webster's and Worcester's. The latter belonged to Webster's onetime business associate Joseph Worcester, with whom he had fallen out. For those at Merriam, the hue and cry of this episode reinforced the lesson that a dictionary needed the documented support of leading public figures. The company sought testimonials from presidents, governors, and notable men of letters. The competition with Worcester also compelled Merriam-Webster to improve its lexicography. Its new editions took account of modern scholarship, even while adding more reference material and illustrations, and becoming more elegant as objects.[3]

A dictionary in the living room became a symbol of genteel aspiration. It was a password for culture, a ticket to knowledge, a compendium of all that was known and worth knowing. Noah Porter, editor of Merriam-Webster's 1864 and 1890 editions—and who, like William Allan Neilson, was by day a college president—said a dictionary should be found in every home and consulted on a regular basis. For no other habit, he wrote, "is at once so eminently the cause and the indication of careful attention to the language which we use, and efficient training to the best kind of culture."[4]

A REPORTER covering the dinner for *Webster's Second* wondered just how universal the dictionary was. "Who was the twenty-sixth president?" he asked. "Who fought the battle of the Marne?" "What is the scoring in contract bridge?" "What is the difference between a porterhouse and a sirloin steak?" "Who was Pocahontas's father?"[5] *Webster's Second* had the answer every time, with lists of battles, presidents, dog breeds, and enough flowers to fill a botanical garden.

It contained basic biographical information on thirteen thousand "noteworthy persons": American presidents, Austrian dukes, Catholic popes, English writers, French kings, and Roman orators. Its pronouncing gazetteer went from Aarhus in Denmark to Zumbo in Mozambique. The main vocabulary identified historical events, characters from Shakespeare's plays, figures from the Bible, literary allusions, and classical epithets. Its entries drew bright lines for all those tricky distinctions between *shall* and *will*, *imply* and *infer*, *lay* and *lie*, carefully tending all those delicate little fences. Words that were slang or vulgar or colloquial were so labeled. Pronunciations were few but prestigious, representing "formal platform speech."

Webster's Second spoke for America's learned classes, represented at the head table by dignitaries from education, publishing, and scholarship. Harvard, once home to a number of anti-Webster partisans, had sent two professors: Albert Bushnell Hart, the "grand old man" of American history only a few days short of his eightieth birthday, who had worked on the 1909 edition, and John Livingstone Lowes, a special editor and a scholar of Coleridge and Chaucer whose Cambridge ties were about as old as those of William Allan Neilson. The Scottish-born Neilson, himself a former Harvard professor, was a protégé of the late former president of Harvard, Charles William Eliot.

And there were no sore feelings associated with the *New York Times*, whose opinions on what belongs in a dictionary had sometimes differed markedly from those of Webster and his successors. The *Times'* own associate editor, John H. Finley, a writer turned graduation speaker who collected honorary degrees by the handful, sat at the head table representing the paper of record. All three hundred guests, according to Merriam's own record of the event, were selected to represent the various professions in a great unified showing of "the country's most intellectual men."

Rising from his chair at the head table, principal William C. Hill of Central High School said that the dictionary, after the teacher, was the most important aid to learning. Noah Webster and his successors deserved much credit, he said, for the great increase in the number of

Americans who had received a high school education since the Civil War.

The spread of education in America was, indeed, astonishing. In 1880, less than 5 percent of the population had any experience with secondary school. By 1934, more than 20 percent of Americans had completed high school.[6] So-called adult education—correspondence schools, vocational training—was exposing growing numbers to a new "lifelong process" of modern education, as editor Neilson said in his introduction. Education and the "best kind of culture," to use Porter's phrase, were less and less the exclusive possessions of a privileged elite like that assembled at the Hotel Kimball.

A great middle class of intellect—male and female, immigrant and native-born, white and increasingly black—was coming into being, built on American progress toward universal schooling. And the culture reflected it. Little more than a high school diploma was required to enjoy middlebrow offerings such as Henry Seidel Canby's *Saturday Review of Literature* and novels from the Book-of-the-Month Club. Radio programs presenting literary discussions became common in the 1930s, as if a popular format built on the art of book reviewing was the most natural thing in the world. *Time* magazine, while trademarking a smart-aleck prose with no small amount of slang, ran cover stories about the Middle Ages and opera stars.

Science, too, was transforming the image of education and knowledge in these years. Mustard gas and other lab-inspired brutalities of World War I had left science with a public image problem, which American scientists combated through an energetic program of publishing and advertisement. But no public relations campaign was more effective than the lives and stories of Albert Einstein and Marie Curie, which the press gratefully reported.[7] Nor could anything so divisive as the Scopes trial and the fight over evolution in the schools rob technological innovation (airplanes, radio) of its power to amaze the public at large.

Still, this middle class of intellect had old-fashioned notions of quality. Their standards were as much Noah Porter as Cole Porter, something President Baker surely had in mind when he asked William Allan Neilson if he objected to it being mentioned on the first page of *Webster's Second* that Neilson had been the associate editor of the well-known and illustrious Harvard Classics.[8] Potential buyers wanted it on good authority that a book was worth buying.

And Merriam was very much in the business of authority. In its own pages, *Webster's Second* was "the Dictionary," with a capital *D* and the definite article as if no other existed. But to continue as the linguistic law of the land, the last word on words, the great "they" from whom all correctness comes, Merriam-Webster needed to remain up-to-date and true to its reputation for completeness and accuracy. Professor Hart put it well when he stood and said, "You've got to be right. Every contributor to the dictionary knows that. That is why Webster's dictionary is what it is."

CHAPTER 2

IN 1961, G. & C. Merriam Company sent out a press release to announce its new dictionary, *Webster's Third*. Along with the press release some journalists received a photo of Betty Grable, whose last movie was *How to Be Very, Very Popular*.[1] The connection was not exactly obvious.

The new dictionary had updated the definition for *leggy*, but the press release did not point this out. Nor did it mention the fact that *sexy* was no longer labeled slang. Or even that *pinup* was one of the new words entered since 1934. But there was this: Betty Grable spoke English.

Twenty-seven years after *Webster's Second*, the *Cold War* (a newish term included in *Webster's Third*) was under way and President Kennedy was in his first year of office. Looking back from the New Frontier to the New Deal, Merriam's president, Gordon J. Gallan, decided against throwing another banquet.[2]

He had been at Merriam for over a decade but was not an old dictionary hand like Asa Baker. He had no editorial experience. Before becoming president, he had been the publisher's advertising manager. And what the new dictionary needed, he thought, was a good promotional campaign. So, instead of renting out the Hotel Kimball, he hired Ruth Millard Associates, a public relations firm in New York City.

Expectations were low, but the story had potential. The press release quoted Gallan, talking up the pretty new words. "The recent explosion of language has forced into everyday usage an avalanche of bewildering new verbal concepts, ranging from *A-bomb, astronaut, beatnik, den mother*, and *fringe benefit* to *satellite, solar house, wage dividend* and *Zen*."[3]

The alphabetical list read like a scat poem of midcentury Americana, suggesting improbable connections. *A-bomb* had first entered the Merriam-Webster files in 1917, described as "fanciful, chemical explosion of an atom"; since Hiroshima and Nagasaki, it was, of course, quite real. *Astronaut* had been around since the twenties, when it also seemed fanciful, but then came the launch of *Sputnik* and Yury Gagarin's trip in orbit earlier in the year. The sound of *Sputnik* had inspired *beatnik*, which Herb Caen of the *San Francisco Chronicle* coined in 1958, and the beatniks, including Jack Kerouac, who that same year published *The Dharma Bums*, helped popularize *Zen* as in Zen Buddhism.

Another angle was the celebrity angle, using famous names and a side-mouth English that no one associated with dictionaries. It was contrary to the tradition of emphasizing Webster's august literary qualities, but such "pungent, lively remarks," editor in chief Dr. Philip B. Gove said, helped the dictionary "come alive."[4] Hence Grable and her lovely gams. She had been quoted under *anymore*: "Every time I even smile at a man *anymore* the papers have me practically married to him."

Mickey Spillane was mentioned. Among the dozen entries quoting the creator of Mike Hammer were *clunk* ("the gun *clunked* to the floor"), *hardcase, shoot out*, and a colorful use of *sugar* ("an operation that cost heavy *sugar*"). Public figures were de rigueur for such an announcement, and former president Eisenhower was mentioned for an unexceptional use of the lighthearted *goof*. Left unmentioned in the press release was Ike's more memorable language for fallen soldiers, cited under the verb form of *exact*: "from them has been *exacted* the ultimate sacrifice," taken from the general's May 1945 Proclamation on Germany's Defeat.

Winston Churchill and Franklin Delano Roosevelt were listed, as their combined public statements had been mined for hundreds of citations, though not as many as came from the Bible and Shakespeare. For a bit of the unexpected, the press release dropped the name Polly Adler, the onetime madam and gossip column item whose 1950s bestseller, *A House Is Not a Home*, was used as evidence for multiple entries, including sense 5A of *shake*: "There was no *shaking* off the press."

The press release quoted Dr. Gove saying that the English language had become less formal since 1934. For an example the PR hands chose the new dictionary's surprisingly tolerant, though oddly worded, entry for *ain't*, which said *ain't* was "used orally in most parts of the U.S. by cultivated speakers."

AFTER TEN years of extremely hard work, there was little appetite to convene major contributors and other esteemed persons for another black-tie party with all those dinner courses and long speeches invoking the founding lexicographer, Noah Webster. Such pomp and circumstance would have seemed *phony*, another word no longer labeled slang in *Webster's Third*, a decade after being wielded like a hatpin by J. D. Salinger's Holden Caulfield against the inflated pretensions of adults, and two decades after the so-called Phony War, when France and England had declared war on Germany but the still-isolationist United States remained uninvolved.

That whole approach seemed the product of another time, a less honest time, when to sell dictionaries you lined up establishment figures to create the appearance of an unquestionable consensus among those in the know. Then everyone else could go around insisting that it was incorrect to speak as you had been raised to speak, because Webster's or some anonymous committee called "they" said it was wrong to split your infinitives or to use *like* as a preposition or to say *due to*, as in "the festival is canceled due to foul weather."

Gove didn't want to be a "they." He thought it a profound mistake that Webster's dictionaries had been called the "supreme authority."

BusinessWeek picked up this thread, reporting that *Webster's Third* had been influenced by the burgeoning science of linguistics, which "strives to describe a language in its present state, without getting into judgments about what's 'correct.'" Gove had told the magazine, "There's no divine sanction in language. It's an instrument of the people who use it."

The people who use it? Exactly. Not some distant authority, always beyond present company and of the best intellectual pedigree. We the English-language speakers. You. The lady down the block. Her ridiculous uncle in Des Moines. Betty Grable. All of us. Us.

The press release did not go this far. It suggested that *Webster's Third* was yet another volume for the enlightenment of the middle class. It was "specifically planned to be read and enjoyed by students, housewives, businessmen, as well as scholars," but this was not Noah Porter's living-room symbol of genteel aspiration.

Webster's Third did not claim to have all the answers. It was not called a universal dictionary. It was shaped by Gove to be something both simpler and more complex: a modern, scholarly dictionary of standard English.

Just as important to Gove was all that his dictionary was not. It was not an encyclopedia, not an atlas, not an international directory of history's big shots, not a dramatis personae of every character in Western literature, not an index of epithets and literary allusions, not a class system that could be counted on to disdain certain kinds of words used by certain kinds of people, not a record of all those misinformed rules of grammar that have no basis in actual usage, not some pompous, overreaching, editorializing, know-it-all windbag of a dictionary that takes its direction from the prejudices of the day while giving short shrift to words, the one thing it should be intensely serious about.

A reader of modern linguistics, Gove knew that even the simplest words defied the neatness of definitions and categories and usage labels, all desperately trying to pinpoint when, where, and under what circumstances *chair* or *apple* or *girl* may be used. Words were much more complicated than they seemed, so complicated that even educated people disagreed on what they meant. And meaning itself was subject to change.

Teachers could correct their students, mothers their children, and bosses their underlings, but the language moved and changed of its own accord. Tracking its vast and hurried adjustments was a great task, a fitting task for a great dictionary, but one made all the harder by the wrongheaded idea that a dictionary was the language in its purest form.

To begin with, there could be no doubt which, the language or the dictionary, was primary. Language was primary; a dictionary was no more than a humble attempt to photograph and itemize the contents. In a way, the basic assumption of dictionary users—that you could check language as real people used it against what the dictionary said—was wrong. It was the other way around. The measure of a good dictionary was its fidelity to the language as real people used it. And the one major claim Gove did not mind making for *Webster's Third* was that it faithfully recorded the standard language of its time.

GOVE—HE WAS Dr. or Mr. Gove to underlings, Philip to his children— threw his own party, for the dictionary staff and their spouses, at his farm, about twenty miles east of Springfield. President Gallan, with whom he got along well enough, declined to attend, saying merely, "It's your day."[5] Which it was.

Guests arrived to find their chief dressed in farming duds and standing atop a hay wagon. He was pouring drinks with a heavy hand that left some of the older editors pie-eyed. The menu was local, including vegetables grown without chemicals on the Gove farm. Dinner was served on the porch.[6]

In the living room, a puppet show was staged: "The Big Book," a jokey skit written by Mrs. Grace Gove with music by her son Norwood. Scene 3 opened on Philip and two other editors stirring a pot, which symbolized *Webster's Third*. The men complained about production costs and section editors holding out on their definitions, hoping to be better compensated for longer words.[7]

Ann Driscoll, Gove's assistant, had quit after being told she would not be listed on the masthead as a managing editor, a final casualty of Gove's impersonal touch as a manager. In the skit, her puppet was a spinster busybody who would not let others be.

She nips at Gove to finish his work on *Webster's Third*, and then clears out the old stock by burning copies of *Webster's Second*. When Gove sees the *Webster's Seconds* on fire, he becomes distraught—the gag being that, in reality, the sight of the old dictionary in flames would not have upset him in the least.

After Driscoll exits, the editors say that what she needed was a lover—that, or she should have taken up golf like the men. This was another bit of irony: Gove kept tenaciously regular hours and spent his weekends working his land, leaving little time to improve his handicap.

In-jokes abounded. A poem in the script cited Mrs. Gove and played on the name of pronunciation editor Ed Artin.

> *If to pronounce you're guessing*
> *Perfection is grace*
> *There's art in expressing*
> *Each phoneme in place*

The banter also touched on what criticisms the dictionary might encounter.

> *We is perfect in grammer*
> *We knows how to spel*
> *So the phobic will clamor*
> *And the damn book will sell*

After the press release went out, the phobic did begin to clamor. Newspapers lunged at the story of the dictionary's shockingly liberal treatment of *ain't*. In Chicago, the *Tribune* and the *Sun-Times* picked up the same newswire item, announcing, "The word 'ain't' ain't a grammatical mistake anymore." The next day, the Toronto *Globe and Mail* weighed in.

"A dictionary's embrace of the word *ain't* will comfort the ignorant, confer approval upon the mediocre, and subtly imply that proper English is the tool only of the snob." But this was something more than your typical lecture from the union of concerned citizens.

We live in a world of problems, the newspaper explained, problems that arise from misunderstandings between individuals and even nations. "Where language is without rules and discipline, there is little understanding, much misunderstanding. How can we convey precise meanings to the Russians, when we cannot convey them to each other?"

The *New York Times* entered the fray. Complaining that *Webster's* had "surrendered to the permissive school that has been busily extending its beachhead on English instruction," the *Times* called on Merriam to preserve the printing plates for *Webster's Second*, so that a new start could be made.

James Parton was thinking the exact same thing. The president of the American Heritage Publishing Company, Parton had been trying to buy enough company shares to gain a majority position in Merriam stock. The dictionary and reference book business had become enormously profitable since the passage of the GI Bill and the baby boom, and nothing had so advanced Parton's takeover efforts as the discovery that Philip Gove had radically altered the dictionary's editorial approach.

Attacked by America's most prestigious newspaper and increasingly vulnerable to a hostile takeover, Merriam suffered yet another blow. Within months, *Webster's Third* became the whipping boy of American literati.

Dwight Macdonald excoriated *Webster's Third* in the pages of the *New Yorker*, producing a classic essay that generated more reader mail than anything else he had written. The aging radical was a traditionalist when it came to literary culture, an Anglophile and a Henry James man. He linked the dictionary's excesses to the principles of "structural linguistics." His essay closed with a Shakespearean lament that this new dictionary might very well represent the end of the world.

In the *Atlantic*, Wilson Follett, a defender of old-fashioned usage, called the new dictionary "a very great calamity." In the *American Scholar*, Follett's friend the elegant historian Jacques Barzun discovered in *Webster's Third* "a subtle attack on The Word"—with *the* and *word* in capital letters, as they were punctuated "in the beginning" of John, chapter 1.

America's greatest language controversy was under way. From Cape Cod to California, the new dictionary was denounced, in the press and from the pulpit, in classrooms and around the kitchen table. As a result, sales of *Webster's Third* greatly exceeded expectations. The permissive dictionary was, indeed, very, very popular. But Noah Webster's ideal of a country unified by his dictionary was in tatters. And forty years later the controversy over *Webster's Third* would be called by David Foster Wallace "the Fort Sumter of the contemporary usage wars."

Not all disagreements, as it happens, can be attributed to what a Paul Newman movie called "a failure to communicate." Some disagreements arise because individuals and nations, or in this case critics and lexicographers, finally understand each other rather well. Facts may indeed suffer along the way, and certainly did in this case, but even after the corrections were made it was clear that the feuding parties just didn't like each other or what each other stood for.

Philip Gove was not merely defending a dictionary when he stood up for *Webster's Third*. He was defending a method of linguistic study and a principle of tolerance for spoken English in all its naturally occurring variety. Dwight Macdonald, similarly, was not merely denouncing an imperfect reference work but attempting to man the ramparts of a civilization whose cultural standards seemed more compromised with every passing year. Gove had unveiled the great shining accomplishment of his life; Dwight Macdonald wrote the best essay of his life, mocking it.

CHAPTER 3

ON JUNE 13, 1918, in the midst of the Great War, Smith College in Northampton, Massachusetts, held its annual graduation ceremony. Charles William Eliot delivered the commencement address. He was eighty-four years old and the very personification of American academia.

He dressed in dark, old-fashioned clothes, befitting his stature as one of those sought-after personages whose views on the latest election or the conduct of life were routinely set in print or aired from a podium for the benefit of well-meaning listeners.

His posture was straight and his hands were clasped in front. He gestured rarely, speaking clearly and evenly. He did not hesitate to state the obvious and would not be heard talking over his audience's heads.[1] But he spoke as if there were no more natural dialect than "formal platform speech."

Smith College was also inaugurating a new president, Eliot's protégé, William Allan Neilson. As simple as the exercises were, out of respect for the many sacrifices borne at home and abroad during wartime, it was a historic moment for the all-women's school. And there was more than a little dramatic interest in Eliot's presence.

At the school's first commencement, in 1879, Eliot had taken the podium and candidly aired his doubts that this experiment in female education would be a success, for its graduates or for society at large. But since then, of course, much had changed.

Eliot said, "The trustees have put at the head of the college, doubtless by well-considered design, a new kind of president."[2] Not a minister, President Neilson was a professional teacher and scholar. Furthermore, he was a "specialist."

The ties between the Protestant church and American colleges were loosening, while knowledge and the very notion of what it meant to be educated had undergone significant transformation since the founding of Smith.

"The original requirements for admission," Eliot noted, "were confined to Latin, Greek, and Mathematics, with some English grammar." Since then, Latin and Greek had come to seem less important, and science more so.

Darwin's theory of evolution had begun to reshape the study of human nature. Ideas such as natural selection and survival of the fittest had come to challenge Victorian moral precepts for the power to explain and justify the existing social order. That ministers ceased to hold leading positions in American colleges was one result.

Science and evolutionary thinking had affected work even in the humanities. A specialist like Neilson, expert in the history of British poetry, was required to study the contributions of nineteenth-century German scholars who had pulled back the cloak of literature to discover in language a self-adjusting system, one quite unlike the rules of grammar and usage immortalized in Victorian-era guides to linguistic etiquette.

A trained chemist, Eliot was familiar with the contributions of scientific research to the changing ideals of knowledge and education. As he told the women of Smith College, he'd spoken at the founding of Johns Hopkins University in 1876, a major turning point for scientific research in America.

And in the realm of science women had done a lot of good. "Women have proved themselves admirable assistants to physicians and surgeons, to public health officials, and in laboratories where scientific researches are conducted."

In 1909, Eliot had retired from the presidency of Harvard after serving for an incredible forty years. And there were any number of educational reforms for which he sought the support of Smith's graduating class, many of whose members, he said, "ought to become teachers in secondary and normal schools."

No longer, he then conceded, did women need to "provide proof" of their fitness to attend college or of the usefulness of separate women's colleges, and no longer did they need to answer questions about the effects of four years of study on their health. "These questions are settled now, and are no longer discussed."

Smith's record of achievement was not to be gainsaid. "The College sends year by year into American society a stream of young women well-fitted to be the equal mates and effective comrades of pure, vigorous, courageous, reasoning, and aspiring young men." Quoting Emerson, he called marriage "a tender and intimate relation of one to one."

Talk of "equal mates" and a "relation of one to one" did not mean, he clarified, "equality in natural gifts." Indeed, he said, "there is no such thing." But now, thanks to Smith College and other schools like it, American women could secure "approximate equality in respect to educational advantages."

WILLIAM ALLAN Neilson, not yet fifty years old, represented a different generation. Born the same year Eliot had become president of Harvard, he was the son of a schoolmaster in Perthshire, Scotland. After an honors in philosophy from the University of Edinburgh he received a traveling fellowship, which had brought him to the United States. He had studied at Harvard, then taught at Bryn Mawr College and Columbia University before returning to Cambridge in 1906 as a professor of English.

At Harvard, the broad humanistic tradition as represented by that other Charles Eliot, Charles Eliot Norton, the Brahmin translator of Dante and editor of the *North American Review*, was still in evidence during those years. But it shared the field with other intellectual strains, including German-style linguistics, the study of speech or language entirely apart from literature.

As one alumnus recalled, "Students were expected to talk in a scholarly way in the classroom and on a final examination about Grimm's or Verner's laws, the differentiating characteristics of Anglo-Saxon among the Teutonic languages, the changes in English phonology, inflection, and syntax from Anglo-Saxon times to the sixteenth century."

The bright light of the younger professors, Neilson was thought likely to succeed as chairman the gaunt, bearded George Lyman Kittredge, who used to say, "A pedant is a person who uses the wrong words in the wrong places." After Neilson presented a paper drawing unlikely comparisons between Shakespearean characters such as Falstaff and Cleopatra, Kittredge asked if all that hard work had kept him from enjoying the plays.

Neilson, however, gave as well as he got. He once dismissed Matthew Arnold, the great Victorian humanist and educator, with a familial bank shot off Arnold's father, Dr. Thomas Arnold of Rugby, "the excellence of whose influence on his students," Neilson said, "was limited only by the fact that they tended to become prigs." Neilson was said to be the one philologist at Harvard with the "requisite combination of humanity, erudition, and cultural finesse to make him a match for the higher critics."[3]

He was a specialist, yes, but one fit for a broader public, as Charles William Eliot must have thought when he enlisted Neilson to be his assistant editor on the so-called five-foot shelf of literary works that came to be known as the Harvard Classics.

Eliot, while addressing what is always described as a group of workingmen, had opined that the formal education his audience lacked was not so elusive, but in fact could be obtained through the purchase of enough classic works to fill a small shelf, so long as these books were read with steady devotion. The commitment need not take up more than fifteen minutes a day, he added breezily. Getting wind of this catchy little pitch, representatives from the publishing house of P. F. Collier offered to bring out such a library of books, and Eliot obtained from the Harvard Corporation permission to use the school's name.

The idea had terrific commercial appeal. Newspapers adored the notion, reporting their suspicions on what books were being chosen for this best-ever list of literary works, speculating about and even criticizing the lineup before it was final. Literacy in America was now commonplace, though higher education was not and books were still precious and hard to come by. Hucksterish pitches for home courses on writing like a gentleman or a lady were advertised in the backs of magazines, as ever more people recognized the financial value of boasting some education. The Harvard Classics promised a shortcut to developing "a rich mental background."[4]

While the literature students under Kittredge took inspiration from the scholars who had labored for years, studying Middle English, to explain a single letter, the final *e* in the writings of Chaucer, Neilson began working on Eliot's publishing venture to bring an Ivy League education within reach of anyone willing to read Plato and Shakespeare for fifteen minutes a day. More than a few Harvardians were furious that their university's name was being implicated in this profit-making scheme, and Neilson bore some of their animus at a faculty meeting. But for his trouble he was rewarded with a stipend of fifty dollars a week.

The Harvard Classics included a vast number of works, but the division of labor was simple: Eliot chose the works, then Neilson selected the exact text, edited the selection, and wrote the introduction and any footnotes. When time grew short and a decision had to be made between filling a volume with Walton's Lives or Locke's treatise on understanding, Eliot delegated the matter to Neilson. When editorial questions turned especially tricky, they were referred up to Eliot. Neilson drew Eliot's attention to some naughty passages in the Elizabethan texts they had chosen, querying whether Eliot thought they should be edited out.[5]

Cutting the dirty parts out of Shakespeare was not unheard of. Almost a century earlier, Thomas Bowdler had published his commercially successful editions of the plays in *The Family Shakespeare*, "omitting those words and expressions . . . which cannot be read aloud in a family."

And in America in 1909, self-censorship was common. The antivice societies were still powerful. Anthony Comstock was no longer a special agent of the U.S. Post Office, licensed to board trains at will in search of mail that violated obscenity laws, but he and his confederates among the Watch and Ward Society still enjoyed a large measure of social prestige, not least through their endorsement by such important social figures as J. P. Morgan, the publisher Alfred Barnes, and Charles William Eliot.

But when Neilson asked Eliot what to do about the naughty language in the Shakespeare, Eliot said that "to cut out of the Elizabethan drama the obscenity which was intended to be amusing would be a large piece of work for you, and it is a kind of work that provokes criticism— particularly when the fundamentally nasty situations cannot be cut out of the plays."

Neilson apparently reengaged the argument because a week later Eliot was still making the case for preserving the ribald humor of the Elizabethans. "If you take the smut out of the obscene passages . . . will they not be left flat and unintelligible. The supposed fun was in the obscenity. Voltaire says, 'we don't laugh in reading a translation.' Will anybody be able to laugh at any part of an expurgated Elizabethan drama?"[6]

Eliot, who is still well known for his Progressive Era preoccupations with physical and moral hygiene, strikes the modern onlooker as the sterner of the pair. With his spectacles and long nineteenth-century sideburns, he lectured the public on the evils of college football and promulgated his own rationalist faith that "in the future" organized religion would outgrow its primitive taboos. Of the two men, he seems, by far, the more dated.

Bearing less history and being not so practiced a commentator on the great issues of the day, Neilson seems less stuffy, less the type to hold forth without warning. More capable of irony, he could be sly, "pawky," to use the Scottish term that was often applied to him. His trim sideburns, neatly coarse mustache, and the stripe of beard running over his chin all make him appear to be the more modern of the two as, in photos, he gazes comfortably toward the camera, not as if he were posing for a statue of himself.

William Allan Neilson always seemed to be the opposite of a prig. Yet he was the one who had looked to bowdlerize the Harvard Classics.

One can imagine Neilson was merely playing the part of the conservative junior partner, making sure his boss knew exactly the risk they were taking—not so great perhaps, since educational materials rarely faced the level of censorious scrutiny applied to dime-store novels—but there is another fact to contend with: In coediting the anthology *Chief British Poets of the Fourteenth and Fifteenth Centuries*, which one modern scholar calls "ruthlessly expurgated,"[7] William Allan Neilson proved he was indeed willing to placate the puritanical mania and sterilize classic literature of its dangerous tendency to coarsen the morals of poor innocent readers.

But the man at the podium, receiving the keys to Smith College, was no philistine. The caricature of the censor in those days was a man or a woman (indeed, ladies played an important role in the history of censorship) who did not know good literature and who, in talking about the filth to be found in some books, ended up quoting, repeating, and otherwise belaboring such filth to the point where one might fairly ask if they were truly cleansing the air or recirculating pollution. That, William Alan Neilson was not. But then what was he?

NEILSON TOOK the podium. He was a serious person, sensitive to the melancholy duties of lauding intellectual achievement as the American soldier faced mortal danger and the young men of Europe died in trenches, attacked by chemical weapons and the first flying warplanes.

He told the class of 1917 that "revolutionary changes, social, industrial, economic, even ethical and religious . . . may be expected from the cataclysm which is even now shaking the world." Among other developments, the common man was coming up. Great Britain, an obvious point of reference for Neilson and his audience, was adopting a new education law, offering to "every child the opportunity of enjoying that form of education most adapted to fashion its qualities to the highest use."

But "the idea of democracy," he said, "does not require the application of the same educational process to all." An education such as the one offered at Smith "can never be enjoyed by more than a small minority." For one thing, it was too expensive, but more important, only those "whose abilities entitle them to this particular opportunity" should be welcomed.

To illustrate, Neilson used a liturgical analogy.

"The old Scottish communion service used to be preceded by a preliminary exercise called 'the fencing of the tables,' in which the unworthy were warned not to approach. These introductory remarks . . . may be regarded as a kind of fencing of the tables. But what is the nature of the feast to which the worthy are invited? How are we to conceive the educational opportunity which such a college as this should offer?"

The true nature of higher education was not easy to describe. "The leading thinkers on such matters were roughly divided into two camps: the scientific and the classical." The division was a "quarrel" that broke out every few years or so. A school need not choose sides, though. "What is needed," Neilson argued, "is an examination by each of the strength rather than the weakness of the contrary position."

The great strength of scientific investigation was its power to "explain the world we live in, to make nature more intelligible." It "gives man an escape from the noisy present into a region of facts which are as they are and not as foolish human beings want them to be," he said, quoting a recent address by the English classicist Gilbert Murray.

Neilson had even more to say about the classical party, as it had been rent by disagreements. There had been of late a "revolt against the classics," which he attributed to "a wide-spread indignation at being cheated." Hundreds of thousands of students had taken up Greek or Latin or both "with the implicit understanding that they would finally have access to the two great civilizations through reading the records in their original tongues." But in the end "they could not read Latin or Greek."

It would have been better, said Neilson, to have spent all that time reading works in translation. For scholars, mastery of the ancient tongues remained necessary. But, he said, "do not let us pretend that a man cannot be cultivated without an accomplishment that most cultivated men will confess they do not possess."

Identifying those things a cultivated person ought to know was only one goal of education. Neilson insisted that a college must also encourage curiosity and doubt, and seek "the full and free development of personality . . . that each person should acquire such power of self-expression as to count for what she is worth in the community."

Personality was an important and fluid word in these years, even as America saw the rise of objective measures to quantify human differences. Smith College among others was just starting to rely on a new standard for admissions, the College Board exam, and 1918 was also the year people began hearing about the Stanford-Binet test for intelligence. But *personality* as Neilson used the term stood to succeed the great Victorian belief in *character*, that virtue so uncompromising it made one's every act and gesture seem like a demonstration in moral superiority. Neilson complemented *personality* with a more novel coinage, *self-*

expression, which had been noticed entering the language twenty-five years earlier.

In closing, Neilson returned to the quarrel, quoting Gilbert Murray again, saying, " 'If we fret and argue and fight one another now, it is mainly because we are so much under the power of the enemy.' "

But the enemy was no foreign power.

" 'The enemy,' " said Neilson, still quoting Murray, " 'has no definite name, though it is certain we all know him; he who puts always the body before the spirit, the dead before the living; who makes things only to sell them; who has forgotten that there is such a thing as truth . . . the Philistine, the vulgarian, the great sophist, the passer of base coin for true, he is all about us and, worse, he has his outposts inside us, persecuting our peace, spoiling our sight, confusing our values, making a man's self seem greater than the race and the present thing more important than the eternal.

" 'From him and his influence we find our escape by means of old books into that calm world of theirs, where stridency and clamor are forgotten in the ancient stillness . . . [and] the great things of the human spirit still shine like stars.' " There, inside old books, we also find " 'beloved and tender and funny and familiar things,' " which " 'beckon across gulfs of death and change with a magic poignancy, the old things that our dead leaders and fore-fathers loved, *viva adhuc et desiderio pulcriora.*' "

A man of his word, Neilson translated the last line of this address for those cultivated listeners who had not mastered Latin: "living still and more beautiful because of our desire."

CHAPTER 4

H. L. MENCKEN DESCENDED from a distinguished line of German academics, but he had little use for the measured tones or intellectual hedging of scholarship. The Baltimorean son of a cigar maker understood that moderation is usually the enemy of a well-wrought argument. Skeptical but curious, he was fully alive to the ideas of his own time, though comically at odds with polite opinion. Everything the moralists and the improvers were for—prohibition, censorship, creationism, and Great Britain—Mencken was against.

He thought Americans were being duped into supporting Britain in World War I,[1] and, when it came to language, the Anglophile prejudices of American highbrows seemed to him yet another example of our national dim-wittedness. Mencken's own use of English was brassy and joyful, drunk with neologisms and seemingly free of inhibition.

He was an all-around champion of the scientific and secular point of view. In the Scopes trial, Mencken pressured Clarence Darrow to use the case to prosecute the beliefs of William Jennings Bryan, counsel for the creationists, and when Bryan died shortly after the trial, Mencken liked to think that he and his allies had hectored him into the grave. Religion was an interesting and sometimes beautiful fraud, Mencken thought. Similarly hollow were the linguistic pretensions of American educators.

In his book on the subject, *The American Language*—first published in 1919, but much augmented in later editions—Mencken began to distinguish our country's idiom from what one learned in school. In those days the National Council of Teachers of English still observed Good Grammar Week, when children were called on to go seven full days without splitting an infinitive. As a reward they were treated to entertaining skits in which Mr. Dictionary vanquished the villain *Ain't*.[2] At home, however, as radios in the 1920s went from being a rare possession to a basic appliance, children might hear "Ain't We Got Fun," a popular foxtrot, "Ain't Misbehavin'," a Fats Waller song, or perhaps even "Ain't She Sweet," another hit song of the time.

American speech was still taught according to "British Received Pronunciation." Few scholars or laymen had ever believed American speech worth defending. In 1905, Henry James, after years of living in England, had lectured at Bryn Mawr on "The Question of Our Speech," saying Americans lacked "good breeding."

Our speech, the novelist said, was utterly lacking in a "tone-standard." It was flat, monotonous, and crude. Instead of yes, we said "yeh-eh" and "yeh-ep." Even teachers added warrantless *r* sounds to words like *idea* (idea-r), *vanilla* (vanilla-r), and *Cuba* (Cuba-r). And we mumbled, neglecting to distinguish "the innumerable differentiated, discriminated units of sound and sense that lend themselves to audible production, to enunciation, to intonation." The National Speech League agreed, and implored children to "say a good American 'yes' and 'no' in place of an Indian grunt 'um-hum' and 'nup-um' or a foreign 'ya' or 'yeh' and 'nope.'"[3]

James said he hardly had time to go beyond pronunciation and tone to discuss the "uncontrolled assault" that American circumstances had imposed on the mother tongue in general, but he assured his audience that its treatment was as barbaric in every other respect. Mark Twain, the other great American writer of the late nineteenth and early twentieth centuries, took the opposite view. The heir of a populist tradition of

American dialectal humor, this literatus wrote with an ear to American speech, inventing characters who said *hain't* and never not minded the double negative.

Of the two tendencies in American—the Twainian and the Jamesian—Mencken was one hundred percent Twainian. He credited the humorist with going further than anyone to Americanize the literary language. Twain's had been a great era for linguistic invention. *Boom* (in the business sense), *crook*, *cussword* (an actual Twainism), *freeze-out*, *grubstake*, *holdup*, *hoodlum*, *light out*, *spellbinder*, to *strike oil*, all came out of the late nineteenth century, Mencken noted. "Racy" was the word he and others settled on when they looked to summarize what was so American about the American language.

In the argument of his book, Mencken roughly sketched a linguistic history of the United States, pitting the shamelessly American against those who still looked to Britain for guidance on how to speak and write. One could certainly see this division in the time of Noah Webster. In the election of 1828, the year Webster's *An American Dictionary of the English Language* was published, Andrew Jackson, that great frontier spirit whose poorly spelt letters crackled with unpredictable native eloquence, defeated the European-educated John Quincy Adams, former president of the American Academy of Language and Belles Lettres, a short-lived organization that sought to protect "the purity and uniformity of the English language" from American "corruptions."[4]

From the Civil War era, Mencken dragged out the example of Richard Grant White, at the time America's most widely read commentator on language, a man so eastern and Anglophile in his tastes that he objected to the Americanism *presidential*. One could only wonder if White preferred the slightly older *colonial*, coined in reference to American subservience to Britain, or maybe the much older and even more established *kingly*.

The presidency of Abraham Lincoln was a historical watershed for plain, unaffected American speech, Mencken noted, while Lincoln himself was often accused of shabbiness, not least when he visited New York City and attended the opera wearing black gloves. Mr. Lincoln (as he was known to many, including his wife) was criticized by Ralph Waldo Emerson and the ex-president John Tyler for his grammar. The New York diarist George Templeton Strong had called him "a barbarian, Scythian, yahoo, or gorilla," but the big-city snob also kinda liked the guy.[5]

Americans often found good sense and even eloquence in low idiom. A well-known speech of the period, attributed to Sojourner Truth, voiced the complaint of the female slave: "I have ploughed, and planted, and gathered into barns, and no man could head me! And ain't I a woman? I could work as much and eat as much as a man—when I could get it—and bear de lash as well! And ain't I a woman? I have borne thirteen chilern, and seen 'em mos' all sold off to slavery, and when I cried out with my mother's grief, none but Jesus heard me! And ain't I a woman?"[6]

Of course this was not the language of polite American usage, which one sought in a good dictionary. Said the *New York Times*, "There are thousands of words used colloquially or in newspapers, or belonging to the depository of slang, whose incorporations in work claiming to be an *arbiter elegantiarum* of speech would be either needless or positively objectionable."[7]

The last two decades of the nineteenth century saw more than one hundred books on usage and grammar published in the United States.[8] The cult of elegance was in full swing. Refined Americans used old-fashioned grammar, wrote in a fancy Spencerian hand, and preferred forks to eat ice cream because spoons were considered vulgar.[9] American pretensions were aristocratic, while the reality was a culture of profound change, shaped by waves of immigration and new urban centers like the fast-growing, multiethnic city of Chicago.

By the time Mencken was writing about the American language, the tide had begun to shift. Among those he credited with undermining the genteel tradition were Theodore Dreiser, Van Wyck Brooks, and

Sinclair Lewis. Mencken was morally and culturally as one with these writers, but another factor helped distinguish his linguistic comments in the 1920s: his simple collecting of words.

Delcevare King, a prohibitionist in Massachusetts, helped coin the decade's most telling neologism by offering a prize of two hundred dollars for the word that best captured the "lawless drinker." Mencken recorded this famous innovation and many others. Amazingly, the winning word, *scofflaw*, formed by the simple addition of *scoff* to *law*, was offered in two separate entries, so the prize was split.

Other favorite words of Mencken's from these years include *debunk* and *debunking* from William E. Woodward's 1923 book, *Bunk*. Mencken noted that *bunk* derived from *Buncombe*, coined a century earlier (the story went) when a North Carolina representative slowly preparing to address Congress deflected his colleagues' calls to get on with it by saying, essentially, *Wait, he had things to say to the people of Buncombe County.* After this *bunkum* referred to any political speech lacking a point except to flatter voters.

No single writer, in Mencken's opinion, was working over the language as much as Walter Winchell, the Broadway critic and gossip columnist whose syndicated slanguage taught Americans, among other things, new phrases for the rise and decline of romance. In love was *on fire, that way,* and *uh-huh; on the merge* meant engaged; *welded and sealed* equaled married; *phfft* could be defined as separated; and *melted* said "divorced" more or less.

More argot from this time can be found in the memoir *A House Is Not a Home,* by Polly Adler, the straight-talking madam who became something of a household name in the 1920s and '30s. The era's motto, according to her, was "anything which is economically right is morally right."[10]

A Polish immigrant who came to the United States as a teenager and worked in garment factories to earn her bread, Adler was taken up by a Broadway actress who asked her to move in with her. The wide-eyed seamstress became acculturated to the fast living of guys and dolls, chorus girls, song-pluggers, gangsters, and hopheads. *Rods* were guns, a *fireman* was a big-deal businessman, an *iron man* was a dollar, and a *yard* was a hundred bucks. Her boyfriend, a bandleader in town, could sometimes be heard performing on the radio. After she made her *wad*, Adler listened from inside the luxury of her new penthouse. The interior design was inspired by the recent King Tut exhibition. Another great word from this time of "wonderful nonsense": *screwball*.

Etiquette books in the twenties licensed the use of slang in polite company for adding "piquancy to our talk," modestly admitting that "even 'swell' and 'sweetie pie' are correct in certain moods." In the conduct of business, however, formality was still preferred: *O.K.* and *all righty* were not to be used when talking to customers.[11]

AT&T hired English instructors during the summer to help improve the literary quality of its correspondence with stockholders. Philip Gove, later editor of *Webster's Third*, who taught composition at New York University, was one such instructor. He thus met Grace Edna Potter, a secretary. Family lore made their meeting sound ever so proper, like a post-Victorian set piece: Philip counseled Grace not to expose her ankles as she bent over the filing cabinet "that way."[12]

For a rejoinder to the gay excitement of the twenties (*gay*, of course, in the old sense: "excited with merriment," according to *Webster's Second*), one could look to the other side of the Atlantic, to the simple declarative sentences and expatriate stoicism in Ernest Hemingway's prose, or to the foreboding poetry of T. S. Eliot and W. B. Yeats. The lingering astonishment at World War I can be recalled in the title of a Ford Madox Ford novel of 1925: *No More Parades*.

But there were happier, more American modes, too. The Harlem Renaissance—of which Mencken was an important champion—was in full swing. Adult education was on the rise, and the economy was growing. The novelist Willa Cather, whose reputation Mencken thought not equal to her merit, was a great admirer of the American character forged in the frontier experience. Though still in the prime of her career, Cather lamented that hers was a middle-aged philosophy in a time of youthful frivolity. She later said, "The world broke in two in 1922 or thereabouts."[13]

In the United States, it was the year of an important and controversial novel of the American everyman, *Babbitt*, by Sinclair Lewis, a close-in portrait of a bumbling, money-loving, self-admiring philistine. And between business and the oppositional culture of literature stood the young popular sensation F. Scott Fitzgerald, unburdening an infatuation with success but finding poetry in the experience of failure and unrequited love.

"Today," Mencken wrote in 1919, "it is no longer necessary for an American writer to apologize for writing American." But where Mencken suggested the passage of time had made such liberty possible, others credited Mencken himself. "American writers were finally able to take flight from the old tree and to trust for the first time their own dialect," his friend Edmund Wilson, the great literary critic, later said. "Mencken showed the positive value of our own vulgar heritage."[14]

CHAPTER 5

PHOTOS OF DWIGHT MACDONALD often show him smoking, usually a cigarette. In one picture from 1924, however, extending from the corner of his mouth and supported by his right hand is a pipe. He wears a morning coat, a waistcoat or vest, adorned by the chain of a pocket watch, and formal sponge-bag trousers. Depending on your whim, the image is thoughtful or pretentious. Young Master Dwight with his glistening, combed-back hair and thin, striking nose appears, deliberately, as the kind of young man who at any moment may be moved to say what *rilly separates curly* Henry James from late Henry James.

He sits across from another young gentleman, this one wearing a pince-nez and holding in his lap a volume, surely of some rather fine verse. A somewhat bolder-looking young man appears behind them both, sitting on the edge of a table, in his fingers a cigarette, unlit.

It is the era of flappers and jazz, of silent movies and Prohibition, half a decade before the stock market crash, but these fellows seem premodern. Their look suggests a highly self-conscious conservatism as one might find in old London clubs or, in America, among the so-called Brahmins of Boston, which is close enough. They are, in fact, New England aristocrats, upperclassmen at Phillips Exeter Academy in New Hampshire, the only members of a student group called the Hedonists

Club. And Dwight Macdonald, dressed like a man of the year, has yet to graduate from prep school.

The trio have their own stationery made with a letterhead reading out their articles of faith: "Cynicism, Estheticism, Criticism, Pessimism." Their motto, in French, is that of the artist who seeks to startle the complacent, middle class, and mediocre: "Pour épater les bourgeois."[1]

His father thinks Dwight precocious and mentions to Henry Seidel Canby, editor of the *Saturday Review of Literature*, that the boy is ready to review books for the paper. Even Dwight thinks this is a bit "thick," but he proudly mentions that his friends also consider him quite the "lion" for the essays he publishes in the school monthly.

His mother is concerned that he is either not socializing enough or not with the right people. Dwight takes up with younger boys at Exeter but is disappointed when they do not value literature as he does. In letters home he mentions giving up the distraction of reading Jonathan Swift so he can begin laying a foundation in Greek. One of the boys he is cultivating is coming over Saturday morning. "I am trying to get him interested in reading."

Very earnest and very bright, he keeps himself busy, works hard at his studies, and yet is no lonely introvert. He has been "talking, talking, talking," he says to his parents. "I should be a more brilliant conversationalist by this time if practice means anything."

LIKE MANY born writers, Macdonald was an incorrigible pronouncer, an unself-conscious and prolific maker of statements. This verbosity came with a great appetite for learning and culture. But pronouncing was also a matter of personal inclination. Like the Bloomsbury set in England at the time, he responded to the cultured person's calling to the fullest possible self-expression, the articulation of one's whole personality, done so unreservedly.

He wrote an amazing number of letters, to his parents and especially his old school chum Dinsmore Wheeler (pictured right, holding pince-nez), which together form a running commentary on life and the world at large, and contain more than a few nuggets that later appear burnished in well-known essays written for much, much larger audiences.

Macdonald got his start working for Henry R. Luce, the publisher of *Time*, *Life*, and *Fortune* magazines, and to whom, after quitting, he became a regular gadfly. And he developed into one of the cast of writers called New York intellectuals. His particular faction was known for its anti-Stalinist politics and its modernist enthusiasms.

He did not go to war, nor end up in Hollywood or Washington, where American popular culture and government were growing explosively, in both size and influence. But in New York City he found himself right smack in the middle of the great intellectual commotions of his era, from the Great Depression through World War II and into the 1960s.

He was an important soloist among America's increasingly noisy chorus of newspapers, magazines, and journals, an essayist about as good as anyone working at the time. He was also an operator, able to help organize and arrange funding for two key journals of the 1930s and '40s, *Partisan Review*, which he wrote for and helped edit, and *Politics*, which he founded and edited alone. Among his friends and correspondents were several of the most important writers and thinkers of his time. Early on, Sherwood Anderson paid him a visit. Mary McCarthy became a close friend. George Orwell and Albert Camus wrote to him from abroad. Hannah Arendt stood up for him.

FROM EXETER he went on to Yale, where he worked hard, wrote a lot, and continued pursuing a "P. of L.," his own shorthand for "philosophy of life," though he also used it in referring to James's *Portrait of a Lady*. When Dinsmore remarked on his fine work ethic, he took offense. "I admit I *do* work, but so did Dickens, so did Carlyle, so did quite a lot of other old boyos that make your tea-for-a-penny Chicago literati look like so many orangutans."

Other traits one notes in the critic as a young man are a lighthearted belligerence and the will to caricature. "I saw the great Henry Seidel Canby in the library," Dwight related once to Dinsmore. The editor Canby, who was also a professor at Yale, was, he said, "very small and insignificant, half bald and half scraggly hair . . . utterly commonplace." He noted the man's "faded, greenish brown suit" and his "funny shirt." Then he drew out a character story to fit: "He looks like the sort of man who would take a pedantic pleasure in collecting pre-revolutionary political pamphlets and in talking about them at great length." Evidence, then verdict: "Another idol shattered!"

In a letter to the president of Yale he protested against compulsory chapel and complained about last Sunday's sermon, unloosing a quick and brutal spray of invective that must have stunned the Honorable James Rowland Angell. The sermonizer, said Dwight, was guilty of "puerile, stupid twaddle" and seemed to have "a remarkable power of hypnotizing himself with magniloquent platitudes."

And so on: "Not one intelligent remark did he make." Lest the university president think the letter a joke of some kind, the writer vouched for every word: "All I have said here I am quite sincere in. Be assured."

He was like a faucet of words that could not be turned off. His mother, always worried about his social and professional prospects, advised that perhaps he should not have so caustically reviewed a faculty member's book in the student newspaper.

He reviewed people, just as he reviewed books and sermons. In 1925, to a girlfriend of Dinsmore's, he addressed a particularly vicious diatribe made all the worse by the smug vanity of its literary style: "I missed in you a certain dignity, an aloofness and sense of personal pride that I fancy is a sign of the lady. . . . Humility is one of the Christian virtues, but as G. K. Chesterton paradoxically points out, humility is merely pride carried to a splendid extreme."

Speaking of religion: "And then too there was the fact that you are a Jewess, and are rather obviously one, to make me react unfavorably. For I dislike rather violently the Jews as a race."

If he sounds villainous on the subject of Jews, he is little better on the subject of blacks. After seeing *The Birth of a Nation*, D. W. Griffith's pioneering silent film of 1915, known even then for its retrograde politics, Macdonald—a future *Today* show film critic—raved, "Its emotional kick is tremendous. You want to tear in pieces the cocky insolent niggers and carpetbaggers of 'after-the-war' days, and when the good old Ku Klux Klan comes sweeping down on horseback and rescues the besieged whites, you want to cheer."

Taking a step back from his initial visceral response, Macdonald writes, "In spite of my prejudice against the modern K.K.K., that was the way I felt."

Such words were, of course, less shocking in the 1920s, though even then the N-word was a "substandard" term, as the 1934 *Webster's Second* put it, "used familiarly, now chiefly contemptuously." Macdonald did sometimes use it unmaliciously, as when he raved to Dinsmore about Fletcher Henderson's jazz band: "Sassy, boy, that's some band . . . those niggers played like men possessed." The air of condescension, though, is quickly gone as he characteristically looks to name the precious qualities that elevated the musical performance: "The disciplined passion they exhibit is the very essence of the greatest art."

The semiprivate mental grapplings of youth, viewed in the harsh light of retrospect, deserve better than snide dismissal. Overall, Macdonald was a riveting if morally dubious specimen: Rare is the person of any age so joyfully committed to the tricky work of self-report.

ODDLY, HE did not immediately seek work as a writer upon graduation from Yale. He made the rounds of advertising firms in New York but accepted a position in the manager training program at Macy's, thinking a year of business experience would make him a more desirable applicant when he did go into advertising. "Up to this time, you know," he told Dinsmore, "literature was my end-all and be-all and my greatest ambition was to one day create it. Well, right now, I don't care much whether I ever set pen to paper again."

He frankly admired the businessmen he'd met, and felt an intemperate curiosity about them. "These men were so cold, so keen, so absolutely sure of themselves and wrapped up in business that I felt like a child before them." If this was the real world, it made campus life seem trivial. "I thought of profs here [at Yale] and back at Exeter who represented culture: they made a poor showing besides these men."

And the larger world of art and letters—whence recently came Eliot's *The Waste Land* and Hemingway's *The Sun Also Rises*, among other masterpieces—looked shrunken and useless. "I tell you, Dinsmore, that American art, letters, music, culture is done. There are hundreds of businessmen, thousands of them, who are better in their line of work than the best poet or painter we have today." Before the letter was sent, however, his excitement died down. "This is all too exaggerated," he said, adding that he had not forgotten his and Dinsmore's dream to live on a farm together. Nor was he shedding his literary ambitions. But business had caught his eye and he wanted to see what it was all about.

The year was 1928, and an infatuation with capitalism was not at all ridiculous. A boom market was on, and stock prices had more than tripled in five years. The American businessman not only seemed awesome to a young man deciding on a career; he seemed awesome to the increasing rolls of middle-class investors. He seemed awesome in general.

But by October the freshly minted Yale grad was growing sardonic. He was working the floor of Macy's, telling customers about the wonderful new fabric called rayon. Coming up was an exhibition from the Rayon Institute of America, intended, he told Dinsmore, "to educate the public about rayon, that is, in order to delude people into believing that rayon is twice as cheap a material as silk, which is true, and also twice as good, which . . . is also true." (Sarcastic ellipses in original.) For his part in the exhibition, trainee Macdonald would stand around and explain how this new wonder fabric was made and tell anyone "who is sap enough to question me that at eleven and three each and every day there will be shown at no charge a motion picture with the title *The Romance of Rayon.*"

Come the new year, he was fully contrite. "Now I realize what a fool I was to go to Macy's and from now on I freely accept that I am an intellectual-artist-man of ideas." In March 1929 Macdonald began a new job in the editorial trenches of Henry Luce's growing media empire.

CHAPTER 6

"SURELY GOODNESS AND MERCY shall follow me all the days of my life; and I will dwell in the house of the Lord forever." So sayeth the King James Bible—wrongly, according to Lindley Murray, writing in the late eighteenth century. The passage was "not translated according to the distinct and proper meaning of the words *shall* and *will*," said Murray. Instead, "it ought to be, *will follow me*, and, *I shall dwell*."[1]

Murray's textbook was the standard reference on grammar in the United States and was popular well into the nineteenth century, when few such books departed from the practice first observed by Johannis Wollis in 1615 that *shall* is to be used in the first person and *will* in the second and third persons.[2] From this came Murray's complaint about Psalm 23, as well as the rule that no one should ever use *will* to ask a question in the first person.

Will I? Never.

In the 1920s, this accumulated wisdom was examined by a professor named Charles Carpenter Fries, originally from Reading, Pennsylvania. He had taught ancient Greek for several years, until the subject was no longer required for admission to elite colleges, and then switched to teaching literature and composition before heading to the University of Michigan to study rhetoric and the history of English.[3]

At Michigan he encountered the scientific view of language. It was, for him, a "new world" that eventually changed his "whole view of language and grammar." His intellectual assumptions were completely overturned. "It seemed to me as revolutionary as the Copernican system in astronomy, the germ theory of disease in medicine, or the study of molecular structure in physics."[4]

Fries (pronounced like *freeze*) sought to observe the barest facts of language: not what might be said in an interpretive spirit, but what could be noticed and taken as physical evidence. Equipped, like many of his breed, with a vast patience for the minutest details, he once wrote a study of punctuation in Shakespeare. The other question that fascinated him concerned how language should be taught.

An enthusiast in temperament, he occasionally delivered sermons at First Baptist Church in Ann Arbor (he had gone to divinity school for two years and almost become a minister), and he was prone to moral exhortation at work, telling younger colleagues to consider the benefits of exercise, swimming in particular.[5] A very clear writer, Fries was uniquely suited to popularizing the findings of his adopted field, linguistics, and applying its lessons to those points of grammar and usage that make elementary students and even professional editors anxious. Full of liberal confidence, he didn't mind reducing the miasma of scholarship to a clear set of truisms the layman can understand.

And it bothered him that the layman didn't understand the lessons of linguistics. For over a hundred years the objective facts of language had been studied comparatively and historically, yet "the modern scientific view of language . . . and the results of scholarly investigations in the English language have not reached the schools."[6] In 1927, he became the president of the National Council of Teachers of English, where he sought to evangelize on behalf of the modern scientific view of grammar.

Teachers didn't seem to realize that pronunciation was enormously variable and there was no such thing as a single correct standard. Some even believed that spelling could be used as a guide to "correct" pronunciation. One teacher he'd encountered was so insistent on this point that she told her students that since *laughter* was spelled just like *daughter* and *slaughter*, it should be pronounced the same way—a ridiculous notion since, in modern English, spelling often provides little or no guidance on pronunciation.

The popular view of language was a primitive view, Fries noticed. People confused words with the things they represented and invented euphemisms to escape harsh realities, such as when they said *passing* to avoid saying *death*. They ascribed mystical powers to words. John Ruskin had said that *wife* truly meant "weaver," telling the womenfolk, "In the deep sense, you either must weave men's fortunes and embroider them, or feed upon them and bring them to decay." Thomas Carlyle saw in *king* a connection to *canning* (an obsolete word meaning ability), adding that the truly "able man" indeed "has a divine right over me."

These moralizing flourishes issued from the assumption that common words could be unmasked to reveal their secret selves and yield insights into the fundamental natures of wives and kings and so on. The next step was for such mistaken beliefs to limit the use of certain words. It had been said that *metropolis*, on the basis of its Greek roots in the words for mother and city, should only be used to refer to cathedral cities, thus "Canterbury is the metropolis of England, but London is not." *Aggravate*, according to Richard Grant White, "is misused . . . in the sense of provoke, irritate, anger." The supposedly correct word in such cases was *irritate*, while the true meaning of *aggravate* only covered situations where something bad was made worse. *Awful*, according to yet another master of the *king*'s English quoted by Fries, could only mean *awe-inspiring*.

But it was not so. "The real meaning of any word," argued Fries, "must be finally determined, not by its original meaning, its source or etymology, but by the content given the word in actual present usage. . . . Even a hardy purist would scarcely dare pronounce a painter's masterpiece *awful*, without explanations."[7]

Language was far more complicated than laymen realized. After he became a father, Fries would illustrate this hidden complexity using the word *chair*. The routine began with Fries asking for a definition. One of his children might answer, "A piece of furniture with four legs for sitting on." Then the questioning began. Do all chairs have four legs? Is a chair always for sitting on? Can a chair not be a thing at all but a word to describe something else? Can a person be a chair? Can a chair be an action?

Of course, not all chairs have four legs and not all chairs are for sitting on. And in *chair cushion*, the word only describes something that is definitely not a chair. And there are, of course, people called chairs, frequently a *chairman* or a *chairwoman* who, indeed, is said to *chair* (verb) a committee or some other body. Then how can the idea of a chair be stated to unify all these permutations of *chair*? Is it even possible? Can *chair* really be defined?

The lesson of the exercise was that no supposedly fixed element of *what a chair really is* could survive interrogation. Everything that seemed to belong to one example of *chair* could be shown to be completely absent from some other *chair*.[8]

When the language proved too elusive for the rules and definitions and principles we devised for it, the only recourse was to evidence. To test the meaning and usage of words, it was necessary to develop extensive empirical records of their appearance in speech and writing. To get to the heart of *shall* and *will*, Fries did just that.

He assembled fifty plays of the English theater, stretching back from the present day to 1550. The choice of literature type was a deft touch, as it offered "the best compromise between the living spoken English and the written English of literature."[9] He identified plays for each decade, and then (with help from his devoted wife, Agnes) tallied nearly twenty thousand usages. Finally, he examined each instance of *will* and *shall* to see how they compared with the rules promulgated by Lindley Murray and others.

Now, as far as Fries was concerned, a rule could only be verified by being widely followed. "There can thus never be in grammar an error that is both very bad and very common. The more common it is, the nearer it comes to being the best of grammar."

A rule of language that was not widely followed was, ipso facto, meaningless, an absurdity, without standing in reality. It was like the "true" meaning of *wife* or *metropolis* or *awful*, something made up by one of those mercurial writers whose opinions were based on a very partial understanding of language history and a most selective interest in the language as used by native speakers.

In first-person usage, Fries found that the traditional rules for *shall* and *will* held up, but examples from the first decades of the twentieth century showed *will* taking over an increasing share of *shall*'s business. And outside of the first person, the traditional rules bore less and less of a resemblance to actual usage. The *Oxford English Dictionary* said that in second-person questions, *shall* is the "normal" word to use. This was not evidenced by Fries's research: "Of the 512 questions in the second person but 7 or 1.3 percent use *shall*; all the rest employ *will*."

Fries looked at *shall* and *will* in British and American plays published since 1900. In several categories, *shall* was perceptibly vanishing. This was especially problematic. In the United States, almost no textbooks acknowledged the existence of any forms of the future tense other than those using *shall* and *will* as auxiliary verbs. *Going to, plan to, desire to, intend to*—there were many in common use, all ignored to reserve room for *shall*, the language's supposed equal partner in the future tense.

Modern usage also called into question the words' standard definitions. Characters in the plays Fries examined frequently used *shall* to express determination or intention and *will* to express simple futurity—the opposite of what many traditional rules prescribed.

In the 1920s, *Shall I?* was still a common usage, but it would not be for long. A few years after Fries's study was released, Bell Telephone allowed a researcher to listen in and count words spoken in the phone conversations of its customers. In the course of 1,900 conversations, *will* as an auxiliary term was used 1,305 times. *Shall* appeared only six times.[10] The long-term trend was obvious. Twenty-five years hence, Alfred Hitchcock fans would leave the theater with the voice of a very proper Doris Day singing in their heads, using *will* in the first person to ask, "Will I be rich? Will I be pretty?"

Fries showed that the roles of *shall* and *will* had changed a great deal since their usage was first described and then encoded in rules—rules that could not be relied on to predict or describe modern usage. Moreover, the conventional understanding of the future tense in English was hopelessly inadequate.

His paper, "The Periphrastic Future with *Shall* and *Will* in Modern English," technical in nature and scientific in method, was one of many flares across the bow of classroom grammar in the 1920s and '30s. The infamous *It's me*, the crime of dangling modifiers, the prohibition on split infinitives, the traditional understanding of subject-verb agreement, the use of double negatives, slang, and many other notions were being subjected to empirical examination to determine their actual status in literature and speech. A rebellion was under way against the rule of rules, and Fries was leading it.

CHAPTER 7

IN 1927, THE AMERICAN editor Henry Seidel Canby attended a conference in London for the Society for Pure English. The society had been founded in 1913 by a band of prominent traditionalists that included the poet Robert Bridges, the essayist Sir Walter Raleigh, Logan Pearsall Smith (an American-born writer living in England whom Dwight Macdonald admired and corresponded with),[1] and Henry Bradley, the second editor of the *Oxford English Dictionary*. Its prospectus called for "preserving all the richness in differentiation in our vocabulary" and holding on to "nice grammatical usage." Assimilationist toward foreign words (wanting them to, please, surrender their funny accents and bad spelling at the border), the society "opposed whatever is slip-slop and careless, and all blurring of hard-won distinctions."[2]

The appearance of an *OED* editor, Bradley, among the society's founding members seems unlikely. No group of scholars had done more than the dictionary's editors and volunteer contributors to win respect for the historical study of language change, an achievement at odds with the society's own view of English as all the more perfect the less it changed.

But Bradley had his bugaboos. *Swashbuckling* he thought a terrible addition to the English language, and, for all his historical perspective, he wondered, When did people start calling the upper part of the human face a for-hed? Everyone knew it was supposed to be pronounced for-id.

In a letter to Bridges, Bradley voiced the conflict of one who accepts change as a fact of life but is not confident that all change is for the good. "Because people used to ignore the fact of language being a natural growth," he wrote, "and to propound futilities about 'improving' it, there has arisen a tendency to run in the opposite extreme."

Canby was no stranger to London, a town he liked and felt comfortable in, and as the co-author of some books on writing and grammar he might even have been received as an authority. He was also one of the first literary scholars to believe that American literature was deserving of serious intellectual attention and not merely a trivial subsidiary of the great British tradition. A graduate course he had created at Yale in 1919 to study American literature had gotten off to a rough start but was possibly the first of its kind.[3]

Attending the conference were a variety of scholars, writers, and other cultural figures: the head of the British Museum, George Bernard Shaw, Sir William A. Craigie, another *OED* editor who later headed the *Dictionary of American English*. Canby and the philologist Louise Pound, among others, represented the old colonies, but, alas, America's most well-known student of language, H. L. Mencken, the great champion of the American language, whose other politics had gotten him into trouble during World War I and would do so again in the next war, did not come. Mencken admired English but not England.

Canby was then developing into a major publishing figure: He was the founding editor of the *Saturday Review of Literature*, a successful weekly newspaper of intelligently written but rarely scathing book reviews. He liked to tell the story of a publisher who claimed that his paper's review of a book had earned him a million dollars. According to Canby, a year later the same publisher complained that a negative review in Canby's paper cost him a million dollars.

Canby's views of books were becoming even more consequential to the fortunes of individual authors and publishing houses. Starting in 1926, he became the chairman of the selection committee for the Book-of-the-Month Club, which began with fewer than five thousand subscribers and reached sixty thousand one year later, hardly slowing down for the next two decades.[4]

Although Canby, to a dandyish undergraduate at Yale, might appear "very small and insignificant, half bald and half scraggly hair . . . utterly commonplace," he was a great example of a slowly fading type, what might be called (though only in retrospect) an establishment intellectual. And not all the undergraduates disdained him. A couple of years ahead of Dwight Macdonald at Yale, Briton Hadden and Henry Luce, the future founders of *Time* magazine, thought Canby sympathetic enough that they showed him drafts of their magazine idea, written in longhand on yellow sheets of paper.

He described himself and his generation of academics as being under an English spell, which had encouraged him to accept an invitation from the British Ministry of Information to visit England during World War I and function as a freelance cultural emissary. Yet there in Britain he began to discern the limits of his Anglophilia and discover within himself a hunger to know more about his own nation's literature.

A Quaker by birth, he became a believer in the League of Nations. Though the 1920s seem notable for youthful nonsense, Canby, very much the responsible adult, prospered and enjoyed the kind of life that appeared, especially to him, illustrative of his own times. He looked back to the nineteenth century as the Age of Confidence, and was perfectly accepting of the philosophical distance between himself and the young writers of the 1920s, whose literature he more than once described as "defeatist," a term coined in the wake of World War I.

He had mixed feelings about the literary tendencies of Hemingway and company. "What the new writers were experimenting with . . . was a fresh use of those words and others drawn from colloquial speech, and still more, new techniques of literary structure." They made "their books read more like men talking well in the nineteen-twenties and less like something called literature."

As students of the language later mapped it out, the rise of colloquial patterns in public speech had been under way since before the Civil War and could be seen in the folksy speech of politicians and the down-home language of some newspapers. But for it to be breaking into the ranks of serious literature was a remarkable change. Here it was affecting the upper registers of usage, where one had expected to find the bookishly correct voice of cultivation. But, increasingly, literary language was no longer the same as formal language.

Such experiments, Canby thought, actually made for a welcome departure from the status quo ante. What he called "the civilized style" of the nineteenth century had become so polished by the 1920s that it was eerily predictable. "A reader could shut his eyes and guess what was coming next."

And so now there was writing that sounded different and kept you guessing, but sometimes it was awful. Witness the very modern prose of Gertrude Stein—one of the first Americans to take up Paris, she was a major influence on the younger writers who came later. Ugh, Canby might have said, were he too becoming more colloquial. "The pages of disintegrated grammar and repetitive diction which she wrote and called fiction, used to upset me like a bad dream." It reminded him of the poet e. e. cummings, who Canby suspected had ceremoniously dispensed with capital letters to distract the reader from the fact that he had so little to say. Stein "picked the English words with color and significant sound, regardless of meaning."

The following sentence by Stein, on the question of repetition, was both an example and a defense of her terrible writing: "Repetition then comes slowly then to be to one who has it to have loving repeating as natural being comes to be a full sound telling all the being in each one such a one is ever knowing."

If this was the new thing in literature, Canby didn't mind being considered a little old-fashioned. But the Society for Pure English conference did not prove to be a gathering of mossbacks. And this was what made it so important, Canby thought.

The conference addressed the international spread of English but settled no controversies of usage. The mother tongue was not declared sacred and in need of defending. Dangling modifiers, though surely an irritation to some, were not recommended for amputation. There were no unanimously passed motions on reuniting the split infinitive. The rule of rules was not upheld. Yet the proceedings "marked the end of one era and the beginning of another."

One simple thing happened. "Without a single dissenting voice we agreed that there was no longer a single ideal standard for the English language except excellence. That the best written and spoken usage of New York or San Francisco were as authoritative as those of London or Oxford if their influences were felt upon the broadening or the strengthening of the tongue."

So, not only were American writers seizing the right to sound like Americans; this esteemed gathering hosted by British scholars and cultural leaders was formally acknowledging that right. The whole thing smacked of Mencken and the spreading influence of new linguistic scholarship. "What we accepted in theory," said Canby, "Mencken was to continue to document in his admirable books."

But his respect for Mencken and American literature didn't save the mainstream Canby from the disdain of the younger generation of writers and poets.[5] A few years later a Harvard student was having his verse torn up by Ezra Pound, who called it "too poetic." Pound suggested he find some other way to make himself useful.

"What is useful?" the apostle asked.

"If you have the guts," said Pound, "you might murder Henry Seidel Canby."

Instead, the young man started New Directions, a successful American publisher of avant-garde literature. It was not the death of Canby or his brand of conventional wisdom but it was a sign of things to come.

CHAPTER 8

SMITH COLLEGE PRESIDENT WILLIAM Allan Neilson waited for Professor Withington to call on him at his office. The two walked across campus together. On their way Neilson asked what the day's topic was. This left fewer than ten minutes to plan the lecture in his head before delivering it.[1] Not a problem. This was Neilson's routine, and he was still at the height of his powers as an educator. Dates and names from literary history were at his fingertips, his trademark wit ready to fire.

He spoke at daily chapel, too. He received faltering students at his house for tea to assure them that whatever their failings in the classroom, they would not be ostracized. In the evenings he attended countless meetings and receptions, but wherever he went, he was always, always setting the tone.

Chapel was "voluntary-compulsory" in the early 1920s. Neilson had made it entirely voluntary but attendance plummeted. The student government then voted to require attendance four days a week, establishing an honor system that relied on students to report their own absences.

President Neilson was intensely popular with the students, whom he rarely called girls. Their budding intellectual and emotional maturity was always foremost in his thoughts, though he had other concerns, too. Smith students, he felt, should avoid upsetting the locals. He did not mind when they cut their hair and wore it in a bob. But women field hockey players were expected to wear skirts over their bloomers on their way to practice. And until it was proven unnecessary, an invisible hat line remained drawn on Main Street, forbidding students from venturing below Beckman's bareheaded.

Many were the rules on campus, though few were overbearing. Students were not permitted to have cars, but an exception was made for second-term seniors in good standing. Dancing the Charleston was prohibited in the upstairs of dormitories, to protect the rickety wooden floors. Smoking cigarettes was permitted, but never in one's room, and smokers had to suffer the intense pleasure of being scolded by President Neilson: "Smoking is a disgusting, expensive, and unhygienic habit," he said with a gleam in his eye, "to which I am devoted."

What really got him going, though, was *how* these young women smoked: "You do not smoke like ladies; you do not even smoke like gentlemen; you smoke like fools."

Neilson was known and admired off campus, too, as an authority on the subject of higher education. When the postwar surge of college enrollment among men began to taper off, he noticed the uptick in female enrollment continued, and wrote about it in the *Nation*, the progressive weekly whose literary and intellectual standards tended to be old-fashioned.

Female education was, indeed, becoming commonplace. "During the last few years," he noted, "the remaining prejudices against the college woman, whether held by young men or old ladies, have been rapidly disappearing."[2]

Like Charles William Eliot, he was a liberal of the superior type: a believer in eugenics and the League of Nations. Where and when a society's leaders were able to come together and think rationally about the problems of their time, it was possible to advance the cause of goodness. Progress was not inevitable, but it was possible. This aristocratic optimism was often reflected in his chapel talks and his conception of the role of a college president as a wise man at large.

In 1924, Asa S. Baker, president of G. & C. Merriam Company, the makers of the Webster's dictionaries, invited William Allan Neilson to become their wise man at large, the titular editor of their forthcoming unabridged dictionary, *Webster's New International Dictionary*, Second Edition.

The idea appealed to Neilson's feeling that while higher education should be reserved for the "fit," education should do more for society than adorn a few lucky individuals. In this light he viewed the legacy of Noah Webster. "There is probably no book that has been written in a hundred years that has done so much in this respect for the country at large as his Dictionary."[3]

Still, Neilson sometimes felt an impatience with the rise of equality in schooling. In 1926, he recalled the pioneers who had made up the first class at Smith. They were "brought into this place because of their appetite for intellectual things." By contrast, "today we have here two thousand students gathered—one must confess—in obedience to a social convention. . . . Education is being defeated by its own success. Education is 'the thing.'"[4]

The work at Merriam took him an hour away to Springfield on alternate Tuesdays. He presided as head of the Editorial Board, which consisted of himself, Mr. Baker, general editor Thomas A. Knott, formerly of the University of Iowa, and managing editor Paul W. Carhart. The board hashed out decisions on innumerable items of style, staffing, and schedule. Discussions were sometimes heated, and the sounds of argument could be heard through the door.

It was not always easy to strike a balance between what could be admitted privately among men of like mind and what it was appropriate to state publicly in a commercial book that might end up sitting in tens, if not hundreds, of thousands of family rooms. Some words had no place in this book or the smaller ones that derived from it. Especially tricky were those words and expressions, seemingly coined five minutes ago, that lacked the dignity of age.

Did *hot dog* belong in the dictionary? This very question the board reportedly debated for over an hour.[5]

The dictionary was a kind of arbiter between the worthy and the unworthy. A person hoping to learn what was correct in a given situation should not be left in the dark or confronted by more information than was useful.

The dictionary user came with questions; the successful dictionary provided answers, clear and unambiguous. The most successful dictionary contained the most answers.

While colleges and universities recognized that specialization had placed increasing amounts of knowledge far beyond the grasp of laymen, the dictionary business continued to operate on the assumption that it was possible to distill all that was worth knowing. Perhaps one reason the work attracted William Allan Neilson was that he was no longer a specialist. He gave up classroom lecturing in 1926, after he found he could no longer answer students' questions about the latest literary theory. The author of several books and the co-editor of several anthologies, he of course knew a great deal about his subject, but his research had been undermined by administrative work.

Yet there was much in his work as a college president that resonated with being the editor of *Webster's Second*. In both cases he was a figurehead, an institutional symbol. Of course he did work, keeping tabs on a hundred little things at the college while giving voice to the intellectual and moral verities the college sought to instill. And at Merriam he presided over the Editorial Board, which routinely asserted its authority over the tiniest details. He personally took charge of two special categories of words: British university terms and Scottishisms. But he was no more a professional lexicographer than he was a full-time literary scholar. And yet to the women on campus and people beyond he personified the worlds of education and scholarship.

This gave him the freedom and credentials to comment on the passing scene. And among all that was going on in the 1920s, two subjects caught his eye.

Despite the decade's well-earned reputation for dissipation, he noticed in 1927 the beginnings of a return to older moral standards. "We have turned the corner and are now moving with our backs to the Jazz Age," he wrote in a letter to the Smith alumnae council. "We are reverting to Victorian formalism." He mentioned that a freshman was said to have "burst" into Northrop House and asked "who that man was with the little gray beard who twice bowed to her on the campus without being introduced!"[6]

Neilson himself was still a Victorian in some important ways. In the new culture of candor he maintained the habits of one more comfortable when much is left unsaid. And not just about sex, vulgarity, and other taboo subjects. For Neilson it might include one's own self. In 1926, in an essay he wrote about the life of Charles William Eliot, he described how Eliot had taken on the job of editing the Harvard Classics. Neilson paused to mention that Eliot had not done this work alone, but had chosen an assistant from the Harvard faculty—and yet Neilson did not mention even parenthetically that he was that assistant.

Nor did an essay on censorship he wrote for the *Atlantic* mention his firsthand experience with editing out "naughty bits."[7] He did make it clear that he felt some sympathy with these efforts to protect man from "pander[ing] to the lower side of his nature."

As a writer, he was a discusser, not a pronouncer, and he labored to appreciate his opponents' arguments. He seemed especially concerned with protecting children from what might be called filth. But he despaired of employing postmasters and policemen as literary critics and could imagine no solid legal or moral ground for "depriving the adult citizen of the privilege of choosing his own books and his own plays and pictures."

Once a self-censorer, Neilson now wrote, more or less, against the practice, his arguments affecting a kind of slow divorce from the opposite thesis only after a demonstration of close familiarity.

He finished by quoting the English literary critic Sir Walter Raleigh, a founding member of the Society for Pure English, on the subject of Henry Fielding, the great eighteenth-century novelist whose scatological comedy would certainly have been a frequent target for censorship were it not so old. "Some literary critics, it is true, with a taste for subdued tones in art, have found some of Fielding's loudest notes too strident for enfeebled ears, but not to the great musician can the whole range of the orchestra, not to the great painter can the strongest contrast of colors, be profitably denied."

As he had in his inaugural address at Smith College, Neilson borrowed his most forthright statements from someone else, and again someone British, underplaying his own rooting interest while giving a preferential nod to the humanists and scholars with whom he kept faith. It was an elaborately dignified gesture, spoken to the like-minded after pages of quietly hearing out the un-like-minded.

The principle he finally embraced could be described thus: For some people—all of them adults—it was important that potentially offensive pictures and language face no restrictions on circulation. But there were always the children to consider, and here William Allan Neilson understood and shared the concerns of mothers and priests and schoolteachers, even if he saw no simple way of addressing the problem.

CHAPTER 9

IN THE SPRING OF 1929, a Yale friend helped Dwight Macdonald land a job writing for the business section of *Time*, the cheeky news digest started by Yalies Henry Luce and Briton Hadden, then only six years old but stunningly successful. Aside from his work in rayon, however, Macdonald actually had few qualifications.

Not that Henry Luce cared. As Macdonald later put it, Luce would "hire poets straight out of Yale or Princeton and set them to work writing about the price of steel rails."

Knowledge was less important than talent. "A smart fellow can do anything he puts his mind to," explained Macdonald, sympathetically, and "a brilliant amateur is likely to be more productive than a prosaic expert."[1]

This smart fellow also became part of the team planning a new magazine, which, he told his friend Dinsmore, would be "devoted to glorifying the American businessman"—work the twenty-three-year-old "intellectual-artist-man of ideas" found "not unpleasant" but ultimately unsatisfying.[2]

Luce himself was not at all ironic about his new magazine, to be called *Fortune*. He stated its mission in a memo to the Time Inc. Board of Directors, using the breathless inverted phrasing that typified his preferred style of journalism. "Accurately, vividly, and concretely to describe Modern business is the greatest journalistic assignment in history."

It was a "saga" with universal appeal. It united Americans of all kinds. Business was "the single common denominator of interest among the active leading citizens of the U.S."

Fortune would be no simpering mouthpiece for industry; it would contain no "ghost-written banalities by Big Names." It would be smart: "If Babbitt doesn't like literature," wrote Luce, evoking Sinclair Lewis's well-known creation (whom Luce actually thought an unfair caricature of the American entrepreneur), "he doesn't have to read it."[3]

Printed on large sheets of thick, expensive paper, with great illustrations and the classic photographs of Walker Evans, *Fortune* would also be gorgeous. But pricey: a dollar an issue at a time when newspapers sold for pennies and *Time* cost fifteen cents. Its writers would include Archibald MacLeish and Dwight's Exeter buddy James Agee, whom he helped get a job.

Proposed in November 1929, as the stock market was crashing—ending a bull market that had lasted six years—the plan for *Fortune* quickly won approval from *Time*'s corporate governors. The magazine debuted in February 1930.[4]

In 1931, the phrase *American Dream* was first recorded—just as the idea was losing its purchase on reality. Macdonald took little notice of the degenerating economy, though he found much to complain of: women who gave him the "go-by" and his job, "8 hours of mental tension" each day that left him famished for reading, conversation, and leisure. There was the consolation of alcohol, which despite Prohibition the young writer had little trouble obtaining. "I went to dinner with the James Hamills, drank 3 cocktails, and just managed to stay above the table."

He berates his friend Dinsmore for being "one of these cover-to-cover readers of *Time*. I thought they were all automobile salesmen or professors of sociology," naming two ultramodern types with a professional interest in American gullibility. He tells Dinsmore that he should be using his free time to read Dante, Cervantes, Plato, or even the great Russian novelists.

The rhetorical conventions of magazine journalism irritate him: the chatty, lighthearted style, the crumbled form of predigested information, the phony familiarity. "Another rule: be personal!" This he thinks inspired by "all these cigarette testimonials written by dukes and sea captains, trying to kid the straphanger, the homo boobiensis, that he is entering into some sort of *personal* relationship with the dukes and captains." But for all his contempt, he is very good at his work, and, increasingly, he earns a handsome salary. Success, however, is neither humbling nor entirely gratifying.

Echoing the antidemocratic prejudices of H. L. Mencken, whose own magazine, the *American Mercury*, was one of several being eclipsed in the fullness of *Time*, Macdonald is drawn to those authors heavily favored by sensitive young men of worldly ambition. He reads Stendhal's *The Red and the Black* and quotes approvingly Stendhal's line that "the Tyranny of public opinion, and what opinion!, is as stupid in the small towns of France as in the United States of America."

Inevitably, Macdonald is soon reading Friedrich Nietzsche, philosophy's love poet to those tormented souls waiting to be hailed by a world they despise. Among a list of maxims he copies down for Dinsmore, one celebrates the spirited contrarian: "A sign of strong character, when once the resolution has been taken, [is] to shut the ear even to the best counterarguments."[5]

The magazine he worked for he called "Lousy Fortune." Each month he wrote one article about four to six thousand words long—which is highly productive for a magazine writer. Paid seventy-five dollars a week, he decided to ask for a raise.

Luce said, "You shouldn't always be thinking about money, Dwight. You should trust us to look out for your interests and see you get well taken care of, so stop worrying and keep your eye on the ball."[6]

But it worked. A raise soon came through. And despite all of Luce's hoorah spirit concerning the saga of American business, the staff, led by the young man of letters Archibald MacLeish, pulled the magazine left. According to Macdonald, "Luce was journalist enough to see that the New Deal was news and that big business, temporarily, wasn't."[7]

Around the time *Hooverville* was coined as a name for the impromptu shack towns sheltering a growing number of homeless families, *Fortune* boldly staked a claim on the little-mentioned story of the growing economic and social crisis. The magazine ran an enormous feature piece, packed with photographs and reports from across the country, shaming the government for failing to address or even gather information on the crisis. Taking its title from Hoover's callous and untrue remark that "No one has starved," the article woke many other newspapers and magazines to the story of the Depression, which had until then been downplayed in the mainstream press.

IN 1933, a year of bank runs and bank closings, of plummeting values and diminishing sales, Franklin Delano Roosevelt takes office, the first Democratic president since Woodrow Wilson, and, again like Wilson, a terrific speechmaker.

With upper-class Ivy League diction familiar to someone of Macdonald's education, the new president sounds like a consummate highbrow as he delivers his inaugural address. He drops his final *r*'s as he promises "this great nation will endure as it has endured" and sounds a bit Shakespearean as he flattens the second *a* in *again*.[8]

He sounds not at all like Gertrude Stein when he repeats a word, but instead grand and classical: "The only thing we have to fear is fear itself." Mixing the biblical and the social, he blames "the money changers" who "have fled from their high seats in the temple of our civilization."

AS THE New Deal begins to address the national tragedy of 23 percent unemployment, Macdonald develops a social conscience, or rather meets one. Nancy Rodman is a society girl with left-wing connections and literary tastes that complement her new boyfriend's. They read Shakespeare together. A graduate of Brearley, the Manhattan prep school, and Vassar College, the former debutante has a grandfather who was president of the stock exchange and a brother who is a fixture on the burgeoning radical scene. "She's a sweet girl," says Dwight, "even if she does let me in for drearily long-winded, left-wing political meetings."

She persuades him to read *The Communist Manifesto* and Trotsky's autobiography. At the same time Macdonald's journalism heads into the problems of labor and economics as a social issue. He has already adopted a stilted view of the great innovators of American business. "Take Ford out of his factory and Edison out of his laboratory, you would have two individuals indistinguishable in spirit, in taste, in intellectual scope, from millions of Americans." Which, of course, is to say "spirit and taste" of a rather low variety. "If these men are the Lincolns and Napoleons of today, the human race has gone to hell."[9]

CHAPTER 10

IN MAY 1931, STERLING Andrus Leonard died in a tragic canoeing accident. He and another passenger hung on to their capsized boat for two hours before Leonard succumbed to the cold, shifting waters of Lake Mendota in Wisconsin. An associate professor of English, the forty-three-year-old scholar was on the verge of publishing a sensational contribution to the language controversies of his time.

His paper, "Current English Usage," commissioned by the National Council of Teachers of English, would be called by the *New York Times* "the most thorough overhauling the English language has had in years."[1] Work on the study was close to done at the time of his death, but it remained for others to finish and bring out the next year.

The canoe's other passenger was I. A. Richards, saved perhaps by his own athleticism. An accomplished mountain climber, Richards was better known as a prominent Cambridge University critic and author of *Practical Criticism*, a penetrating look at how we actually react to literature—as opposed to what we are taught to think. Richards was rescued and remained an active scholar for decades to come. Today he is best remembered for announcing the dawn of New Criticism, which in the 1930s and '40s taught English departments to focus above all on the literary text through the process of "close reading." Its motto—and Richards's, too—could have been "Take nothing for granted."

Leonard was present at the dawn of a different intellectual development, one every bit as stirring: the new linguistics. In the 1920s and '30s, American scholars of the English language staged a well-coordinated rebellion against traditional authorities of grammar and usage: British example and the rules of classroom grammar. From the time of the founding, America's relationship toward its language suffered an *inferiority complex*—a term that dates to 1922 in the Merriam files. The new attitude was summed up (overstated, better yet) by the chest-thumping title of H. L. Mencken's polemic, *The American Language*. But the new attitude was not genuinely anti-British, it was empiricist, concerned with how the language is actually used as opposed to how it is taught.

The two men made a curious pair, and not because of their nationalities. Richards is known for his endlessly complicated account of what happens when a person reads a piece of literature and arrives at something called meaning. Leonard's work on grammar and usage seems lighthearted and even a little naïve by comparison. Yet linguists and literary critics were departmental colleagues on most college faculties. They spoke a common language and reviewed each other's work. A linguist might even see himself, as both Leonard and Charles C. Fries did, as not merely a student of the realities of language, particularly speech, but also as a scholar of, or even champion of, literature.

The unlucky canoeists also had this in common: an interest in linguistic experiments that tested common assumptions against real-world experience. Every week for an academic term Richards had assigned his honors literature students at Cambridge poems to read. The poems—some great, some minor—were presented anonymously, without any information about the authors or periods. The readers were required to describe their reactions. What followed was, in Richards's estimation, the queerest brew of nonsense: stock opinions, hopeless guesses, and a good deal of ignorant, defensive, interpretive flailing.

Not only could the students not identify the authors, they could not distinguish important poetry from the commonplace. Richards used the word *obtuse* to describe their reactions. Few students evinced even the slightest feel for poetry. The technical clues of structure and diction were beyond the noticing of these young scholars. Evidence of genius, there on the page in black and white, went undetected. Their fancy education hadn't actually trained these students to recognize Shakespeare by the quality of his writing.

This exercise taught students, above all, to consider their almost complete dependence on past scholarship and received opinion when forming judgments about works of literary art. And, in turn, it helped inspire a new method of study whose goal was to reconnect literary scholarship to the simple act of reading carefully.

Leonard's experiment also concerned tricky questions of language and opinion. But instead of teaching a wary regard for received opinion and traditional standards, it sought to overturn them.

He impaneled a distinguished cast of linguists, educators, authors, and businessmen. Henry Seidel Canby and H. L. Mencken were among its litterateurs, while its linguists included Edward Sapir, Otto Jespersen, and George Philip Krapp, all leading names in the study of language.[2] And judging from the quoted comments of its businessmen, these smooth-tongued Babbitts were far from your average Rotarians.

This was no bottom-up study organized to examine the language in the unrestrained variety of its au naturel state. Yet asking people what they believed instead of asking what the rulebooks decreed was, all by itself, considered radical. Said the *Times* about Leonard's study, "The King's English is going democratic nowadays, in a revolution led by no other people than some of the teachers of English themselves." This last was a reference to Leonard's publisher, the National Council of Teachers of English, which had come a long way from the cheery days of Good Grammar Week.

Only the year before Leonard's study came out, a *Times* reporter had collected much more typical material, in Milwaukee, at the annual teachers' conference. The superintendent of English in the Newark, New Jersey, public schools had haughtily insisted there was but one way to pronounce *vagary*, and it rhymed with Mary. A teacher had rattled off—with his eyes closed, one imagines—a list of the most common grammatical mistakes made by students: *ain't, I done, I seen, them things*, and the notorious double negative *I didn't do nothing*.[3]

With "Current English Usage," however, the teachers' association would join the vanguard of linguistic opinion in which words like "mistake" and "correctness" were, more and more, being handled with ironic quotation marks.[4]

Leonard's panelists were shown over two hundred English-language expressions "of whose standing there might be some question." The goal was to show how far from the rules these VIPs of culture strayed in their own thinking about what was proper and acceptable. Another was to show how the opinions of linguists, singled out in Leonard's survey as "expert" opinion, differed from lay opinion.

Like Richards's experiment, Leonard's shone an unflattering light on many of its test subjects. The laymen just didn't understand what the experts knew to be true. Their opinions were restrained by the prejudices of their educational background.

Less intentionally, the study also showed that its well-known linguists were no cold-blooded rationalists, but in fact as capable of flip and catty comment as the ignorant snobs of old, whose authority they sought to topple.

Shown the sentence *One rarely enjoys one's luncheon when one is tired*, the linguists agreed the sentence was, alas, without blemish. But there is correct and then there is "correct," not wrong exactly but too fussy to be considered worthy. One linguist called the sentence's clothesline of *ones* "semi-literate straining for correctness."

The sentence *The man was very amused* was rebuked for its gratuitous *very*, with a linguist commenting, "'There seems to be a touch of shadowy elegance about that which can be justified no more than the carrying of a stick or the wearing of spats." Take that.

In a footnote, Leonard himself commented on the use of *an* (instead of *a*) before *historical* as "one of a number of expressions among the 'established usages' which might be called *hyper-urbanisms*—artificial, trite, pedantic, or stilted attempts at correctness."

Other examples might have been described as hyper-dubious: *You was mistaken about that, John*. On this occasion, dry humor and historical perspective won out, as a linguist commented, "Good 100 years ago."

An expression using *different than* (as opposed to the more respectable *different from*) made a British linguist quite irate. Not that he objected; he objected to the objections.

The poor persecuted *different than* was, he said, "good as literary or formal (but wrong for colloquial use). 'From, to, than, all in best authors'—Concise Oxf. Dict. *Differs* plus dative (Tacitus and elsewhere. Tell the purists Tacitus was a Roman historian and Latin was his native language)."

And he wasn't finished. "The reference to *differ* is as superficial as most puristic rubbish (speaking dispassionately). The logical analogies of opposite to, contrary to, dissimilar to, would never have occurred to those boneheads."[5]

"Current English Usage" did not examine the speech and writing of its subjects; it examined their opinions. Authors were "the most severe group of judges." Businessmen were sometimes all about correctness, and other times, as with the split infinitive, as liberal as any linguist. English teachers, "possibly influenced by the pronouncements of sundry handbooks," tended to puritanism, wrote Leonard, as when they condemned the slang but timely expression *busted* in "The stock market collapse left me *busted*."

The study was well designed to pose provocative questions, for instance, Did you know that over a third of linguists say *don't* is acceptable colloquial English in *Martha don't sew as well as she used to*? Well, it was true. And that six of seventeen prominent linguists gave the okay to *ain't*, calling it colloquial and acceptable in educated speech in *I suppose I'm wrong, ain't I*?

Fifteen years before Winston Churchill stirred a fuss by saying, "It is me" (instead of *It is I*), the usage was considered by these linguists to be *all right*, which they also considered all right. The redundant expressions *from whence* and *reason why* were given a pass. The fading of the subjunctive form was acknowledged but hardly mourned as *I wish I was wonderful*, quoted from a J. M. Barrie comedy, slid by with two-thirds of the judges describing it as good informal English. (The formal rule on this would have led to *I wish I were wonderful*.) The line on singular-plural ambiguities was not entirely upheld as *None of them are here* was approved. An unorthodox use of *shall* was considered acceptable, but Leonard commented, "The whole [*will*-versus-*shall*] matter is at present surrounded by a cloud of uncertainty."

"Current English Usage" became a promotional piece for the new linguistics, especially its open hostility to classroom grammar. Leonard himself, a student of both educational history and modern pedagogical methods, was pitiless when it came to the teaching of rules not supported by actual usage.

"Probably no study is allotted more time and is more barren of results than that from which our grammar schools derive their name. After five or six years of grammar work in the elementary schools; after endless diagramming (which is but parsing in pictorial imagination); after painful memorizing of rules and definitions; and after constant composition of illustrative exercises, many a high school freshman cannot write or speak a decent English sentence."[6]

From the time of Samuel Johnson and Jonathan Swift, it had been common to bemoan the state of the language, but with the rise of the new linguistics, the complainers were put on notice to show cause, to buttress their suppositions about what was correct with real-world evidence. This did not, however, bring an end to such complaints. Rather, the complaints had to become far more selective, made with an eye to the historical record. So, bitching about the terrible language of others did not go out of style, even among linguists. On the contrary, language snobbery now required a much finer sense of actual usage.

CHAPTER 11

DWIGHT MACDONALD GREW A goatee and traded his vested shirt-and-tie for a chambray work shirt, which he wore to the office. Yet Macdonald did not all of a sudden hand his heart to the unionists, the communists, or other radicals. Covering the Communist Party of the U.S.A. for *Fortune*, he found the communists to be a "maddening race for an outsider because of the great air of mystery and conspiracy they adopt."[1] In July 1934, he, Walker Evans, and another writer, Geoffrey Hellman, visited Camp Nitgedaiget, a Communist Party training center in Westchester County, just outside the city.

The weekend "came near making a fascist out of me." After bathing with the communists and eating off their dirty dishes, he notes, "the comrades were 99 44/100 percent pure Yiddish and they had that peculiar Yiddish love of living in each other's laps that you can observe any day at Coney Island." By Sunday noon, he could take no more of the "squirming mass." He and his companions, he tells Nancy, "stole away to the Westchester Embassy Club . . . where we bathed in a clean if capitalistic pool and drank a couple of Tom Collinses in capitalistic solitude."

This story of comic misadventure does not go over well with Nancy.

Four days later, Dwight is backpedaling. "Yes, I agree entirely. . . . Last weekend didn't change my belief that, all else aside, communism is the only way out of the mess our society is in." Not only that, he wants her to know that he has been flying his political flag at the office. "The other day I had a two-hour argument with Luce about *Fortune* not having enough social consciousness."

That fall, after an announcement in the *New York Times*, Dwight Macdonald married Nancy Rodman. The tension with Luce, however, did not pass. Dwight's feelings about *Time*'s political coverage, which seemed to be lurching rightward along with the Roosevelt administration, did not go unexpressed.

He wrote the staunchly Republican Luce a letter. *Time*, he said, was not as impartial as it should be and even showed a "bias toward the right." The initial tone was reasonable. Macdonald said his own politics "happen to be liberal," but that did not mean he thought *Time* should have a liberal bias either. Rather, *Time* should seek to be "truly objective and impartial."[2]

After what he called a "few hours' review" of recent issues, Macdonald had assembled seven examples of *Time*'s political slant, adding that he thought he could find even more examples of a clear bias if he had the raw material from which other stories had been written. The lecture went on for several pages—about half of it solid criticism, with the other half taken up by sideline whining of the If-I-had-written-this-article variety. But what stands out is the fact that Dwight Macdonald—a thirty-year-old writer who was paid a lordly $10,000 a year (over $150,000 in today's dollars) at a time of great hardship and want nationwide—doesn't care in the least if his boss finds him annoying.

Principles were at stake, but for Macdonald, protest was also personal indulgence. As he put it on another occasion, "I can work up a moral indignation quicker than a fat tennis player can work up a sweat."[3]

And much of his indignation was on behalf of neither journalistic nor even liberal values. The seventh and last example he drew forth to demonstrate *Time*'s bias—"Exhibit G," he called it—concerned a brief article recounting a strange near car accident turned fracas involving the French socialist leader Leon Blum and a funeral procession of monarchists yearning for the restoration of their exiled "king."

"Pieces like this," he wrote to Luce, "are one reason for the charge of fascism so frequently made against *Time*."

A chaotic incident that would have required Evelyn Waugh to conjure, the near collision and bizarre episode of violence that followed was captured on film by an amateur cameraman, allowing *Time*'s writer to describe the whole thing rather vividly in the February 24, 1936, issue. Long on caricature and farce, the article seemed vulgar to Macdonald for its retailing of physical violence. And though its treatment of the monarchists was far from sympathetic, what angered him was its insufficient respect for the leftists involved, who were described as "screaming" with rage on the victim Blum's behalf.

"Why must radicals always be presented as screaming or howling? Do their protests seem so silly to *Time*? If so, small wonder *Time* appears silly to them."

Take that.

IN 1936, the fourth installment of Macdonald's book-length opus on the U.S. Steel Corporation for *Fortune* ran into heavy editing. His sardonic though sympathetic article on the Communist Party had not been bowdlerized before publication—which had surprised him. But for this conclusive chapter on U.S. Steel, he'd gone for broke, opening the article with a long quotation from *Imperialism*, by V. I. Lenin.

U.S. Steel's managers were described as too stupid and monopolistic to be good capitalists. Nor were they communists, for they were too vicious and cruelly indifferent to the fate of the worker. More like fascists, thought Macdonald, cycling through one ism after another, and definitely dictatorial.

This attempt to report on American business from the inchoate point of view of a recently converted Marxist was likely never intended to succeed. Predictably, long stretches of theoretical anticapitalist commentary were cut. Macdonald played the role of the offended party. "If stories are to be edited like this," he asked, "why hire writers at all?"[4]

Afterward, he took six months off, confident of never returning. "A weight has been lifted off my shoulders. I feel free, free to see what life is all about, to really read scores of books that I've long wanted to. Especially I hope to orient myself politically. I know that I don't believe in capitalism, but I'm still hazy as to what course to take from there."[5]

CHAPTER 12

IN THE 1930S, LINGUISTICS was in some ways still a young discipline. But, after more than a century, it was possible to write a unifying treatise of its history, methods, and assumptions, as the American scholar Leonard Bloomfield did. He titled the work, very simply, *Language*.

Bloomfield taught at the University of Chicago, not the best home for a linguist at the time. He complained of "the snobberies and imbecilities which make a byword of the American college."[1] His supervisor, Dean of the Humanities Richard McKeon, an administrator working under President Robert Hutchins, once dismissed linguistic research as "counting prepositions."[2] McKeon later did his best to keep Bloomfield from going to Yale, but he could not convince Bloomfield, who had gotten stuck chairing his department and teaching introductory German year after year, that Chicago was truly interested in its linguistics program.

The center of gravity at Chicago in those days was to be found in its burgeoning great books curriculum, a descendant of the liberal education conceived by Charles William Eliot and marketed as the Harvard Classics. The handsome and young Hutchins, a media darling, was declaring war on specialization. "The gadgeteers and data collectors," Hutchins wrote, "masquerading as scientists, have threatened to become the supreme chieftains of the scholarly world."[3]

The goal of undergraduate education, thought Hutchins, should be loftier than the assimilation of facts; it should be the attainment of wisdom, discovered through personal engagement with timeless works of great literature.

Bloomfield, a quiet man, did not speak the same language. He had more in common with the scholars who had labored for years to work out a doctrine of the final *e* in Chaucer. The nephew of another prominent linguist, an expert in Sanskrit, he was born into a German-speaking household with two other intellectually gifted children. According to his biographer (also a linguist), he spoke with an "inimitable uvular trill" for certain *r* sounds.

A dull classroom instructor, he was a bit of a mystery to many who knew him. To some colleagues he seemed insufficiently anti-German during World War I as Americans took to renaming their sauerkraut "liberty cabbage." More outspoken during the 1930s, he said that if a Hitler were to come to power here in the United States, he, Bloomfield, would apply to the University of Mexico for a job—and if he wasn't offered one in two weeks' time, he would promptly commit suicide.

He greatly admired the Menominee Indians, whose language he studied and recorded, lamenting the loss of their native eloquence and their entrapment in the substandard English of the American underclass. He also bore a marked sympathy for American blacks, saying once that the United States could not rightly be called a democracy until the day it elected a black president. But it was not for his political views—which were rarely on offer, even to his closer friends and colleagues—that Bloomfield became known.

A socially inept intellectual—his idea of humor, when friends came to stay, was to plant fake bedbugs in his guest room and wait for the inevitable screams—he would become one of the most celebrated linguists of his time, a key spokesman (at least in print) for his discipline and its contribution to the sum of human knowledge.[4]

Hoping to explain linguistics to the outside world, Bloomfield began his treatise with the conventional point of view of the educated layman. "Occasionally he"—the layman, that is—"debates questions of 'correctness'—whether it is 'better,' for instance, to say *It's I* or *It's me*." To settle such issues the layman might refer to a grammar or a dictionary, or, more likely, he'll try to reason his way to an answer, using those grammatical terms he learned in school: subject, object, predicate, and so on.

"This is the common-sense way of dealing with linguistic matters. Like much else that masquerades as common sense, it is in fact highly sophisticated." By sophisticated, Bloomfield did not mean intelligent so much as complicated and bearing assumptions the layman did not even recognize.

Bloomfield's layman also believed in the authority of experts when it came to language. He showed a humble faith "that the grammarian or lexicographer, fortified by his powers of reasoning, can ascertain the logical basis of language and prescribe how people ought to speak."

There was more than a little politics behind the beliefs of this layman. His ideas—that language could be rationally explained and that grammarians were rightful authorities—were traceable to the antidemocratic assumptions of the eighteenth century, when "the spread of education led many dialect speakers to learn the upper-class forms of speech."[5]

With an air of persecution, Bloomfield continued: "This gave the authoritarians their chance: they wrote *normative grammars*, in which they often ignored actual usage in favor of speculative notions. Both the belief in 'authority' and some of the fanciful rules (as, for instance, about the use of *shall* and *will*) still prevail in our schools."

The normative grammars, Bloomfield argued, helped cement a mental block of class prejudice and intellectual failure that kept Europeans from faithfully recording the facts of language and appreciating its natural spoken form. But not forever. Around the turn of the nineteenth century, European scholars learned about the study of Sanskrit.

The Hindu tradition collected ancient hymns in the Rig-Veda, which dated to 1200 BC or perhaps even earlier. As the spoken language evolved, it became the work "of a special class of learned men" to read and interpret the sacred text, preserving knowledge of correct pronunciation and the like. "We find the Hindu grammarians," said Bloomfield, "making rules and lists of forms descriptive of the correct type of speech, which they called *Sanskrit*."

The oldest treatise of Sanskrit dated to the third or fourth century BC. Written by a man named Panini, "it describes, with the minutest detail, every inflection, derivation, and composition, and every syntactic usage of its author's speech. No other language, to this day, has been so perfectly described."

The difference between Sanskrit and modern attempts to catalog socially preferred English was in method. "The Indian grammar presented to European eyes, for the first time, a complete and accurate description of a language based not upon theory but observation."

After the European discovery of Sanskrit came the comparison of Indo-European languages. The scholar and fable writer Jacob Grimm discovered what came to be known as Grimm's law: a system of corresponding sound shifts among Germanic and other Indo-European languages. These correspondences, said Bloomfield, "showed that human action, in the mass, is not altogether haphazard, but may proceed with regularity even in so unimportant a matter as the manner of pronouncing the individual sounds within the flow of speech."

It also showed that language was properly, if not exclusively, an object of scientific investigation. But while fundamental laws of language change were being discovered in the nineteenth century, the layman continued to worry about secondary issues of correctness.

Of course, it was part of the linguist's task, according to Bloomfield, "to find out under what circumstances the speakers label a form in one way or the other"—good or bad—"and, in the case of each particular form, why they label it as they do: why, for example, many people say that *ain't* is 'bad' and *am not* is 'good.'"

About what was truly good and truly bad, however, the linguist had to remain unprejudiced. And within large speech communities, the student of language should observe that standards for good and bad language change with class.[6]

In the United States, "children who are born into homes of privilege . . . become native speakers of what is popularly known as 'good' English; the linguist prefers to give it the noncommittal name of *standard* English. Less fortunate children become native speakers of 'bad' or 'vulgar' or, as the linguist prefers to call it, *non-standard* English."

There were the literary standards of formal discourse, the colloquial standards of the privileged class, and middle-class public school standards. There was also "nonstandard" language. And there was, rather confusingly, something else called "substandard," which Bloomfield described as used widely in the United States but not by adherents of privileged-class standards or middle-class standards. Bloomfield used the same example for nonstandard as he did for substandard: *I ain't got none.*[7]

The double negative was, of course, verboten in standard English. And whatever *ain't* was—substandard or nonstandard—it was not standard. It was not "good." This did not mean that *ain't* was not a word, only that it was out of favor in standard English.

Linguistics was also neutral among the different standards of different times. Speaking for his profession, Bloomfield accepted without qualification that language change is normal. Change was "unceasing," and "constantly going on in every language." It was not even to be lamented.

And not only did Bloomfield and the new linguistics put words like "good" and "bad" in quotes; they put the word "authority" in quotes. There was no authority, no wise man who knows all about this stuff; there was only the record of usage, partly known and widely misunderstood. Dictionaries might attempt to combat "personal deviations" in the language or slow the pace of linguistic change, but they could not hold back the tide.

The discovery that language was better understood when better observed led to a reevaluation of writing, which had dominated and, according to Bloomfield, distorted the European understanding of language. Writing, said Bloomfield, was "a relatively recent invention, and . . . its use has been confined, until quite recently, to a very few persons."

To study writing was not to study language. "All languages were spoken through nearly all of their history by people who did not read or write; the languages of such people are just as stable, regular, and rich as the languages of literate nations." This was not just Bloomfield's view; it was a matter of doctrine among linguists. Writing was "merely a way of recording speech by visible marks."

And just as usage and grammar were relative, so was pronunciation—more so, even. It was infinitely variable. Phoneticians needed to be warned not to record too much information about pronunciation. "Having learned to discriminate many kinds of sounds, the phonetician may turn to some language, new or familiar, and insist upon recording all the distinctions he has learned to discriminate," even when they "have no bearing whatsoever."

Discussing slang, Bloomfield, always the reticent scholar, sounded gently reproachful as he cited the types of person who indulged in "facetious and unrestrained language." These included "young persons, sportsmen, gamblers, vagrants, criminals" and "most other speakers in their relaxed and unpretentious moods." So, just about everyone.

Bloomfield was certainly aware of taboo language, taking the Lord's name in vain, or using words that referred to sexual and execratory functions, but his attitude remained scientific, even anthropological. It was simply not for the linguist to justify allowances and prohibitions; only to observe and record. The whole subjective aspect of language seemed to be of little interest to Bloomfield or to linguists as he represented them.

Literature did not appear in Bloomfield's book as within the jurisdiction of linguistics. Nor was it the linguist's task to determine meaning beyond what was knowable from the speech act itself.

As so much of what stirs people to take an interest in the study of language relates to meaning, Bloomfield's scrupulousness was hard for many readers to comprehend. In discussing meaning, he made it sound at times as if he thought the subject too nebulous to be approached. He called "the statement of meanings" the "weak point in language-study." Meaning was so hard to pinpoint that the dictionary definition of *apple* could only be "roundabout."

The linguist could, however, extrapolate from known meanings. Starting with the known meanings of *one* and *add*, for example, he could then define *two* as "one added to one" and *three* as "one added to two."[8] But, for the linguist, the liberties to be taken with meaning appeared to be few and grudging.

As the University of Chicago became better known for Hutchins's broad ambitions, and later plans to market the lessons of great literature into a successful series of commercial books à la the Harvard Classics, the delicately chiseled assertions of Leonard Bloomfield would seem out of place. Thinking he had failed in his quest to teach the layman to understand and appreciate linguistics, he told Charles Carpenter Fries to give it a try. And in 1940 Bloomfield left Chicago

CHAPTER 13

AFTER *WEBSTER'S SECOND* WAS published, William Allan Neilson was often called on to defend the "universal" dictionary. In doing so, he could be rather modest about its powers of correctness.

To Leon Scott of the National Association for the Advancement of Colored People, who wanted to know why *negro* had not been capitalized in *Webster's Second*, he wrote, "All that a dictionary like Webster's can do is to record actual usage and when opinion differs show its own preference." To another correspondent, who complained about a technical inaccuracy, Neilson pleaded helplessness: "One of the embarrassing things . . . about a dictionary is that one is not free to state merely what one is convinced is correct but one has to record usages which are widespread even when they are unscholarly and inaccurate."[1]

Usage, of course, was not everything. Naughty words and phrases were left out of dictionaries of the time, including *Webster's Second*, which had found room for minor dukes, Austrian generals, and Turkish pashas but not such common scatological terms as *cunt*, *dick*, or *shit*. Nor did it allow *fuck*, *penetrate* in the sexual sense, *hump* in the sexual sense, or *pecker* in the nonwoodpecker sense.

Some words that referred to dirty matters were allowed into *Webster's Second* but made to clean up their act first. The definition for *peep show* made it sound respectable; the definition for *orgy* mentioned Bacchus and "carousal" but avoided the issue of arousal. *Horny* had something to do with actual horns but not much else. Both George Bernard Shaw and D. H. Lawrence had used *ménage à trois* to describe love triangles, but in *Webster's Second* the entry for *ménage* was limited to "a household"—no more, no less.

Neilson's dictionary claimed to represent "the civilization of today," but its concept of civilization excluded large stretches of American and international life. The reporter who said it contained the answer to every question he could think of should have asked about show business.

Movie had elbowed out *film*, an Americanism that was thriving abroad, but *the movies* was considered slang in *Webster's Second*. *Bit, extra, gag, grip, stuntman*, and numerous others from the silent and *talkie* eras made it in. Some terms hailed from elsewhere but gained currency with the rise of cinema: *Fan* originated in baseball and *star* had been used figuratively for a long time but both became associated with *Hollywood*, which itself entered the files in 1923, and by 1934 was shorthand for "the American motion-picture industry."[2]

But if he had looked for marquee names, the reporter would have found biographical entries for Douglas Fairbanks and Charlie Chaplin and none for Mary Pickford. None of the pioneering directors or daring businessmen who built and ran the Hollywood studios were listed.

Nor did the reporter ask about sports figures. The Editorial Board had decided not to include even Babe Ruth, who had set the home run record in 1927 and carried the New York Yankees to seven pennants and four World Series victories.[3] The great boxers of the era were not named. Jack Dempsey and Gene Tunney went unmentioned. The great Joe Louis was left out, while room was found for thirteen different French kings named Louis.

And never mind Louis Armstrong. There was no entry for what was called at the time *race music* (though there was one for *race riot*). There was no entry for Countee Cullen, Duke Ellington, Fletcher Henderson,

Ma Rainey, or Bessie Smith. "Morton, Jelly Roll" was not on this honor roll. Harlem was listed, but one could not tell that it was the birthplace of the "New Negro Movement." W. E. B. Du Bois and Booker T. Washington got in, but not Marcus Garvey.

Darky was labeled colloquial in *Webster's Second*, which sadly may not have been unthinkable in the 1930s, when the no-nonsense Rhett Butler asked Scarlett O'Hara, "Do you think you can parade through the Yankee army with a sick woman, a baby, and a simple-minded darky?"

Clearly whiteness did not make you civilized, or even mentionable in polite company. Eugene O'Neill, Somerset Maugham, and Oscar Wilde were all listed, rightly, in the pronouncing biographical section, but none of their works or characters were given entries, while hundreds of lines were devoted to entering the titles of and characters from Charles Dickens's works. William Allan Neilson had arranged for Merriam to hire a few girls from Smith, at forty cents a hour, to read and mark up contemporary prose for *Webster's Second*, but it may have been too much to ask a young woman to page her way through *Desire Under the Elms* or *Of Human Bondage* or *The Picture of Dorian Gray*.[4]

Sometimes *Webster's Second* did not seem to be of the twentieth century. Under *wrath* were four illustrative quotations, not one of which had been written after the sixteenth century.[5] Faced with the choice of being up-to-date or safely behind the times, the editors often chose the latter. The dictionary embraced "formal platform speech" just as radio and microphones were making it possible to spare one's vocal cords and address the public in a more conversational tone and style, as Roosevelt did in his fireside chats, speaking usually in the first person and cozily calling his listeners "my friends." *Ballyhoo* they labeled slang, even after FDR used the term, not without dignity, saying, "We cannot ballyhoo ourselves back to prosperity."[6]

Yet it was the great American dictionary of its day, and it did cover a major expansion of the standard lexicon. From *Armistice Day* (when the Allies and Central Powers ceased fighting) to *zero hour* (the moment when a military plan is enacted), world war had contributed many new phrases. *Flame thrower* and *mustard gas* were newly entered, used in the battles that moved Wilfred Owen to write of "blood come gargling from the froth-corrupted lungs." *Webster's Second* even translated "Dulce et Decorum est pro patria mori"—a line from Homer that Owen borrowed with bitter irony, meaning "It is sweet and seemly to die for one's country"—because it was the kind of thing cultured people want to know. *Shock troops*, meaning a highly disciplined advance guard, was in the new dictionary, dated 1917 in Merriam's files, though *shock* as a term of war went back to Shakespeare's time. *Defeatism* summed up the postwar mood in Europe; so did *shell-shocked*, a term of psychiatry coined early in the Great War to categorize numerous symptoms appearing in veterans.

The answers to war were also in *Webster's Second*. Woodrow Wilson's optimistic *Fourteen Points* were described, one by one, starting with its famous demand for covenants of peace and ending with the proposed creation of the *League of Nations*, also defined in *Webster's Second*. More lasting than either was the developing concept of the *nation-state*, which entered Merriam's files in 1918 and became a fundamental principle of the international system, giving all peoples with a historic national identity a presumptive case for statehood.

The dictionary's preface referred to "the increased pace in scientific knowledge in the past generation." *Blood sugar, continental drift, radio frequency, sac fungus,* and countless scientific and technical terms much less recognizable had joined the language. The twentieth century's interest in the mental self had begun taking shape as a raft of important psychological terms—*collective unconscious, extrovert, gestalt psychology, id, superego*—appeared while *Sigmund Freud* still lived and breathed and himself appeared in the main vocabulary as well as the list of noteworthy persons in *Webster's Second*.

Jazz was one of the great new words to enter the language (its first citation dated 1913 in Merriam's files), while its derivatives *jazzy* and *jazz* as a verb were labeled slang in *Webster's Second*. *Flapper*, once a young woman trained to prostitution, was labeled colloquial for "a young girl of about fifteen to eighteen years of age, esp. one who is not yet 'out' socially." The very next sense, labeled slang, was the quintessential 1920s usage: "a girl or young woman whose behavior or costume are characterized by daring freedom or boldness."

With the *Nineteenth Amendment*, entered in the dictionary like all the other constitutional amendments, the flapper, or at least her mother and older sisters, got the vote. With the *Eighteenth* and *Twenty-first Amendments*, alcohol was banned and re-legalized. *Speakeasy*—labeled slang, of course—dated to the nineteenth century but had gained new relevance in the twenties as the *Anti-Saloon League* (itself an entry) won passage of the laws that banned the sale of alcoholic spirits. *Wet* and *dry* were prominent colloquialisms in the twenties, as adjectives referring to potables, moral attitudes, and political sides of *prohibition*, itself also defined in *Webster's Second*.

The economic meaning of *depression*, an old usage, was included, but America's economic troubles had not yet earned the definitive article *the* or come to be known as "great." President Roosevelt's *New Deal* made for an entry, defined as the policy of the National Industrial Recovery Act of 1933.

Grammar was handled delicately, so as not to offend. Under *split infinitive*, the editors wrote that it was "widely objected to, but it is sometimes desirable or necessary, esp. to avert ambiguity." Holding the line on *shall* and *will* required an enormously complicated usage note, and under *future* the entry noted that "this tense is formed with *shall* and *will*"—the findings of Charles C. Fries notwithstanding. As *Webster's Second* instructed readers on correct usage, it sought to avoid the nagging tone of the schoolmarm, but sometimes it could not be helped.

"The forms of *lie* are ignorantly or carelessly confounded with those of the transitive verb *lay*," said the dictionary. Elsewhere the editors reported actual usage while acknowledging the rules such usage violated. Under *got*, the dictionary said, "the phrase 'have got' . . . is objected to by many grammarians but is common in colloquial use." Under *me* could be found a usage note for "It is me," saying, "although avoided in formal writing and by precise speakers is frequent in colloquial and dialectal speech." *Different from* was preferred to *different than*, and *than him* was "generally regarded as incorrect."

Under *genteel*, *Webster's Second* said the word was "now regarded as at least inelegant, except when used humorously or somewhat sarcastically." Such was the fate of *genteel* some twenty years after the writer George Santayana decried the "genteel tradition in America" and Van Wyck Brooks followed by criticizing the separation in American life of a prissy, respectable, academic culture of "highbrows" from the popular, streetwise culture of "lowbrows." In this division, William Allan Neilson was certainly on the side of the highbrows, but in its packaging and retailing of high culture *Webster's Second* was also an example of what would come to be called middlebrow culture. And *genteel* was, in fact, an excellent word to describe its editorial intentions, especially in the first sense listed: "free from vulgarity."

CHAPTER 14

ON A TRIP TO Paris, carrying a letter of introduction from a mutual acquaintance, Dwight Macdonald met James Joyce. Macdonald was accompanied by his good friend George L. K. Morris.

Recalling the "famous meeting," Macdonald said "JJ" looked "like a haggard race-track tout." Actually, he could not remember what the man was wearing, but he did remember that the conversation was halting. The famous author "seemed quite content to sit there in silence until we left."

When the visiting Americans began to make their exit, Joyce suddenly came to life. He turned to Macdonald and said, "I understand you're on *Fortune* magazine." "Yes," replied Macdonald. Then Joyce, by some lights the greatest writer in the English language at the time, asked Macdonald, a mere journalist not even thirty years old, if he might put in a word for a writer friend of his who was moving to New York and needed work. Macdonald said he would. Then Joyce "ushered us out—with considerably more cordiality than he had let us in."[1]

Twenty-seven years later, the episode still struck Macdonald as bizarre. In more than one way, it was. Macdonald's own feelings toward gainful employment were, in fact, a little eccentric.

~~~~~~

STARTING IN 1935, writers across the country were being given jobs to keep them busy, at miserly rates, producing state guides for the Federal Writers Project. John Cheever and Richard Wright and Ralph Ellison were on the literary dole, as was Jim Thompson, later author of *The Grifters*. Thompson was an Oklahoman who thought John Steinbeck a fine writer but that *The Grapes of Wrath* showed he actually knew little about the state.[2] For her sojourns into swampy hideaways in Florida, the inimitable anthropologist-novelist Zora Neale Hurston collected a government check, as did the poet Kenneth Rexroth in San Francisco and a young Saul Bellow in Chicago. Few were too proud to be taking assignments, no matter how dull or unremunerative.

Dwight Macdonald, surely alone at the time, was slowly abandoning a lucrative position at a well-known and well-regarded publication to stalk the literary breadlines as a freelancer. He took umbrage at the suggestion that his great salary at *Fortune* meant anything to him. He and Nancy could very happily live on a fifth of such largesse, he proudly announced as they moved out of a posh apartment on Forty-Fourth Street and into a dark walk-up in Greenwich Village, which at the time well fit Lionel Abel's description of New York City as the most interesting part of the Soviet Union.[3]

The literary light of the 1920s, F. Scott Fitzgerald, had "cracked up" and was now making hungover confessions of what success had been like. Money and gilt-edged prose had given way to a drier landscape of dirt roads and American grit. Erskine Caldwell and John Steinbeck made hunger and survival their subjects. The modernism of Joyce was imported and redistributed by Faulkner, whose Bundrens knew poverty but not common sense as they carried their mother's coffin on a horse-drawn southern journey, with crows flying overhead, to a final resting place. *Fortune* sent Macdonald's friend James Agee to write about tenant farmers and Walker Evans to photograph them. But the magazine rejected Agee's piece, later published with Evans's photos as *Let Us Now Praise Famous Men*.[4] The new great satirist of American literature,

Nathanael West, largely disregarded at the time, took aim not at the small-souledness of country club Republicans (à la Sinclair Lewis) but at the teary-eyed human animal and his utter naked frailty. In the earnest version, human existence was rendered tragic; in the less earnest version, it was pathetic to the point of embarrassment.

In this atmosphere, patriotism was "morally suspect" and "intellectually unfashionable." There seemed to be "no reason to believe in the 'viability' of American capitalism."[5] Immediately after leaving *Fortune*, Macdonald wrote a three-part siege on Henry Luce in the pages of the left-wing magazine the *Nation*.[6] He was now a confirmed member of those radicals to whom, as he had put it in his letter to Luce, small wonder, *Time* looked rather silly.

He met the fetching young troublemaker Mary McCarthy, who became an important friend. She described him in her short story "Portrait of the Intellectual as a Yale Man." His fictional version was shallow, bumbling, and likable, buoyed along by good looks, Ivy League bona fides, and the decency to be a radical without rubbing it in anyone's face.

Macdonald threw parties, including one for the sharecroppers, serving cocktails "for free and in glasses," noted McCarthy. After a few drinks, he would get into fights with Geoffrey Hellman of the *New Yorker*, whom he considered a Tory. Just as predictably, the two would make up during the week and reunite over drinks the next weekend. It was McCarthy, along with Margaret Marshall of the *Nation*, whose chance comments on the fraudulence of the Stalin trials prompted Macdonald to purchase a transcript and read them for himself.[7]

Macdonald was shocked that the Soviets hadn't taken more care in framing the defendant Leon Trotsky. "Witnesses" made the absentee defendant out to be the perfect straw man, a living antithesis to every single policy Stalin undertook, a murderous villain bent on undoing the Russian Revolution. It was uncanny.

"Has *Pravda* been plugging for the newly won higher standard of living? Trotsky was plotting to lower it. Are Soviet citizens justly proud of their collectivized farms? Trotsky would break them up. . . . The Five-Year Plan? Trotskyites tried to wreck it. The Stakhanovite heroes? Trotsky murdered them. . . . Trotsky even planned to liquidate the intelligentsia, beginning presumably with himself."

Macdonald joined the masthead of *Partisan Review*, then being revived by Philip Rahv and William Phillips as an anti-Stalinist literary journal after being set aside by the John Reed Clubs that used to fund it. He also brought in his friend Morris, who was a painter and a leading member of the American Abstract Artists—abstract painting at the time was still a fledgling movement in American art, where Thomas Hart Benton's masculine, anti-European realism reigned supreme.

Morris's wealth helped underwrite the revived literary journal. Macdonald also talked of ponying up money. There was much excitement and planning. Macdonald joined the Workers' Party and began writing a mediocre political column for the *New International*, mostly on the American press. More skillfully, he picked fights.

To the editor of the *New Republic*, he addressed a rebuttal to Malcolm Cowley, the magazine's literary editor and a committed fellow traveler, who, in his review of a book about the Stalin trials, seemed to be giving the benefit of every doubt to Stalin, even after what Macdonald called "the most baffling state trial in history."

"Mr. Cowley," wrote Macdonald, "began his article by confessing, with disarming candor, a personal prejudice against Trotsky. Perhaps it is not too late to try to match his honesty by confessing, on my part, an equally deep-seated prejudice in Trotsky's favor. It's hardly necessary to give my reasons. They are about the same as Mr. Cowley's."[8] Take that.

Trotsky was an almost papal figure among the anti-Stalinists, every bit the revolutionary but also an intellectual and the exiled scapegoat of Stalin's murderous purging. As communists in the West made common cause with liberals of all stripes—including many they had formerly denounced—the Trotskyites became an embittered minority. Sidney Hook, a philosophy professor at the City College of New York who had turned against the Communist Party some years earlier, organized a committee, headed by the celebrated American philosopher John Dewey, to consider the case against Trotsky.

Next Macdonald was taking it to the *Nation*, for skipping a Trotsky Commission meeting; for playing nice with New Deal Democrats; and for avoiding the question of whether Stalinism was building socialism or destroying it. Shrewdly, Macdonald realized the left's vulnerabilities on the matter of Stalin's brutality, but with extravagant outspokenness he used his own personal experience, his own life story, as warm-up for his attacks.

"While I was at *Fortune*," he wrote to the *Nation*, "the *Nation* was always to me the great symbol of honest, truthful, intelligent journalism—everything that I missed at *Fortune*. But it now appears that the *Nation*, too, has its commitments, its investments, so to speak, just like *Fortune*."[9]

All the world was a magazine, and working for Luce had made him a man of the world. It didn't occur to Macdonald, for starters, to question whether a magazine résumé could double as a compass for locating the right and the good in politics. Or that it was simply naïve to believe any magazine was without prior commitments. And yet in some ways his guilelessness served him well, as a writer. The revelation of dark truths is made all the more shocking if you can play innocent first.

HENRY SEIDEL Canby had noted in the early 1920s the growing numbers of communists in New York's literary hangouts. *Red-baiting*, which most people associate with the 1940s and '50s, is dated 1928 in the Merriam-Webster files. *Fascism* is noticed entering the English lexicon in 1921, *Stalinism* in 1927, and *Nazism* in 1934—words and ideas that were, of course, needed to recognize the political tumult enveloping Europe.

The thought that the United States would go the way of militarized dictatorship, amid economic problems at home and another major war brewing in Europe, struck many on the left as plausible. Sinclair Lewis wrote a dystopian alternative history in which a presidential election yields a fascist takeover of the United States government, led by a folksy, great-books-loving media mogul whose "Minute Men" shock troops quickly wrest control of private property and empower thugs to persecute Jews, blacks, and intellectuals nationwide. The detail about the dictator's love of classic literature is a hilarious if unfair thrust in the direction of the Harvard Classics and other such programs in the best kind of culture.

Macdonald too imagined the United States was on the verge of a fascist transformation. It was a simple thing, he wrote, for "the old-fashioned liberal [to] shade off into the fascist apologist."[10] But the urge to centralize power was widespread. Even the Trotskyites were hierarchical and undemocratic.

After his call for greater transparency and a new voting system for party decisions went ignored, Macdonald resigned from the Workers' Party in July 1941, complaining of "the interminable rehash of stale platitudes and catchwords with which the party leadership covers up (or rather, reveals) its political bankruptcy."[11]

It was not the first time Macdonald took on the party, one versus all. While writing for the *New International*, he also wrote a letter to the editor of the very same Marxist sheet, calling an article by Trotsky himself "disappointing and embarrassing."[12]

The feeling was, at times, mutual. Macdonald's "intellectual vanity," noted Hook, "suffered at the hands of his fellow professional revolutionists, who regarded him as a literary journeyman rather than as a schooled Marxist capable of coming to grips with the nature of the Soviet Union under Stalin."[13] Trotsky complained (in words that improved in their retelling) that "everyone has a right to be stupid but Comrade Macdonald abuses the privilege"—a line that must have wounded Macdonald but that he also laughingly circulated.

Partisan Review, meanwhile, was publishing work that would make the little-known journal legendary. Clement Greenberg, a Macdonald ally, typified the *Review*'s anti-Stalinism and enthusiasm for modernism. In 1939, he published a profoundly influential essay on the meaning of *kitsch*, which also endorsed the then-novel idea of an avant-garde that creates art for a cultural elite, in opposition to the cheaply reproduced culture of the masses. Even as the radicals at *Partisan Review* opposed capitalism and the inequalities it created, they were careful to tend distinctions between high and low culture.

And in the idea of an *avant-garde*—a word that appears in English only a few decades earlier—they found a ruling-class mentality in the important but neglected realms of taste and culture. *Kitsch* itself was a new concept and new word in English, broached for the first time only in the 1920s but used by Greenberg to describe a "gigantic apparition" of Hollywood movies and Tin Pan Alley music and Norman Rockwell covers on the *Saturday Evening Post*. Kitsch saved one from the hard work of looking at Picassos; it "predigested" art.

Greenberg, foreshadowing arguments that Macdonald would recirculate in the 1950s, blamed cheap reproduction and universal literacy. Now that everyone could read, literacy became a "minor skill" and no longer the "exclusive concomitant of refined tastes." In the age of radio and Hollywood movies and universal literacy, kitsch was the "universal culture"—and the death of high culture.[14]

After Hitler invaded the Soviet Union, Macdonald and Greenberg wrote up ten propositions about the coming war for *Partisan Review*. It was an unintentional parody of intellectual style. Forthright bullet points were qualified by tendentious explanations that grew longer and longer, some sprouting their own internal arguments and thus requiring footnotes, one of which concerned an elaborate set of literary references to Cervantes's *Don Quixote*. The authors sought to refocus attention on the possibility of a Marxist revolution, for only revolution would save America. "In the war or out of it, the United States faces only one future under capitalism: fascism."[15]

As World War II developed, Macdonald was at odds with "the boys" at *Partisan Review*, Philip Rahv and William Phillips. After his and Greenberg's ten propositions, the journal abruptly announced it would have no editorial line on the war since its own editors were not in agreement. This vote of no confidence in the article they had just published, an article written by one of their own editors, created a bitter divide in the masthead.

The poet Delmore Schwartz, a good friend, dismissed the brouhaha as further evidence that Macdonald was a "congenial sorehead." Actually, it was deeply frustrating to Macdonald, who told Schwartz that "my political beliefs, which I take seriously, are not based on mere love of brawling and being 'different' but on some experience (mostly my years on *Fortune*), on sympathy for human beings (who are being brutalized and oppressed in every way in the social system we have), and on intellectual conviction which I've arrived at by a wide (and still continuing) reading in politics and economics."

Schwartz was younger than Macdonald and the butt of some advice, which continued here. "As I told you a long time ago (a prediction that has come true), you're ruining your career (not to speak of your moral being as a man) by trimming your sails to prevailing winds, by keeping silent on any hot, controversial issues, by excessive diplomacy and a hush-hush attitude toward all the fakery and shoddiness that's for years been growing in our whole intellectual atmosphere."[16]

Sometimes these intellectuals referred to their own circle as "the family." Like the members of many families, they always presumed to know and understand each other so well, too well, actually, and, as with Macdonald's friendly advice to Schwartz, were rather mean about it. But friction was routine, with cutting commentary being part of the fun and, in fact, an essential part of the intellectual training.

McCarthy was the source of much friction. When still a lover to Philip Rahv, she, an upper-class Catholic girl, and he, a Ukrainian-born Jew of little means, bickered a great deal. There was a recurring joke

between them—a riff on an old Marxist debate—about the impossibil-
ity of achieving socialism in a single country when they couldn't even
achieve it in a single apartment.

McCarthy soon left the *Partisan Review* editor to marry the much
older literary critic Edmund Wilson—"because he had a better prose
style," the comment went around. It was a typically mean thing to
say, and McCarthy disputed it, saying that Wilson's prose style was not
really or always better than Rahv's.[17]

And, indeed, there was much to be said for Rahv's prose. In 1939,
Rahv published a seminal essay on American literature, "Paleface and
Redskin," dividing American writers into these two camps representing
the cerebral and mannered art of Henry James, among others, and the
more boisterous, earthy passion of Walt Whitman, a division that in
many cases pit the Anglophile against the Americanist.

Like Clement Greenberg's essay on kitsch, which came out the same
year, it boldly seized upon the broadest possible categories, provoking
the reader, not with the writer's politics or curious readings of important
works, but with powerful assertions about the true nature of culture. By
today's more academic standards, Rahv's two types of American writers
seem crude, overdetermined, and (the ultimate campus put-down these
days) facile. But as an impression of the literary mind at work, entertaining an interesting and historically supportable thesis, the essay is about
as satisfying as any literary essay written in the twentieth century.

This was the *Partisan Review* crowd at their best, placing culture
before politics. Frustrated, Dwight Macdonald decided to start his own
journal, inverting that formula. Macdonald's magazine, called simply
Politics, would not ignore cultural issues but in fact "integrate them
with—and, yes, subordinate them to—the analysis of those deeper
trends of which they are an expression."[18]

At *Partisan Review* he was replaced by Delmore Schwartz.

CHAPTER 15

IN AUGUST 1936, *TIME* magazine published an article about the research of Miller McClintock, the first person ever awarded a doctorate in traffic. With the rise of automobiles came the rise of traffic accidents. Analyzing what factors led in 1935, for instance, to 37,000 deaths and property loss equal to more than $1.5 billion was the job of McClintock and his traffic bureau, which were funded by the Automobile Manufacturers Association.[1]

Almost 100 percent of accidents, reported *Time*, were caused by 15 percent of drivers, a group the magazine described colloquially as "speed maniacs, psychopaths, drunks, or morons." Expecting these folks to shape up and become safer drivers was unrealistic, according to McClintock and other "experts." Instead, "the driver must be externally restrained from killing himself."

McClintock classified accidents into four types: head-on collisions; collisions at intersections; those "generated by road shoulders, abrupt curves, faulty banking . . . trees, parked vehicles or pedestrians"; and rear-end collisions. These four he called, respectively, "medial," "intersectional," "marginal," and "internal-stream."

The solution was to build better roads. McClintock envisioned a now-familiar system for highways, with a clear division between opposing streams of traffic; three lanes in each direction, including one for passing and one for one slower driving; and finally, cloverleaf turnoffs. The aim, said McClintock, was to channel automobiles "in a sealed conduit past all conflicting eddies."

There was something so funny about jargon and its pseudoscientific rhetoric, thought Philip Gove, who was still teaching composition at NYU, where witnessing the forced march of students through the constant writing of class papers had made him an authority on insincere prose. The article in *Time* with its overdressed categories and suspiciously credentialed expert moved him to mock.

"Sirs," he wrote in a letter to the editor, "From my unpublished thesis on bicycle accidents I give the following digest. There are five principal kinds: vectorial (when two vehicles coming from different directions alter each other's subsequent position); intervenient (sudden appearance of immovable obstacles); interplanetary (leaving the road, as when riding off a bridge or an embankment); subcutaneous (loss of concentration caused by bees, dogs, etc.); and exhibitionist (passenger on handle bars, standing on head, etc.). Consequently, build one-way, one-wheel, walled-in alleyways for one cyclist at a time: when he exits, green light flashes, and entrance gates admit cyclist No. 2, etc. Please to give me an honorary LL.D. and two columns in TIME (with cut). . . ."[2]

Gove was indeed working on a dissertation, but its real subject was a subgenre of English fictional narrative he called "imaginary voyages," such as those Gulliver undertakes in Jonathan Swift's classic. It was a bibliographic work involving little to no literary interpretation. Bright enough but not exactly an academic star in the making, Gove struck one colleague as being under the impression that his career would be advanced by the excellence of his classroom teaching, which was not only mistaken but naïve.[3] Yet in the late 1930s he got smart and focused his efforts on projects that would lead to his degree and to publications.

It was important that he figure these things out. He had married Grace, the pretty young woman he had met while trying to improve the quality of correspondence at AT&T. And they had two children, Norwood and Susan.

Another area of eighteenth-century literature that interested Gove was Samuel Johnson's dictionary. But this work, which represents a milestone in both the history of dictionaries and the history of English literature, had already been the subject of extensive scholarship, so Gove turned his eye to various subtle, underexplored aspects. One was how the serialization of Johnson's dictionary, begun two months after its original publication as a single volume, inspired the almost simultaneous serialization of Nathan Bailey's much older dictionary, which had been updated using Johnson's dictionary and was now competing with it.

The second question that interested Gove was how the bank of citations Johnson relied on to write his dictionary reflected Johnson's own mind and affected the literary views of his dictionary. To know Johnson's dictionary better, it would help to know more about the exact authors he had read and the exact editions he had read them in.

These were both highly technical areas of research, requiring detailed knowledge of the book business of Johnson's time and the precise contents of Johnson's library. The first reflected a surprising interest in competition among dictionaries (a potentially nasty business, all in all), and the second an important but only partial truth: that a dictionary comes down to the evidence collected by the lexicographer, those countless little passages copied out from countless, usually unseen, sources. While there is much to be said for it, this view tends to underrate the influence of the lexicographer, who, like any editor, must finally insist on what goes in and what stays out, whether for good intellectual reasons or practical necessity or to anticipate the desires of the marketplace or in deference to the prejudices of the age. The impetus for Gove's project emphasized the purity of process at the expense of editorial prerogative—such as that exercised by Johnson himself and, in Gove's own day, the Editorial Board of Merriam-Webster.

In early 1939, Gove defended his dissertation but was not ready to deposit the required seventy-five copies in the Columbia University library in order to receive his doctorate. He wished to travel to France and England to expand his painstaking catalog of all known examples of imaginary voyages between 1700 and 1800. A fellowship worth two thousand dollars came through, which Gove would use to put finishing touches on his dissertation and, while he was at it, perform research for a book he was planning on Samuel Johnson's dictionary. Disappointed to learn that NYU had rejected his request for a sabbatical at half pay— an unpaid leave was his only option—he decided to go abroad with his family all the same.[4]

Philip spent the summer in London, while Grace and the children made do, lonesome, far away in Cornwall, on the southern tip of England. The family stayed in touch by letter, these messages intensely affectionate and always yearning. Grace recounts how Norwood "came in from meeting the postman at the gate with a letter and three packages. He said, 'This is a day, isn't it?' Susie was proud that she had a possession to share, and she and Nod became such good fellows over their game of dominoes that when Nod left to get the milk she insisted on coming with him even though it was raining."[5]

Gove busied himself with research, getting to know London, and getting to know Johnson scholars and lexicographers. At the end of the summer, he rejoined his family, and, after placing the children in a school, he and Grace "spent a few quiet days in a bungalow on the banks of the English river Looe, surrounded by the calm green tops of Cornwall hills."[6] Years later Gove recalled the details of these weeks in a poignant memoir.

The bungalow owner's son was an Air Raid Precautions warden who liked to regale his guests with stories about local preparations for war. "The gas squad, urgently called out to assist the Plymouth fire squad in the practice burning of slum quarters, had themselves been so overcome by mere woodsmoke that it was necessary to call out the first aid squad to carry them off on emergency stretchers." Gove savored the grim humor of these practice episodes: "One 'casualty,' assigned to be badly wounded, having given up all hope after interminable wait, left a note on his spot, reading, 'Have bled to death and gone home to bed.'"

In late August, Philip and Grace set out for London, learning at the nearby train station that, in fact, the city was being evacuated. The next day, September 1, the poet Auden noted "the clever hopes expire of a low dishonest decade." With their luggage and gas masks from Her Majesty's government, the Goves bought tickets to go as far as Reading. "The train was crowded. People seemed uneasy, apprehensive, and uncommonly concerned about soldiers and sailors who filled the station platforms."

A day later they visited the city, "impelled by curiosity." Philip and Grace hoped to encounter American acquaintances, someone with information on what was really going on. Like hapless tourists, they made their way to the American Embassy, which was thronged. "I do not know why such a visit seemed desirable," recalled Gove, "or what we would have said even if we could have talked to Ambassador Joseph P. Kennedy himself. I think what we both wanted was for someone— anyone at all—to tell us to run along, and not worry."

They joined the evacuation of London, heading back to Reading, and then on to Oxford the next day. The morning of Sunday, September 3, Grace and Philip took a walk "along Iffley Road to look at a Norman church with its dogtooth carving and the yew trees in the church-yard." Their stroll led into fields where children were playing. The married couple admired the town's "neat rows of brick houses, garden plots bright in the sunlight, and cheerful-looking people." When they returned to their boardinghouse, the landlady greeted them. "'Did you have a nice walk? And see the church? Well, we are at war.'"

The Goves stayed abroad nonetheless, and it was a productive year for Philip, who published four journal articles on Johnson. In reviewing the competition between Bailey's serialized dictionary and Johnson's, he noted that Bailey's updaters had relied more than a little on Johnson's newer dictionary, borrowings that struck the modern eye as dubious: Wrote Gove, "A glance at any page of Bailey will reveal that line after line is rankly plagiarized" from Johnson.[7]

This argument drew interest from other Johnsonians, mainly for its lack of context: Copying among lexicographers had been more common in the eighteenth century, and even Johnson could be shown to have borrowed from Bailey's original dictionary. On the bicentennial of Johnson's dictionary, the American scholars James Sledd and Gwin J. Kolb returned to the issue, quoting Gove and commenting that "indignation at a lexicographer's raids on his predecessors is a little utopian."

The problem with Gove's very earnest argument was that it expected too much originality, and even integrity, from a mere dictionary, that repository of traditions, including the minor tradition of imitating one's predecessors. On the upside, his career was showing signs of life and his work was finally winning some attention.

CHAPTER 16

IN ONE OF THE classic parodies of vulgar American English, H. L. Mencken rewrote the Declaration of Independence.

The original text begins with a handsome specimen of eighteenth-century British English rhetoric, written from a lofty, transcendent point of view and filled with beautiful noun phrases that must have taken hours to assemble: "When in the course of human events, it becomes necessary for one people to dissolve the political bands which have connected them with another, and to assume among the powers of the earth, the separate and equal station to which the laws of nature and of nature's God entitle them, a decent respect to the opinions of mankind requires that they should declare the causes which impel them to the separation."

Mencken's comic translation is written as the passionate speech of an American philistine, with an ear to the shifting standards of American English to favor street-corner slang and simple pronouns: "When things get so balled up that the people of a country have to cut loose from some other country, and go it on their own hook, without asking no permission from nobody, except maybe God Almighty, then they ought to let everybody know why they done it, so that everybody can see that they are on the level, and not trying to put nothing over nobody."

The famous next sentence of the original says, "We hold these truths to be self-evident, that all men are created equal, that they are endowed by their Creator with certain unalienable rights, that among these are life, liberty and the pursuit of happiness."

Mencken's version: "All we got to say on this proposition is this: first, you and me is as good as anybody else, and maybe a damn sight better; second, nobody ain't got no right to take away none of our rights; every man has a got a right to live, to come and go as he pleases, and to have a good time however he likes, so long as he don't interfere with nobody else."[1]

And so on. In 1936, Mencken removed the parody from the fourth edition of *The American Language*—to avoid any confusion. He said that outraged purists had mistaken it for a model of how American English should be written.

INTEREST IN the varieties of American English was certainly on the rise. Alan Lomax, following in his father's footsteps, was recording songs and stories directly from the mouths of hillbillies, field hands, and rural preachers. Woody Guthrie, an Okie who had learned songs on the migrant worker circuit, was recording folk music for a major record label. Zora Neale Hurston was touring the depths of Florida to record the words and sounds of African Americans whose speech reflected not the rules of the classroom but cultural isolation and even sounds of the Middle Passage. John Steinbeck, sometime newspaper reporter, was writing about farmhands and grape-pickers to call forth the unglamorous lives of real people. *The Grapes of Wrath* was chosen by Henry Seidel Canby as a selection for the Book-of-the-Month Club, and then it won a Pulitzer and became a celebrated movie. The true American, Roosevelt's "Forgotten Man," was everywhere being stalked and made to show himself. In music, literature, and the movies that Americans now routinely watched, the Voice of the People, with varying degrees of authenticity, was being spoken. Even President Roosevelt—who could sound like the world's greatest WASP standing atop a stack of Harvard Classics—had gotten in on the act, adopting a less formal persona and simpler language in his fireside chats on the radio.

In his own way, Charles C. Fries was listening. Through the efforts of the Modern Language Association and the Linguistic Society of America, he had gained access to three thousand letters to the United States government, all written by native speakers whose parents and grandparents were also native speakers of American English. Until now every "corpus" study in linguistics had involved edited material written for a public audience—in short, literary writing. Fries wanted material that did not sound like essays or novels, language conceived without any intent to enlighten, flatter, or amaze. And these letters to the federal government were as plain as the words one might address to a clerk at the Department of Motor Vehicles.

The language was simple, honest, and prosaic. Still it was not ideal.

The letters were written to the U.S. Army and came from military family members. Much of the language was informal, but all of it was rather serious, at times desperate. Much better, thought Fries, would have been a large body of mechanical recordings of American speech. "The use of any kind of *written* material for the purpose of investigating the living language is always a compromise," he wrote, "but at present an unavoidable one."[2]

At least the letters were spontaneous, all "personal letters written to accomplish an immediate purpose with presumably no thought that they might ever be read by any other than the particular person to whom they were directed." Fries knew the writers' biographical specifics: age, current address, relevant family information, and, most important, occupation and educational background. The last two pieces of information he used to categorize the letter-writers into groups.

The first group consisted of urban professionals with a degree from "one of our reputable colleges" whose spelling, capitalization, and punctuation conformed "completely to the usual conventions of written material." Their letters were used as examples of "standard English." The other important group comprised individuals with eight years of schooling or less, who held manual jobs making less than ninety dollars a month, and whose spelling, capitalization, and punctuation showed them to be "semi-illiterate."[3] Their letters represented "vulgar English." In between was a middle group of people with at least some high school education who held skilled jobs, but the goal of the study was to document differences between standard and vulgar English.

Fries's method was as radical as his choice of materials: He defined standard English by the people who used it, not by a preordained set of rules that could have been used to measure just how standard the language of the letter-writers was. In this, he was completely inverting the traditional method of popular grammar-writing, in which a rule was set forth, followed by examples of written or spoken English that violated the rules.

The National Council of Teachers of English, where he had served as president, had commissioned the study, which was called *American English Grammar*. Begun many years prior to its publication in 1940, it asked the reader to put aside his assumption that the "language practices of formal writing are the best or at least that they are of a higher level than those of colloquial or conversational English." Fries dwelled on this point. Too many people, he said, when "they find an expression marked 'colloquial' in a dictionary, as in the phrase 'to get on one's nerves' in Webster's *New International Dictionary*, they frown upon its use."

But *colloquial* did not mean bad or wrong. The word "is used to mark those words and constructions whose range of use is primarily that of the polite conversation of cultivated people, of their familiar letters and informal speeches." Such informality was claiming an increasing share of public discourse: "Even the language of our better magazines and of public addresses has, during the last generation, moved away from the formal toward the informal."

Another bias that had to be put aside was the presumption that standard English, the language spoken by educated people in positions of influence, was better English. Historically, it was "a local dialect, which was used to carry on the major affairs of English life and which gained thereby a social prestige." In the United States, the usages of New England predominated "because of the fact that New England so long dominated our intellectual life." There was now, however, a broad American standard that was identifiable and coherent despite regional differences.

But the most important thing to remember was that standard English—American or British—was not standard because it was "any more correct or beautiful or more capable than other varieties of English." Instead, it was standard because it was the language "used in the conduct in the important affairs of our people."

Standard English was the language of the socially powerful, and that was why it was standard. It enjoyed no divine right. Its selection as the standard language was simply a by-product of historical and political evolution. The double negative, for example, was no longer a part of English not because it was redundant or irrational, but because the double negative was not a characteristic of the English spoken by those whom history had favored with social and political power. A grammar of the language spoken in the United States—standard and nonstandard alike—had to overcome this bias by identifying the linguistic tendencies of all, including "the great mass of people in most of our communities" and especially the poor and uneducated.

Fries did not, however, conclude from these premises that all varieties of English were equal. He accepted without qualification that it was a proper educational aim to fit children with the means to speak standard English. The problem was that the language taught in classrooms was not standard English.

"Seldom have school authorities understood the precise nature of the language task they have assumed and very frequently have directed their energies to teaching not 'standard' English realistically described, but a 'make-believe' correctness which contained some true forms of real 'standard' English and many forms that had and have practically no currency outside the classroom."[4]

So, it was necessary to look for examples of how and to what degree standard English differed from vulgar English. And this is where the letters came in.

Fries examined the letters for grammar only, never commenting on their contents. From the scientific point of view, what the letters said was irrelevant, but one can hardly pass here without observing the strange tonal effect of so clinical an approach. It is similar to that of a head doctor who is making rounds with residents in tow, observing patients in great distress but never letting on that he is personally affected. Letter 8288 says, *"there* will be Six little orphans in the Street if my Son doesn't come back home soon," but Dr. Fries wants us to merely see that the patient, a speaker of vulgar English, has used an "adverb of locality" in the opening word *there*—a usage that occurs, actually, twice as frequently in standard English. Elsewhere Fries points out that letter 8296, another example of standard English, employs *and* to introduce a consequence: "he was living in hell all the time *and* had to drink to keep from going crazy." Of course, with a whole F. Scott Fitzgerald–style breakdown going on in that sentence, the layman is to be forgiven if his eyes aren't instantly drawn to its grammatical qualities.

Personal tragedies aside, the letters did provide Fries with an impressive catalog of verbal tells of differences between vulgar and standard English. Examining plurals in vulgar English, Fries noted that *s*-less forms were common: "16 year of age," "2 mile down the road," "ten gallon of water." So were certain plus-*s* forms: "a lots of," "youse," "in regards to."

The quirks of standard English number forms were of a different order. "Concord or agreement in number has . . . nearly passed out of the language," Fries stated. Then he showed that *none, any*, and *neither* and *either*, with only one exception, all appeared with plural verb forms, in flagrant contradiction of the traditional rule, which insisted that all of these be accompanied by a singular verb.[5]

Elsewhere Fries had argued that complaints about *he don't* were all too typical of the misplaced priorities of the purists, but the letters examined for *American English Grammar* demonstrated this was indeed a signature usage of vulgar English. *He don't* appeared not even once in the letters of standard English; in vulgar English the use of *doesn't* was "exceedingly rare."

In their treatment of such verbs as *be* and *do*, the vulgar English letter-writers sounded like Ma Joad or a Zora Neale Hurston character. "My children is on starvation," lamented the writer of letter 8037. "The dirt floors requires continual work," said 6413. Letter 8293 voiced the perennial line about misfortune: "Times is so hard." Said 8275, "Father . . . don't make but a small salary."

Double subject nouns connected by *and* were, even in standard English, frequently used with a singular verb when the sense of the noun subject suggested a one-ness. Singular noun subjects were used with plural verbs when intervening words suggested a plural-ness. Another grammatical misdemeanor often found in standard English was the split infinitive. Eighteen of the twenty split infinitives Fries found were from the standard English letters.

In similar amounts of writing, the letters of standard English "contained nearly four times as many participles as did the Vulgar English." And the vulgar examples included past participles without -*ed* endings ("The people *ain't* never *discharge* my son") and mixed past-tense forms ("My folks may *have wrote* you").

The standard English letters yielded many examples of genitives ("possessives" in layman's terms) followed by gerunds (-*ing* verbs that function like nouns) that did not follow classroom rule. By many lights, these phrases all required an *'s* but did not have one: "due to the *instruments* being out of adjustment," "Another reason for the *War Department* crediting my war service to West Virginia," and "There is no record of this *officer* having been attached."[6]

Fries demonstrated that standard English was less traditional than vulgar English, contrary to popular assumptions. Along with the notions that standard English was standard because it was more beautiful and more correct, the received wisdom held that it was also more conservative of linguistic tradition—which had long been one of its selling points.

For example, the standard English letters contained four times as many examples of past participles, which was typical of later patterns in modern English. In the use of the inflected endings -*er* and -*est*, the vulgar English letter-writers were far more traditional, avoiding the newer tendency to use such comparative "function words" as *more* and *most*.

A *function word*—a standard linguistic term coined by Fries in this book—was a word that had no actual content but expressed a grammatical relation. The educated layman to whom Fries addressed *American English Grammar* surely found this to be one of its most difficult concepts. The function word helped to illustrate the increasingly abstract relationships among certain words and usages, especially in standard English. These were always words, many of them prepositions, whose contributions seemed to be nil outside of the phrases they were a part of, linguistic zeros that expressed a relationship but nothing in themselves.

Standard English showed three times as many instances of the adjective–plus–function word phrases *according to, owing to, relating to,* and the sometimes controversial *due to.* Certain kinds of relational word groups appeared only in the standard English letters: *In as much as, In case, In the event that, in order that.*[7]

The standard language appeared rife with such phrases made up of otherwise familiar words whose distinct meanings could not be individually plucked from their context. The common criticism, then, that modern language was becoming a mumbo-jumbo of pompous, ritualized, technical-sounding phrases was a complaint to be set at the door of the standard language and educated speakers.

Again and again, Fries emphasized context and grammatical patterns over and above the values of individual words with individual meanings. Inflectional languages, he pointed out, allowed more freedom of word order. Modern English was mostly uninflected, and word order was critical. Meaning depended on context. Differences in grammar were subtle and sometimes difficult to comprehend, but the evidence Fries had gathered described a virtual class system of the language spoken in the United States.

Vulgar English, like Mencken's parody, relied heavily on pronouns. It also used many fewer adjectives, and much less frequently used a noun as an adjective preceding another noun. Like the Declaration of Independence, "the standard English materials contain many more nouns in the subject and object relation than do those of vulgar English."

Vulgar English omitted many function words like *that* and *which*, and made less use of relational terms such as *provided* and *since* in their conditional meanings, *yet*, and *however*. Most standard English writers failed to use *whom* in the interrogative according to rule (like parts of *shall*, another usage that was fading from the language), but the word *whom* did not appear even once in the letters of vulgar English. Structurally, vulgar English was not less complicated than standard English, but lexically it was very different.

Get, that humble and irritating everyword that never refuses a task, especially in the language of children, appeared "ten times as frequently in vulgar English." The word *so*, in the meaning of "therefore," appeared six times as frequently in vulgar English. Vulgar English strove much less often to express an "analysis and emphasis of the precise meaning relationship involved," as in what Fries called "expanded forms"—phrasings that could, in theory, be simplified but were instead aired out to allow for subtle pinpointing. Vulgar English (like, one might note, a lot of professional, intentionally colloquial writing) tended in the opposite direction. "In vocabulary and in grammar the mark of the language of the uneducated is its poverty. The user of vulgar English seems less sensitive in his impressions, less keen in his realizations, and more incomplete in his representations." The cure for this, Fries would argue elsewhere, was less language study and more language in general, foreshadowing contemporary findings that emphasize the numbers of words and books to which children in educated households are exposed, compared to their economically less fortunate peers.

In *American English Grammar*, Fries ignored literary standards to examine the grammar of the people, but his study did not romanticize the people's language. Unlike the litterateurs of the time, he did not vouch for its ingenuity (as did Hurston) or dignity (Steinbeck), but instead wanted educators to notice its actual structure and a few distinguishing characteristics in order to address its failings. And this required clearing away rubbish like the traditional lessons on *lie* and *lay*, which had never reversed the habit among educated people of saying *laid* instead of *lay* for the past tense and instead of *lain* for the past participle. It also required admitting that the actual difference in underlying grammar between vulgar and standard was, in reality, quite small.

Pompous formality about the rightness of standard English was not going to work. "The experience of at least two hundred years shows that we cannot hope to change the practices of a language; we can only help students learn what those practices are."

Certain speech habits could be supported by social pressure, but "it must be the vigorous social pressure of a living speech, the forms of which can be constantly verified upon the lips of actual speakers."[8]

Rather than go on teaching make-believe rules that were supposed to govern *lie* and *lay*, or the old business about *shall* and *will*, or insisting that *neither, either, none*, and *any* always take a singular verb, or any number of other crotchets of textbook writers, it should be the business of the schools, Fries argued in 1940 and throughout his career, to teach the language of modern professionals, increasingly informal, though still polite, and typical of the educated speaker, language that a child might actually hear in the world outside the classroom.

After sending off his manuscript to the publisher, however, Fries did not hear back for a long while. Finally, about twelve months later, the revised manuscript came back, and it was a shock to look at. Every single instance of uneducated grammar that Fries had quoted in his study—hundreds of passages painstakingly transcribed from those handwritten letters—had been corrected for grammar and usage by some well-meaning copy editor.[9] Luckily Fries had another copy of his original manuscript.

CHAPTER 17

WOODROW WILSON HAD BEEN a great speechmaker, as much when he was president of Princeton University as when he was president of the United States and lecturing Europe on how to put an end to war forever. With his Fourteen Points, America began to lead the world, though more in speech than in deed. Under Franklin Delano Roosevelt, the United States withdrew from the world stage, tending once again to isolationism. Presidential rhetoric remained, with some exceptions, old-fashioned, while American linguists and litterateurs became much more invested in the genuine American idiom.

In World War II, the United States began to genuinely lead the world, this time not with the eloquence of college presidents but with the courage of soldiers and the know-how of engineers. War was a kind of school for American culture, and its graduates spoke less and less like Woodrow Wilson or FDR and more like Dwight D. Eisenhower. Manly bluntness and technical jargon replaced High Church eloquence. Our leaders went from talking of "fear itself" to coining "the military-industrial complex."

Any number of lives from this era might illustrate some of what this implied, but the journalist and publisher James Parton happens to be an important figure in the larger story of this book. And while many observers noted the war's effect on American English, Parton noticed how a Texan's use of American English changed the course of the war.

Fresh out of college, Parton worked as an assistant to the legendary Edward L. Bernays, a nephew of Sigmund Freud who looked to use his uncle's theories to manipulate public opinion. Bernays is quoted in the *Oxford English Dictionary* under *public relations*, an activity he personally helped transform into a profession and industry: "To some the public relations counsel is known by the term *propagandist*."

A cynic might say it was logical for Parton to go from the manipulations of PR—an abbreviation that begins to appear in the coming decade—to working for Henry Luce. But, in Parton's case, writing for a general audience was a family tradition.

His grandfather James Parton had been one of the great popular American historians of the nineteenth century, writing biographies of Ben Franklin, Thomas Jefferson, and other prominent Americans before penning two books about "captains of industry," whom he also called "the rightful successors of the feudal lords of another time." Several of these men (and all were men) had risen from humble beginnings and made their mark upon the world through hard work and ingenuity.

The younger James Parton rose from the Harvard Class of 1934, and, after a year of working for Bernays, took a job at *Fortune*, from which he slid over to *Time*. He was promoted to aviation editor. *Time* had consistently shown great interest in the derring-do of pilots flying *monoplanes* and *biplanes* and other *flyers* in the 1920s. *Airplane* makes its first appearance in *Webster's* in 1929, another generic term being *airship*, yet another being *aëroplane*. Like the language it gave rise to (*flyboy*, *wingman*), aeronautics was a reliable source of novelty and excitement. In 1927, *Time* published a harrowing first-person account of a double plane crash in Buenos Aires that took place during a goodwill tour by the U.S. Army Air Corps.[1] The article was written by Ira C. Eaker, one of the surviving pilots.

Eaker was a propagandist in his own right: for the military potential of airplanes. During the isolationist 1930s, he asked the army to send him to journalism school so he might better craft his message, which he formulated in a series of popular books, cowritten with Colonel Henry H. Arnold, about the romance and adventure of military flying. Born in Llano County, Texas, Eaker wrote like a graduate of the James Parton School of Writing.

"The fighter pilot is a throw-back to the knights of King Arthur. His safety, his success, his survival lie in his own keen eyes, steady arm and stout heart. . . . Here the principles of mass warfare have broken down, we are back to the tournament joust, to the mailed knight on the great charger."[2]

But propaganda was not enough. The United States refused to cultivate airpower and paid a dear price for it in Pearl Harbor, where, Parton thought, "long-range land-based air patrols could have thwarted the Japanese surprise."

In January 1942, Colonel Eaker was promoted to command the American bombing effort in Europe, to be run out of Britain. Parton joined his staff, which was made up of civilian lawyers and journalists, a group that came to be known as "Eaker's Amateurs." That spring, they set up headquarters at the Wycombe Abbey School for Girls, a residence with cooks and waitresses as well as tennis courts both grass and clay. Eaker was keen on fitness. He ordered his officers to exercise for an hour a day, and often joined them with a cigar still in his mouth.

Eaker's military duties required a good deal of diplomacy, but he did not talk like an ambassador. And he did not talk the way he wrote. At a dinner with High Wycombe's mayor, city council, and some two thousand other people, he was called on to give a speech.

Rising reluctantly from his chair, he delivered an address only two sentences long. Its tone was informal and its language was colloquial. It contained no literary or historical allusions, no medieval imagery, and no calls to arms. The word *honor* did not cross Eaker's lips even once. All he said was this: "We won't do much talking until we've done more fighting. After we've gone we hope you'll be glad we came."

The speech was a hit. Like a Hemingway character (or, later, one played by John Wayne), Eaker had found simple American eloquence in the rejection of old-fashioned speechmaking. It was of a piece with the famous story of General Anthony McAuliffe of the 101st Airborne Division, who later held the Belgian town of Bastogne against superior German forces. Given a chance to surrender, McAuliffe refused and sent the Germans a one-word reply: "Nuts."

Airpower was, of course, critical in the European Theater. In less than two years, the Eighth Air Force grew from a handful of officers with no equipment to 185,000 officers and 4,000 planes. Their job was to cooperate with the Royal Air Force to execute a lethal counterattack against Hitler.

Churchill was saying, though not publicly, that "the severe ruthless bombing of Germany on an ever-increasing scale will not only cripple her war effort, including U-Boat and aircraft production, but will also create conditions intolerable to the mass of the German population."

Parton relished a story about Eaker's British counterpart, Sir Arthur Harris, who had been stopped by a policeman for speeding. "You might have killed someone," the officer said. "Young man," the commander replied, "I kill thousands of people every night!"

The Americans, in Parton's telling, were chary of the British taste—acquired during Hitler's savage bombing of London—for taking the fight to the front doors of the German people. But they were overwhelmed by the cooperative spirit of their British hosts and allies. A disagreement meanwhile developed over a common strategy.

The *OED* gives a 1939 citation for *precision bombing*, which *Webster's Third* later defines as "the dropping of aerial bombs by means of a bombsight on a narrowly defined target." In 1942, the phrase was still more of a rhetorical conjuring than a military reality.

The British flew only at night, which, before radar, made it impossible to be discriminating in target selection. The reality of aerial targeting in World War II was better described by another term popularized by the war: *carpet bombing*. This was accomplished by massive formations of bomber planes. Parton, in a biography of Eaker he wrote many years later, dramatically described the coordination this required.

"Each B-17 or B-24 had a crew of ten, and each crew member was a specialist—gunner, navigator, radio operator, bombardier, pilot. Each had to be taught procedures not included in the flying schools of Texas. How, for example, to take off along with as many as 2,000 other planes from 43 airfields crammed in an area the size of Rhode Island, spiral up through as much as 10,000 feet of heavy clouds with constant risk of collision, then assemble above the overcast behind their own squadron and group commanders, rendezvous with fighter escort over the Channel and proceed in huge formations in prescribed sequence to assigned targets and back, a trip often requiring ten hours in the air, much of the time on oxygen."

It was no joust. The defeat of Hitler depended on the success of extraordinary technical undertakings and helped introduce any number of aeronautics acronyms into dictionaries and, to some extent, the standard lexicon: *VHF* for Very High Frequency radio sets for communication among planes, *IFF* for Identification—Friend or Foe, and *ILS* for instrument landing system. But the most critical phrase in the Allied attack on Germany was much less technical-sounding: *round-the-clock bombing, which Eaker made up.*

Around the clock had been around for over a century, but Merriam-Webster dates the *a*-less version to 1938. Eaker used the *a*-less version. He thought that while the British continued to hit Germany at night, his American forces should attack in daylight hours, when it was easier to see a target though also easier to become one.

Working on Eaker's staff brought Parton, only thirty years old, into contact with a number of prominent military and political leaders. He briefed General Eisenhower in the war room at Wycombe Abbey. Though remembered by later generations for his reservations about modern warfare, Ike was a believer in the Eighth Air Force's potential to devastate Germany.

Eleanor Roosevelt passed through, shaking hands with every single one of the three hundred officers present to greet her. Parton escorted her on a tour of a B-17, watching as the first lady "nimbly shoehorned her lanky body" through the bomber's small door near the rear. From the inside, she examined its guns, navigation, and radio systems, and "then gamely insisted on tottering on high heels up the narrow steel catwalk through the bomb bay to the pilot's and bombardier stations."

On her way out, "her eye was caught by a black rubber funnel and hose clamped to the rear bulkhead. 'What is that?' she asked." Parton said it was "for the convenience of the crews during long flights."

"How clever," ER replied.

Parton was promoted to captain and became Eaker's aide-de-camp. On January 15, 1943, he flew with his boss to Casablanca for a major war conference. At dinner Eaker learned from his old co-author General Arnold that the plan to bomb Germany by day was in danger of being overruled.

Parton wrote in his diary, "The president is under pressure from the Prime Minister to abandon day bombing and put all our bomber force in England into night operations with (and preferably under the control of) the RAF." Eaker thought it would lead to disaster. "We'll lose more planes landing on that fog-shrouded island [Britain] in darkness than we lose now over German targets."

It fell to Eaker to meet with Churchill and persuade him to withdraw his opposition. To prepare, he got down to writing. The first draft of his memo, "The Case for Day Bombing," was "completed with journalistic fluency in about three hours," wrote Parton.

"Day bombing," Eaker argued, "is the bold, the aggressive, the offensive thing to do." For Churchill he prepared a one-page "minute," listing seven reasons for day bombing, while handing off another sixteen pages of supporting argumentation to General Arnold to be used in other meetings.

Churchill knew Eaker and liked him, and he knew Eaker was

unhappy. Arriving in his air commodore's uniform, which he wore to meetings with air force personnel, the prime minister said, "Young man, I am half American; my mother was a U.S. citizen. The tragic losses of so many of our gallant crews tears my heart."

Day bombing was not working out, said Churchill, because American losses were double those endured by RAF forces flying at night. Eaker might have rebutted this claim. The Eighth Air Force had, according to Parton, recently lost planes at a rate much lower than the RAF. But rather than argue numbers, the Texan stuck with his one-pager, handing it to Churchill, who motioned for Eaker to take a seat.

The prime minister read the memo half aloud. "When he came to the line about the advantages of round-the-clock bombing," according to Eaker, "he rolled the words off his tongue as if they were tasty morsels."

"How fortuitous it would be," said Churchill, "if we could, as you say, bomb the devils around the clock. When I see your president at lunch today, I shall tell him that I withdraw my suggestion that U.S. bombers join the RAF in night bombing."[3]

The prime minister may not have been persuaded that daytime bombing would work, but the idea of bombing Hitler every hour without reprieve had, as Edward Bernays would have understood, great psychological appeal. The phrase, which would also preserve the equal status of American leadership vis-à-vis the British, had that impressive aspect of just sounding right.

Among the new words popularized by the war, *snafu* was a humorous play on acronyms and later defined as "systems normal all fouled up" in *Webster's Third*. *Blitz* was German, as was *flak*. Screenwriters collected colorful slang while Mencken complained that the bloated prose of New Dealers had become the officialese of the American soldier. The well-named Maury Maverick, an American defense contractor, was irate about the war's effects on American English: "Let's stop *pointing up* programs, *finalizing* contracts that *stem from* district, regional, or Washington *levels*. No more *patterns, effectuating, dynamics*. Anyone using the words *activation* or *implementation* will be shot."[4]

Technical and mathematical language were quite common. *Operations analysis* applied the statistical methods of social science to questions of readiness and strategy. One of Eaker's preoccupations was the soldiers' diet, which analysts strove to correlate to illness and readiness to report for duty. *Operations* was very much a term du jour, used so often it was abbreviated in *SOP* or *standard operating procedure*.

Come March, the Eighth Air Force accomplished one of its signal successes, bombing a submarine plant in Vegesack, near Bremen, Germany. Ninety-seven bombers dropped 268 bombs, each weighing a thousand pounds, on an area no larger than sixty acres. Only two planes were lost in the attack, despite heavy defenses, and the damage to the submarine plant was significant.

Churchill sent Eaker his compliments: "to you and your officers and men on your brilliant exploit." Sir Charles Portal, another of Eaker's doubters, called it "the complete answer to criticism of high altitude, daylight, precision bombing."

The Eighth had used AFCE or *automatic flight control equipment* and measured their effect with a PRU, a *photo reconnaissance unit*—two terms that would end up in Webster's. With the aid of such technology, it was determined that 76 percent of the bombs landed within a thousand feet of their intended target.

Critics moaned about the swollen language, but much of it was due to the changing nature of government and war itself. Modern warfare required modern thinking. And soon the daring of daylight bombing was brought together with the analytical methods of modern military thought. A bombing intelligence group in Washington, D.C., issued a new air doctrine based on the principle that "it is better to cause a high degree of destruction in a few really essential industries or services than to cause a small degree of destruction in many."[5]

It was now more important to bomb Germany's petroleum supplies and ball bearing factories than its cities. From this line of thought came the idea for the simultaneous attacks on Regensburg and Schweinfurt by the Eighth and Fifteenth Air Forces, which resulted in language and drama that soon became familiar back home.

A battle in military jargon was a *show* and this mission, code-named Pointblank, was the *Big Show*. It became the basis of a wildly successful novel, *Twelve O'Clock High* by Beirne Lay Jr. and Sy Bartlett—later a film starring Gregory Peck and then a TV series. In the novel, one of the generals laconically explains the new targeting doctrine:

> *He reached into his pocket and brought out a shiny red object which he held in hand so all could see it. "Approximately half of these German ball bearings are manufactured at [Schweinfurt]," he said. "Last night, Air Chief Marshal, Lord Charles Portal, handed me this one. I'll repeat what he said to me: 'If you can stop the Jerries from making these things, it's going to be a much shorter war.'"* [6]

The only problem with this (in fact) American strategy may have been that the Allies didn't carry it far enough. Years later Albert Speer, Hitler's minister of armament production, told Eaker, "If you had repeated your bombing attacks and destroyed our ball-bearing industry, the war would have been over a year earlier."[7] It was a little more complicated than that, actually, but the Allied air campaign had opened a second front well before the invasion of the continent, and the American contribution was enormous.

CHAPTER 18

AFTER *WEBSTER'S SECOND*, WILLIAM Allan Neilson oversaw the making of a biographical dictionary, extending Merriam's coverage of "noteworthy persons" into a stand-alone volume. While the left talked of the working class, and Hollywood made films about the common man, Neilson's plan for a dictionary of biography conceded little to the new order of who and what mattered.

Only two movie stars had made the cut for *Webster's Second*. Many more motion picture actors were considered for the biographical dictionary, but their social status was clear even in the planning stages when Neilson and others estimated that perhaps fifty movie actors warranted notice, compared to a thousand legitimate-stage performers. Baseball players too were to be included, starting with Hall of Fame members, since by the late 1930s leaving out Babe Ruth and Ty Cobb no longer made sense, but there was much less confidence about reserving space for, say, female tennis professionals.

The relative significance of countries was familiar: First came American figures, next those of the British Empire, and then "other countries and classes." The Editorial Board had decided that "in the case of foreigners of second-rate and lesser importance, it will not be considered necessary to devote much time or effort to the running down of birthplaces when the information is not available in the first source or two consulted."[1]

MERRIAM PRESIDENT Robert C. Munroe, successor to Asa Baker, and a handful of editors, including general editor J. P. Bethel, began tinkering with various plans for *Webster's Third*. Updating their big book, it appeared, could only come at the expense of the great load of encyclopedic facts that had helped make dictionaries one-stop reference works. A universal dictionary like *Webster's Second* that tried to be everything to everyone was still fashionable but no longer possible.

Since 1864, every new revision of the company's largest dictionary had brought a significant increase in the overall size of the book. *Webster's Second* was 26 percent larger than the 1909 edition, which was 41 percent larger than the 1890 dictionary. But such growth could not go on indefinitely. A new edition that increased as much, measuring even 15 to 25 percent larger, "would hardly be practical."

Bethel drew up a memo stating the nature of the problem as the current leadership saw it: "Mr. Munroe and some of the editors . . . concur in the opinion that W1934 [*Webster's Second*] represents in physical size (number of pages, bulk, weight) and in its list price the top limit of a one-volume dictionary."[2]

How to proceed? Two basic alternatives presented themselves: a new edition in multiple volumes or a smaller, less complete edition in one volume.

No one at Merriam thought it commercially wise to make *Webster's Third* a multivolume dictionary. The most likely solution was always a smaller, and less comprehensive, *Webster's Third*.

If so, the very idea for Merriam's largest dictionary would have to change. The unabridged had always been the source of Merriam's other dictionaries. More than any other book, it represented the value of the firm's total holdings, all its lexicographical assets. But already

Merriam was developing smaller, specialized dictionaries, such as the dictionary of biography that Neilson had edited and a dictionary of geography. Would *Webster's Third* become something less than a comprehensive collection whose coverage "blanketed" all the firm's smaller dictionaries?

Of course, one of the great advantages Merriam enjoyed was that its citation files had been growing steadily for well over a century to become the most extensive in the world. And now editors would have to find ways to prune that advantage. If *Webster's Third* was to fit between two covers, the range of possible material had to be reduced. And the biographical section along with the pronouncing gazetteer were among the first items to be mentioned for likely sacrifice. Not that money wasn't to be made selling such material. The dictionary of biography performed very well in the marketplace.

It was simply no longer possible to build on the great tradition of big Webster's dictionaries by adding ever more material. There was simply too much that could be added. Bethel's memo, which he sent to Neilson, mentioned a number of specialized dictionaries—chemistry, law, medicine, and so on—that Merriam might undertake as profitable standalone projects. But a single-volume dictionary that comprehended all that growth in specialized language in addition to the ever-growing lists of words from all the other categories included in *Webster's Second* could no longer serve as the firm's ideal. This system—a hierarchy of information and books in some ways mirroring the world at large—had to change. The next big dictionary would have to be somehow leaner, if not simply less, than *Webster's Second*.

Few were prepared to accept the lamentable necessity of dumping profitable material that dictionary users had come to expect, yet there was already talk of *Webster's Second* as a golden era not to be seen again. Reviewing possible scenarios for the next big dictionary, Bethel gave voice to a minority opinion that called *Webster's Second* the "ultimate in comprehensiveness of editorial content possible." According to this view, only ten years after its publication, *Webster's Second* was "a sort of monument to a closed era of lexicography."

IN LATE 1944, the Editorial Board met to discuss the problem. Dr. Neilson asked what competition *Webster's Second* faced in the marketplace. He also wanted to know if there were any competing large dictionaries on the horizon. President Munroe responded that competition today was "practically nil."

The lovely old multivolume *Century Dictionary* had not been updated in many years. A two-volume edition was for sale but out of date. The short version of the *Oxford English Dictionary* "has never been a real competitor." And Funk & Wagnalls hadn't revised its big *Standard Dictionary* since 1913. The only competition they faced came from the "spurious Webster" put out by the Syndicate Publishing Company in Cleveland, a dictionary that had never been thoroughly revised but sold at a much better price than *Webster's Second*.

This other Webster's dictionary was spurious because it did not descend directly from Noah Webster, but it took advantage of Merriam's lack of a monopoly on the Webster name. There was always a chance that this bastard Webster's might assemble a large staff and make a big book of its own to compete with Merriam's unabridged, but President Munroe thought it highly unlikely.

The editors and President Munroe had already discussed the problem extensively with each other. What they wanted to know was, What did the great William Allan Neilson think?

"Regardless of the competition," it seemed to him that "we have an obligation to the public to continue the publication of a dictionary comparable in size and content" to *Webster's Second*. Furthermore, he believed, "we owe it to ourselves as a matter of prestige to continue the publication of such a work."

It was a matter of prestige. Like the Harvard Classics, the Webster name ought to suggest the absolute highest quality. However, the board was willing to consider some changes.

They were open to the publication of more specialized dictionaries, which made sense given the pace of specialization and advances in professional knowledge. Exactly how those related to the big dictionary was not clear, but it was possible that such work would aid in the eventual full-scale effort of *Webster's Third*. If space in the next big dictionary were indeed so precious, well, perhaps some room could be saved by shortening the pronunciation guide. Reduce a little here and there, and the problem did not seem so large.

"It was suggested," according to the official record, "that the omission of the Gazetteer and Biography sections and such other savings as are made in the front matter will probably be sufficient to take care of the necessary 'new matter' for the Third Edition."

This was not really true. What research had so far been done on the problem showed that much larger cuts were needed.

Neilson seemed to realize this. He asked the board to discuss whether some of the encyclopedic material from the main vocabulary should be cut, but Munroe and Lucius Holt, who had been on the staff of both *Webster's Second* and the 1909 edition, objected. Everyone objected, in fact, even Neilson, who did, however, say that perhaps the table of archery rounds could be left out. And, once he was on the subject, he asked, What about all those history tables? Of battles, of wars, of treaties? The others were sympathetic but no one seconded his suggestions. It was easy, everyone knew, to single out a handful of items that might be jettisoned, but it was all too much to think what those discrete excisions would mean once translated into whole categories of material.

And what about the countless pictures? Neilson said he thought many of the illustrations not very good to begin with: "The pictures of birds, beasts, and fish could virtually all be thrown out without loss." President Munroe said he actually thought the dog illustrations were very good.

The board would stir, as if to take action, but then dither. Biblical names might be left out, and so perhaps obsolete spelling variants. The historical time line for vocabulary might be adjusted. But after a long meeting the only decision made was "that all of these matters would have to be taken up in detail at future meetings of the Board."[3]

Come spring Munroe and the senior editors of Merriam were still hemming and hawing. President Munroe spoke to a meeting of the Editorial Board members and some of the sales staff, returning to the great issue stalking them. "We have reached the limits of physical size in this single-volume unabridged dictionary: What shall we do now?"

Again the discussion turned to the role of the smaller specialized dictionaries, which presented various problems, including the need for specialized sales forces and the possibility that the books might compete with the next unabridged dictionary. Then an even bigger problem was raised, this time framed as a matter of definition: If the unabridged dictionary did not "blanket" the coverage of these other dictionaries, their great big dictionary could not be said to be "unabridged" and Merriam could not go on calling the big dictionary the "supreme authority."

For everyone in the room this was a *sticking point*, to use a phrase dated 1946 in the Merriam-Webster files.

The progress of science and the specialization of knowledge had taken them far, far from the nineteenth-century moment when it seemed possible for a small team of well-educated men to build an unstumpable dictionary, a dictionary to answer any and every question. But the marketing of Webster's dictionaries and Merriam's sense of identity were still beholden to this claim. Rather than surrender the title of "supreme authority," the board and its sales staff even preferred to envision a multivolume dictionary, which no one believed could be anywhere near as profitable.

The meeting took a vote and everyone present agreed that, yes, at some point in the vagueness of time Merriam might be forced to make their unabridged dictionary a multivolume publication. That was unfortunate but acceptable, all agreed. So long as they could call it the "supreme authority."[4]

ON FEBRUARY 13, 1946, in Northampton, Massachusetts, William Allan Neilson, former president of Smith College, passed away. Or, as a euphemism-disapproving linguist might put it, he died.

His name adorned a standard collection of Shakespeare, the Harvard Classics, the *Cambridge History of Literature*, and *Webster's Second*. He was, said the *New York Times*, a man of "executive ability, liberality, and recognized scholarship." Recognized, indeed. Though he had long stopped trying to keep up with new research and methods, his "voice was heard beyond academic limits in the sphere of world affairs." A true successor of Charles William Eliot.

In the uncharitable light of retrospect, Neilson is also remembered as an unusually late Victorian—Mr. Clean Language, Mr. Hygiene, Mr. Fencing of the Tables, warning "the unworthy" not to approach. But the unworthy—in colleges, in the military, and elsewhere—no longer included women, a development he had in many ways championed. For that and many other favors, Neilson was revered and doted on by the students and alumnae of Smith.

And in his pawky manner, Neilson returned that affection without ever surrendering his light touch. On the road he had sometimes fallen into conversation with salesmen, gregarious types who were always glad to advertise their wares. Asked what line of business he was in, Neilson liked to say "skirts"—an inspired usage though labeled slang in the dictionary he had overseen.[5]

"I AM NOT a linguist and have no claim to being a lexicographer," wrote Philip Gove at the close of World War II, in a letter to G. &

C. Merriam Company, inquiring about employment opportunities.

Gove had volunteered for the navy when war was declared and had been stationed as an officer at naval air bases in San Diego and Seattle. It had been a comparatively serene war for him, with time to take a host of correspondence courses in ordnance, gunnery, and other matters of naval operations. Rising to lieutenant commander, he thought about pursuing a postwar military career but too often bristled at the infelicities of bureaucratic life. In a letter to Grace he poked fun at the government prose he was suffering. The use of weather reports had been described as "the effective utilization of meteorological advice," and he had to wonder "whether I could put up with it."

His occasional dissatisfaction with standard operating procedures was visible to others. A commanding officer described Gove incompletely but well in an official report: "He has rather definite convictions and at times is not tactful or diplomatic."

Gove could have returned to teaching at New York University but he had not been treated well there. And elsewhere there seemed to be few opportunities for midcareer academics.

On the plus side, Gove wrote in his letter to Merriam, he had done "considerable research on 17th and 18th century dictionaries" and as a result possessed "about as much knowledge as an outsider could acquire . . . of how dictionaries are made."

J. P. Bethel asked Gove for references, and received letters describing "an extremely capable man in all respects." One shortcoming mentioned was that Gove had, at NYU, been "under the delusion that good teaching would bring advancement."[6]

In August 1946, Gove—principled, but a tad naïve—was offered a position, paying one hundred dollars a week, as an assistant editor.[7] Around this same time higher-ups at Merriam were thinking about how to fill the position once held by the late William Allan Neilson.

~~~~~~

PRESIDENT MUNROE asked Bethel and senior editor Edward F. Oakes to estimate the duties and potential time commitment of a new editor in chief. Their response was thoroughgoing but pointed. The most important duty the new editor in chief could perform was "to sit in a semi-judicial capacity over discussions of editorial policy."[8]

In particular, the new editor in chief should help Merriam loosen the knot they were tied in. "We are building a new and different dictionary for the use of a new generation," wrote Bethel, "but at the same time we are not discarding the scholarship, features, or methods of New International Second Edition that have proved their adequacy."

Opinions differed on many questions, especially on "the essentiality of different features and the desirability of radical change in method." But editorial policy must represent a consensus, Bethel insisted, reached by way of open discussion, and it must result from compromises made to ensure "the best completed product."

The editor in chief must also serve as a representative figure, "the unprejudiced spokesman for the learned class, the leaders of the professions on whose approval, in the opinion of many persons, the prestige of the dictionary depends." Such personages as William Allan Neilson and Noah Porter had not required lessons in speaking as men of the world, so the memo discussed at much greater length the "umpiring capacity" of the new editor in chief, who would have "to sit back as arbitrator" and finally "to act as a brake on personal idiosyncrasies, excessive zeal, unnecessary refinement of editorial material, and anything else that threatens to prove detrimental to the intelligent consultant of the revised dictionary."

CHAPTER 19

IN A WORD, PRESTIGE. The consensus at Merriam was that the new editor in chief should be "a man not only of established reputation in his own field but one whose name is known fairly widely among the public at large." President Munroe wrote to Percy Long, who had worked as an editor on *Webster's Second* and on the 1909 edition. Long said the primary contribution of an editor in chief was "prestige," especially academic prestige.

Yet "there is almost always a choice," Long added, "between actual qualifications and public *réclame*." Quoting Long's letter in a typewritten memo, Bethel inserted by hand four separate phonetic marks on *réclame*, using a pen to do so.

One area of academe possessing a remarkable degree of prestige in these years was science. Bethel and Long agreed that "the day of paramount emphasis in academic circles upon the humanities has passed."[1] Therefore "it might be a shrewd move on our part to select a scientist," a physical scientist, yet not a biologist and not a social scientist.

Not everyone thought so. Harold Bender, who had been in charge of etymologies for *Webster's Second*, felt Merriam should hire another editor in chief whose training was in philology. Said Bender: "I have given further consideration to the suggestion that the next editor in chief should be a scientist," but "the more I think about it the more I am opposed to the idea. It would be a sop to current popular interest, but would, I think, serve no other good purpose."

Popular interest in science was, indeed, enormous, and the publishing industry had been paying great attention to it. Newspapers had been building this appetite for years with reports on the lives and findings of Albert Einstein and Marie Curie—and Curie had even been the subject of a successful Hollywood biopic in 1943. A whole industry of for-profit scientific and technical publishing had developed since World War I, coming on the heels of an explosive growth in the number of university-sponsored science journals in America. Before there was a Book-of-the-Month Club, there was a Scientific Book Club, founded in 1921 and bought out in the 1940s by Henry Holt & Company.

In the last few generations the American intellect had turned increasingly scientific. When Johns Hopkins University was founded in 1876, the United States was a late-to-the-party imitator of European, especially German, scientific research. By the 1930s, American journals were at the forefront of international science publishing. And academic publishing accounted for only a small fraction of all scientific and technical publishing in the United States.

American literary figures found themselves enthralled by the discoveries of modern science. In 1925, the same year that the Scopes trial exposed fundamental tensions between science and scripture, Sinclair Lewis made a scientist the hero of his novel *Arrowsmith*. For this book Lewis had sought the advice of the microbiologist Paul de Kruif, who in 1926 published the bestselling *Microbe Hunters* about Louis Pasteur and the early history of bacteriology. Its dust jacket displayed a blurb from H. L. Mencken, who called its story "one of the noblest chapters in the history of mankind."

Technical publishing addressed both highly specialized professional markets and amateur enthusiasts. During World War II, the publishing industry's Council on Books in Wartime declared that "books are weapons" and responded to the enormous and precipitous demand for technical manuals. At Macmillan, six thousand pages of manuscript became an eighteen-volume series for aeronautical training in little over a month.

Civilians too wanted to know more about the science and engineering contributions to the war effort. The physicist Henry DeWolf Smyth produced the official report of the Manhattan Project for the U.S. Government Printing Office after it was rejected by commercial publishers. Their mistake. *Atomic Energy for Military Purposes* became an instant bestseller and, after being taken over by Princeton University Press, was soon in its fifth printing.[2]

Science equaled prestige. Which is why J. Robert Oppenheimer ended up on the list of names that had been suggested for the position of editor in chief of *Webster's Third*. Such lists are always a potluck, yet the very first name on Bethel's list, the dream candidate, was another scientist, the chemist James Bryant Conant, president of Harvard University. He would "best fill the bill if you could get him; but I doubt if you could," said the recommender.

Several people on the list subscribed to what Charles C. Fries and others called the scientific view of language. Hans Kurath, editor of the *Middle English Dictionary*, which Fries had also worked on, was "known in academic circles for his work in English grammar." Only Kurath was a bit of a stiff and incapable of small talk, which Bethel had noted when seeing him at Modern Language Association meetings. H. L. Mencken, whose extremely modern views on language were shaped by correspondence with language scholars, was also on the list. Mencken was, however, too old, and did not live anywhere near Springfield.

Also, Bethel said, "some of us . . . feel that regardless of age, geographical location, and national reputation, we shall be well advised *not* to select our editor in chief from among journalists and publicists." Although the misbegotten definition of *journalistic* in *Webster's Second* had already caused much embarrassment ("characteristic of journalism . . . hence of a style characterized by evidence of haste, superficiality of thought, inaccuracies of detail, colloquialisms, and sensationalism, journalese"), it apparently reflected strongly held feelings.

Jacques Barzun was recommended by one confidant.[3] Not a scientist, Barzun was just the opposite, a supremely eloquent historian and a de facto spokesman for the humanities in their classical mold. He possessed a significant amount of prestige as a Columbia University professor, the author of several widely noted books, and literary editor of *Harper's* magazine. According to some people, Barzun even looked prestigious, with a prominent nose, straight hair parted neatly on the side, and the patrician bearing of a European aristocrat. "He looked like his name," someone said.[4] The suggestion to try to hire the Paris-born professor was not seriously considered. One wonders if the person who mentioned Barzun's name had taken notice of his views of language, circulated through the recent success of his book *Teacher in America*.

Barzun had said that "we in the twentieth century must offset not only the constant influence of careless speech and the indifference of parents, but the tremendous output of jargon issuing from the new mechanical means at man's disposal. Worst of all, circumstances have conspired to put the most corrupting force at the very heart of the school system."[5]

Barzun was more likely to wield his pen against the proliferation of technical language than seek to profit from it. And he despised the *hokum* (which Merriam-Webster attributes to a combination of *hocus-pocus* and *bunkum* and dates to 1909) of educated writing. This hokum, with its intentional abstractions, amounted to a terrible new language that he called Desperanto.

From a recent master's thesis Barzun drew an example of this new awful lingo: "In the proposed study I wish to describe and evaluate representative programs in these fields as a means of documenting what seems to me a trend of increasing concern with the role of higher education in the improvement of interpersonal and intergroup relations and of calling attention in this way to outstanding contributions in practice."

The passage was bloated from those "expanded forms" that Charles C. Fries found only in standard English. But Barzun did not think such language signaled a careful attempt to draw out abstract relations among words. No, its problem was vagueness. It "says nothing definite. It only embodies the disinclination to think."

Barzun especially loathed the phrase *in terms of*, which he thought epitomized the chronic failure of Desperanto to establish vivid mental connections. Perfectly acceptable as a mathematical shorthand, *in terms of* had become sloppy cant, meaning "any connection between any two things." And it was spreading beyond campus. "The objectionable phrase is now to be found in newspapers, business reports, and private correspondence. It is a menace *in terms of* the whole nation."

Barzun cited the increase in public schooling since 1870. Always from the middle class and below, these strivers have "shown worthy intentions. They want to be right and even elegant, and so become at once suspicious of plainness and pedantic. They purchase all sorts of handbooks that make a fetish of spelling, of avoiding split infinitives, of saying 'It is I' (with the common result of 'between you and I')—in short, dwelling on trivialities or vulgarisms which do not affect style or thought in the slightest."

And now they had become victims of progressive education, "the desire to be kind, to sound new, to foster useful attitudes, to appear 'scientific.'" A pathetic ideology, it resulted in bland textbooks incapable of dramatic effect. These invited not reading but the routinized search for "THREE MAIN RESULTS." Books written by individuals, Barzun noted with Gallic contempt, that reflected the author's unscripted search for wisdom across all disciplines, these were simply not the stock in trade of the growing textbook business.

Jacques Barzun was simply not a dictionary man, not in the modern sense, despite all his learning—or it might even be said, *because* of all his learning. He was a throwback to nineteenth-century ideals of unbounded knowledge. "In the realm of mind as represented by great men, there is no such things as separate isolated 'subjects.' . . . The great philosophers and scientists are—or were until recently—universal minds, not in the sense that they knew everything but that they sought to unite all they knew into a mental vision of the universe."

Columbia University, like the University of Chicago but even earlier, had institutionalized its own curriculum of classic texts. Barzun was a designer, champion, and teacher of the famed Colloquium on Important Books. Discussing the reading habits of students in *Teacher in America*, he turned to the question of what books students found at home.

American parents, especially those recently emigrated to the United States, would gladly pay for anything labeled art or culture, he observed. Especially gullible to the false promises of modern marketing and public relations, they were suckers for books with *snob appeal*, a term the Merriam-Webster files date to 1933. Barzun called *snob appeal* "a recognized trade term," which he thought "should have been in use as far back as Dr. Eliot's 'Five-Foot Shelf.' "

The Harvard Classics, observed Barzun, had brought together the expectation that reading would be easy and "that it shall bring prestige." There was more than a little hucksterism in the whole enterprise, but one great thing could be said for it: "The family that buys the Five Foot Shelf not to read—for it is hard work—but to dazzle their friends, will in time bring forth offspring for whom these books were intended."

THE NEXT editor in chief would not be identifiable with anything so prestigious as the Harvard Classics. The job was offered to Frederic Cassidy, a former student of Charles C. Fries who had worked on the *Linguistic Atlas of New England*, a pioneering study of regional dialect in the United States.[6] This research project sought linguistic evidence in the usage of ordinary people, eschewing literary sources in favor of authentic speech. An affable scholar in his early forties, Cassidy had also produced a charming yet expert study of place names of Dane County,

Wisconsin. He lacked public *réclame* but possessed actual qualifications, which he would later put to use editing the celebrated *Dictionary of American Regional English.*

Cassidy turned down the job. Merriam also approached Albert Marckwardt, another student of Charles C. Fries. Marckwardt, who once said that his name was spelled with as many letters as possible, was best known for a study he co-authored that followed up on Sterling Leonard's pioneering examination of linguistic opinion.[7] Where Leonard had compared the opinions of educated users to the rules of classroom grammar, Marckwardt compared these opinions to what could be discovered about the facts of actual usage in the citations and usage notes of the *Oxford English Dictionary, Webster's Second,* and other sources.

Isolating a list of 121 disputed uses that had not passed muster with a majority of judges in Leonard's study, Marckwardt and co-author Fred G. Walcott found that 87 percent of these apparently dubious uses were perfectly established, in far better standing than Leonard's judges, in particular the severe laymen, had allowed. This helped to map a new reality of correctness, as understood by linguists. After Leonard had discovered that educated opinion was more liberal than classroom grammar, Marckwardt and Walcott found that opinions were still not liberal enough, given the record of actual usage. In practice we English-speakers were more tolerant of deviation from classroom standards than our own stated opinions indicated.

Marckwardt's attitude toward the language could be gleaned from the first sentence of his recently published *Introduction to the English Language*: "The study of language is a science." The inspiration for this book, he said, was a 1928 committee report from the National Council of Teachers of English declaring that college instruction would be deficient if it did not convey "a scientific point of view toward the language."

Cassidy and Marckwardt knew each other well, and had even written a book together, the *Scribner Handbook of English.*[8] It too advanced the scientific view of language, but it was far more congenial to the expectations of consumers than the authors' more scholarly works. The handbook was, in a word, *prescriptivist*. Its business was to tell student writers how they ought to write. "Avoid trite or hackneyed expressions," read one section heading, above a list of clichés such as *breakneck speed*, *budding genius*, and *captain of industry*.

Marckwardt and Cassidy provided a list of the "worst errors of usage," based, interestingly, on the vulgar set of letters examined in Fries's *American English Grammar*. "Many points of usage are disputed or variable but there is no question about those included in this list." There was the failure to add an *s* to make a noun plural (*five mile away*) and the misuse of an apostrophe to make a noun plural; next came *we was*, *you was*, *them people*, *he did it hisself*. The list condemned the confusion of *lay* and *lie*, which Fries had, in fact, singled out as a typical grammar lesson not worth spending any time on. Apparently neither of these students of his agreed.

In the book's glossary of usage, the authors gave an uncompromising entry for *ain't*, writing, "Not acceptable, except possibly in one situation, the first person singular interrogative, *ain't I*, where it may be considered only as a possible colloquial form." The alternatives, Marckwardt and Cassidy explained, were also problematic: *Aren't I?* mixed plural and singular forms while *Am I not?* was rather stilted. But this liberal attitude toward *ain't* began and ended with the first-person interrogative: "Remember that any other use of *ain't* is wholly without justification, and that *ain't* should never be used in any formal situation either in speech or writing."

CHAPTER 20

UNDER MACDONALD'S OWN BYLINE, *Politics* journeyed into the messy theoretical heart of the uncommitted radical, a kind of revolutionary without a country. In his most searching piece from this period, a long two-part essay called "The Root Is Man," Macdonald began to turn away from the Marxist view of injustice as the systematic result of capitalism. He then tended toward a more humanistic view, in which, darkly, man himself is at fault but also, rather optimistically, the only hope.

Macdonald had come to loathe all systems of government. He saw a keen resemblance between the modern capitalistic state and its Nazi and Soviet competitors. Each deprived the individual of the economic and moral power to define his own existence.

In a great passage, the once-blatant anti-Semite described the crushing experience of reading about the horrors of the war, especially the concentration camps. "Let us not only accept these horrors; let us insist on them. Let us not turn aside from the greatest of them all: the execution of half the Jewish population of Europe." One also had to reserve moral revulsion for the Soviet Union, where millions had been starved to death or left to die in state prisons. And still this would not be enough.

The moral conscience must also be stirred, Macdonald argued, by the American firebombing of Dresden and other German cities, and its atom-bombing of Japan, too. And yet it would not do to merely denounce such enormities, for they were as much the result of scientific progress as of modern social organization. In collective action—that of corporations, of armies, of the state—everyone was involved but no one was responsible. "If everyone is guilty, no one is guilty."

It was an overwhelming, unforgiving vision of political fault, so idealistic, so insistent on denouncing the sins of the United States beside those of the Soviet Union and Nazi Germany that it diminished their moral differences and left the radical without a side of his own. In the modern bureaucratic world, the only morally acceptable role was that of the permanent dissident, for he alone is released from the compromises required by living and working with others.

Macdonald was serious about confronting evil but less serious about the other challenges of being in this world. He seemed to lack the humility necessary to reconcile himself to organizations small and large—magazines, marriages, countries—whose wrongdoings and rightdoings somehow become our own. Idealism is a one-man operation, and it was a useful creed for Macdonald, chosen, one suspects, for the support it gave to the pleasant and gratifying work of playing critic at large, a role he always played well.

As a theorist, Macdonald was unimpressive. Pages and pages he devoted to working through his Marxist education and applying it philosophically to the class struggle and the war. As much as he had tried since first laying eyes on *The Communist Manifesto*, he never showed a talent for dialectical work. And his grasp of American history was poor. Though he strove to prove himself as a thinker, he was more successful as a writer, a journalist, a magazine essayist—which this writer certainly does not mean as faint praise. A long, malicious attack he wrote on Henry Wallace, the Soviet apologist and Progressive Party candidate for president, did far more for Macdonald's reputation than any of his more theoretical work.[1]

To the picky, discriminating writer, there is nothing so revealing of a person's true character as the words they favor, and Wallace's vocabulary revealed to Macdonald a dopey liberalism of high motives and low intelligence. He described Wallace as having his own idiom, "*Wallese*, a debased provincial dialect," in which good people are always " 'forward-looking,' 'freedom-loving,' 'clear-thinking,' and, of course, 'democratic' and 'progressive.' " Bad people "were always 'reactionaries' or 'Red-baiters.' "[2]

The major part of Macdonald's still-developing literary gift consisted in finding bumptious nonsense that could be parlayed as journalistic material, at once comic and stimulating. He was a master of the telling detail that not only entertains a reader but silently congratulates him for being smarter than the idiot he is reading about. There is art to such writing, the art of verbal caricature, and there is sport: the fun of making fun and the pleasure of watching blowhards and know-it-alls get their due. But there is always the feeling that a minor injustice is being perpetrated; what saves the reader from being repelled is his confidence that this injustice is somehow deserved—in the end, more right than wrong.

Amid the riches of New York's literary scene, there were other notable styles, also compelling, of intellectual writing about matters of public interest. Less entertaining, less stylish, but altogether more serious, for example, was Lionel Trilling's essay in *Partisan Review* on the first Kinsey report. *Sexual Behavior in the Human Male* sold two hundred thousand copies in its first two months and suggested that a new consensus on sex was taking shape amid the ashes of nineteenth-century reticence.

Sex was above all natural, according to the report, and the more frequent the better. "American popular culture has surely been made richer by the Report's gift of a new folk hero," Trilling dryly commented, "the 'scholarly and skilled lawyer' who for thirty years has had an orgasmic frequency of thirty times a week."[3]

Trilling astutely noted "an awkwardness in the handling of ideas" that required a careful rethinking not of the report's scientific evidence, which he left for others to examine, but of its cultural and moral implications. The report's findings on masturbation contradicted the traditional view codified in *Webster's Second*, where masturbation was memorably defined as "onanism; self-pollution." Kinsey and company sought to defend sex from such traditionalist moralizing and separate sex from character. But, Trilling noted, this did not stop the Kinsey Report from pursuing its own ideas about sex and character, sometimes at the cost of its principles.

According to the report, masturbation was common among upper-class males who found "an insufficient outlet through heterosexual coitus." But it also represented an "escape from reality" and was therefore potentially harmful to the pent-up individual's "personality." What kept the report's authors from entirely countenancing masturbation, Trilling ably showed, was its prior commitment to the sexually uninhibited individual.

"Much in the report is to be understood as having been dictated by a recoil from the crude and often brutal rejection which society has made of persons it calls sexually aberrant." And this was a "good impulse," said Trilling, but it was pursued thoughtlessly.

The report rejected the altogether sinister view that homosexuality was evidence of "psychopathic personality." Fair enough, said Trilling, but the authors had not by this simple gracious act won social equality for homosexuality. In short, the fact of homosexuality did not save scientists and other thinkers from the work of thinking about how it might be accommodated.

Trilling had been educated at Columbia University in the 1920s, first in the general studies course developed by John Erskine, who had studied under Charles Eliot Norton. His essay showed how a classically trained mind was equipped to address questions, difficult moral and social questions, too subtle for scientific evidence-gathering. It was a style capable of humor and especially strong at making careful distinctions between fact and interpretation, between the is and the ought. It could be generous to other disciplines and views it opposed (speaking humanistically and quite ably to the authority of science), but it assumed a burden of seriousness, preferring classic categories to catchy handles while eschewing the pleasures of mockery and making one's opponents out to be fools.

The two writers—Trilling and Macdonald—took an interest in what was only recently being referred to as "popular culture." In 1944, Dwight Macdonald had written, "surprisingly little attention has been paid to Popular Culture by American intellectuals," capitalizing a phrase that he also used with quotation marks in the title of an article in *Politics*, indicating its novelty.[4] A Google Ngram search shows *popular culture* to be exceedingly rare before the 1950s. If Clement Greenberg's argument about kitsch showed the difference between cheap reproduction and high art, Macdonald's essay began the work of cataloging examples of popular culture, from the popular science of Paul de Kruif and the popular philosophy of Will Durant to the literary criticism of Henry Seidel Canby and the journalism of *Reader's Digest*, which typified for Macdonald all that was wrong with literary culture in America.

"Here is a magazine which in a few years has attracted an enormous circulation simply by reducing to even lower terms the already superficial formula of commercial periodicals. Where *Harpers* treats in six pages a theme requiring twelve, *Reader's Digest* cuts the six pages to two, making it three times as 'readable' and three times as superficial."

Success of this order practically required the diminution of smaller, nobler efforts such as *Partisan Review* and *Kenyon Review*. A cultural version of Gresham's law took effect, and the bad drove out the good. Macdonald had long been a cultural pessimist, yet he paused to reflect on one especially novel example of popular culture: superheroes. Just a few years after the introduction of *Superman*, a striking response of American imagination to the despair of the 1930s, Macdonald was recommending that radicals pay attention to such "synthetic" folk heroes.

But as with Greenberg's essay on kitsch, which mapped the cultural distance between the avant-garde and the rear guard, Macdonald looked to separate the high from the low. One sees the beginning of a recurring lament for Macdonald, that fairly serious culture that could be taken for granted in Paris or London was not available in America except on the margins. Typical of this period, however, Macdonald treats the question as a political one, asking about the exploitative aspects of American capitalism. But even here one sees the roots of a cultural critique that would soon be caricatured in popular discussions of highbrow versus middlebrow versus lowbrow culture, in *Harper's* (though in fewer pages, of course) and other magazines.

BY THE end of the 1940s, Dwight Macdonald was depressed about politics and exhausted by *Politics*, which he not only wrote for, but edited, proofread, and laid out all by himself. And he began to part ways with his social conscience, Nancy. His approach to life changed. Political abstractions gave way to matters of the self. He started recording his dreams and liking his children and exploring a newfound sensuality in extramarital affairs.

All the while he kept a busy schedule of organization-joining and -supporting, lecturing, and correspondence. To George Orwell, he wrote, "I wonder if you share my private enthusiasm for Dr. Johnson?"[5]

The Macdonalds finally moved out of Greenwich Village to an apartment in Midtown. In 1949, Mary McCarthy published *The Oasis*, an anti-utopian satire of "the family," the circle of anti-Stalinist New York intellectuals bound to each other through *Partisan Review* and other publications. Dwight Macdonald appeared as Macdougal McDermott, who had "sacrificed $20,000 a year and a secure career as a paid journalist. . . . He had moved down town into Bohemia, painted his walls indigo, dropped the use of capital letters and the practice of wearing a vest."[6]

He is one of the leaders of a group of intellectuals who flee the city to start a utopian colony in the mountains. The first sign of trouble comes when the colonists have to decide what to do about Joe, a successful businessman, a "well-intentioned Babbitt" who has latched on to the scene in order to pursue his passion for painting but quickly runs afoul of the local gods.

For its transparent depictions of the family, *The Oasis* became the scandal of the year. "More rows, clashes, feuds, and factional conflicts in the NYC literary world this winter than at any time in the past—maybe it's all breaking up—rather frightening really," thought Macdonald.[7]

CHAPTER 21

IN 1950, *COLD WAR* and thirty-six pages of other new terms appeared in a special addendum, inserted into the latest reprinting of *Webster's Second* just before the main vocabulary. The once-"fanciful" *A-bomb* was thus entered, along with a definition for *Manhattan Project*. Words to describe the challenge of the USSR gave rise to entries for *commie, hammer and sickle, red, red-bait, NKVD,* and *soviet.*

The Soviet threat colored other additions. A *stooge* was a dim-witted foil on the stage and screen. Larry, Moe, and Curly were not mentioned, but communism was. In the third sense a *stooge* was "a group outside the USSR that plays a completely obedient and obsequious role to Soviet dictation." In defining this pointed term, the lexicographer adopted the point of view of the word itself. Similarly, communism was left out of the newly added definition of *witch hunt*: "A searching out of victims professedly for exposure on charges of subversion, disloyalty, or the like . . . esp. liberals." This same year Alger Hiss was convicted of perjury. Communists in the State Department? "Fanciful," the dictionary seemed to say.

War had contributed much new vocabulary that needed defining: *beachhead, biological warfare, combat fatigue, flak, sack time, sad sack, snafu.* And older words and phrases found new meanings and relevance: *bombardier, dogfight, ground crew, scuttlebutt.* Entries for *Marshall Plan,*

National Security Act, the *Social Security Act,* and *Truman Doctrine* were added. Room was made for all the wartime abbreviations: *V E Day, V J Day, WASP, WAAF,* and so on. *GI* was defined to include both *GI Joe* and *GI Jane.* An entry for *World War Two* itself was added.

Keeping up with the language required keeping up with the culture, itself reshaped by newfound leisure time and the tastes of young Americans. *Teenage* and *teenaged* had been around since the 1920s, and other forms of the words much, much longer, but in recent years these adjectives grew into persons and the cultural figure known as the *teenager* had to be entered in the dictionary and defined.

What he or she chose from the *jukebox* might suggest they were a *bobby-soxer.* The jazz-inspired *jive* was finally entered, after decades of nonrecognition. *Round the clock* was added, two years before Max C. Freeman and Jimmy De Knight wrote the quintessential "Rock Around the Clock," made into a resounding hit by Bill Haley and the Comets in 1954.

Dwight Macdonald's favorite fabric, *rayon,* had made it into *Webster's Second* in 1934; *polyester* was entered in 1950 in the new addendum, where the *new look* was described as "the 1947 mode in women's clothing calling especially for much longer fuller skirts, and narrower waistlines, following relaxation of the material shortages of World War II." *Pinball* was added, as were *pizza* and *hamburger.* Pizza had been around for a long, long time, of course, but now English-speaking people, Americans especially, were eating it, in *pizzerias,* some decades after waves of Italian immigrants had arrived. *Webster's Second* had only an entry for *Hamburg steak,* sounding like some Teutonic pensioner who might have sworn fealty to the Kaiser. For drink service, *jerk* and *soda jerk* were now being yanked into the pages of Webster's.

A new image of American domesticity was coming into view. With television ownership on the rise, the abbreviation *TV* needed consideration. As Levittown on New York's Long Island was still under construction, *prefab* shows up in the addendum. And what would suburbia be like without the *station wagon*? This car was driven on the *expressway* or the *superhighway*, either way likely to be one of those *cloverleaf* roads Dr. McClintock had discussed in *Time* magazine. What to do when a young couple wanted to go for a ride? Hire a *babysitter*, a term Merriam-Webster dates only to 1947. The "tender relation of one to one" was already netting a great many babies to sit, but *baby boom*, dated 1941 in the Merriam-Webster files, did not yet rate.

CHAPTER 22

IN 1950, W. FREEMAN Twaddell, a professor of German on leave from Brown University, joined G. & C. Merriam Company as a resident editor responsible for *Webster's Third*. He stayed long enough to determine that he was not needed.

J. P. Bethel continued as general editor. And after Twaddell had been on board for a year or so, Bethel asked him as a relative newcomer to write down his impressions of the staff. It was not a casual suggestion, but a request for a statement that could be circulated to the president and the Editorial Board. Nor was the exchange spontaneous; Bethel knew what Twaddell would say and wanted him to say it.

"My strongest impression," wrote Twaddell, "is that the Editorial Department, thanks to the wise policies and careful administration of the past couple of decades, has come of age; it is a force of the first order—anonymous and somewhat awe-inspiring."[1]

Twaddell compared himself to the swallow in a story told in the eighth century by the Venerable Bede, a church historian. The swallow flies through an open door and into a house where people are peaceably eating dinner, then immediately leaves by another door. After so brief a visit, Twaddell had not developed an insider's view of Merriam, full of history dating back to Webster himself. He nevertheless felt confident in his observations and ready to argue for the reversal of a major long-standing policy.

"It is no longer necessary or even desirable to import or borrow the prestige of an eminent outsider for any product of the Editorial Department." The reason was simple: "No one personage, in scholarship, combines high reputation and balanced versatility as the Merriam-Webster editorial staff does."

The search for a "name," a spokesman for the learned professions, was actually self-defeating, Twaddell argued. Should there be a controversy, the dictionary would too easily be cast as an extension of that one person's predilections. "That one name is far more likely to arouse suspicions of one-sidedness, of this or that over-emphasis, than the reverse."

It was an argument for actual qualifications over public *réclame*, questioning the power of figureheads to lend majesty to those humble clerks and middle managers who do the actual work. Those names that flit about from government commissions to the presidential offices of colleges and universities to the covers of major anthologies, the William Allan Neilsons of the world, they did not deserve what rightly belonged to the staff lexicographer, who, like the forgotten man of Rooseveltian rhetoric, possessed all the experience, all the skill, Merriam wanted.

Beyond this, the passing swallow saw a set of problems essentially practical in nature. In making *Webster's Third*, he said, "there are two evils that the Editorial Department has to avoid." The first was "lost motion, needless disturbance of the smoothly functioning machinery by the ignorance and inexperience of a newcomer." This problem could be avoided "only by turning over administration to a Merriam editor who knows the ropes and knows the deficiencies of individual staff members."

The second "evil" was "the ever-present danger of being un-self-critical, ingrown, tradition-bound." This Twaddell did not consider a real problem, since the editorial staff was "anything but stodgy." But this criticism was sometimes heard from competitors.

To undermine the suggestion and perhaps even address the felt need for a little outside prestige, Twaddell recommended that Merriam assemble a board of paid advisers, including some of the people who had been considered for the job of editor in chief. These individuals would be in a position to make genuine specialized contributions in their areas of expertise but, more important, their opinions could be separately polled for any innovations Merriam was contemplating. Then their advice could be ignored if necessary.

As a parting word, Twaddell mentioned another action that could be taken instead of wasting time in search of a prestigious editor in chief: An assistant could be hired for Bethel, the man who asked Twaddell to write up his impressions. Too much of Bethel's time, Twaddell had noticed, was taken up by routine reports, correspondence with the printer, and company records. If the editorial staff was what distinguished Merriam, then its time needed to be used more carefully.

Bethel's exact reaction to this last suggestion is not known, but it seems safe to say that he approved.

ONE OF the first changes to the traditional design for *Webster's Third*, for which there was already broad support, was the end of the split page, in which minor words were relegated to a footer that staff called the "downstairs." By crediting Merriam's editors and definers with all the necessary intellectual authority, Twaddell helped reverse another upstairs-downstairs hierarchy, that which dignified the prestigious outsider who stopped in for meetings every couple of weeks at the expense of the hardworking insider who showed up every day.

Two months after receiving Twaddell's memo, acting president Robert Munroe gave Associate Editor Philip Gove a promotion. "You have been selected to have full responsibility, under the Editorial Board, for the editing and production of the next edition of the Merriam-Webster Unabridged Dictionary." Hired in 1946 at a salary of $5,200,

Gove would now receive $8,000 per year, "extra compensation if business returns warrant," a pension, and "the privileges of the services of the Blue Cross and Blue Shield."[2] His title, for the time being, was managing editor, but he was the most senior individual working on *Webster's Third*. He was the new person in charge.

CHAPTER 23

SHORTLY AFTER BEING PROMOTED, Philip Gove indulged an urge that would have seemed out of character to many people who later came to know his name. He politely, grammatically, and ever so carefully told someone off—someone who had offended his highly discriminating sense of what was right and appropriate in the use of language.

Gove was at home, recalling the circumstances. Home was a house on a farm in Massachusetts, twenty miles east of Springfield. A slim man almost fifty years of age with close-cropped, graying hair, drawn neatly in a middle part, Gove was sitting at a typewriter and working from handwritten notes, as was his custom.

His daughter Doris had brought home a note from her second-grade teacher. It was "a familiar purplish-blue stencil, faint and wrinkled."[1] He called the note's appearance "familiar" because, as the father of three children, among whom Doris was the youngest, he'd seen many of its kind. And as examples of written communication they were uniformly disappointing. "When these notes turn up . . . I never know whether I am being queried by the child's teacher, by a student helper learning to type, or by the truant officer."

His wife, Grace, usually referred such notes, forms, and permission slips to him, so "my signature shows up rather often; their mother might be nobody in particular." Yet he was no longer the parent who wrote excuses for when a child was absent. "I never could bring myself to write, 'Please excuse Doris for being absent yesterday.' Instead I would write, 'Doris was absent yesterday because she didn't go to school.'" Such a message was intended not to be rude but truthful.

Explained Gove, "I didn't care whether the child was excused or not." So, asking that the child be excused would have been insincere, a lie. No wonder, he said, "my excuses kept coming back to me for a revise."

The latest note was about transportation to and from school. It asked, "On what bus do you ride to school?" Since the note was addressed to him, Gove considered writing "none." Instead, he shrugged off the problem and asked his daughter about the bus, but she too insisted that queries be phrased in just such a way. He parried by asking if it was maybe the East End bus or the number 2.

"How should I know?" said Doris.

Well, Gove continued, "what do you call it?"

"We don't call it," Doris answered. "It just comes." And, besides, "It isn't a bus at all."

As it happened, the vehicle that picked her up was a car. Gove kept at it though. "We'll skip the first one. What time does it, the bus, I mean the car, leave your stop?"

Doris asked, "What's a stop?"

With this Gove decided it was no longer worth playing along with this stupid, misaddressed, ambiguous note from the teacher. He folded it over and wrote on the back, "I am sorry but no one in my house seems to know the answers to any of these questions," and because what he had written was true, he signed his name.

"Next night the note was back home," he recalled. "Written in pencil beneath my writing was the following, unsigned: 'Would you please fill in the name, residence, and the approximate time that Doris has to leave the house and the time that she usually arrives home in the afternoon. Please sign your name. Thank you.'"

This request seemed a little more straightforward. Gove re-interviewed Doris and a half hour later began to write the teacher a reply that surely went through several drafts before ending up almost four pages long. It was the kind of letter you write to let someone know that they are a perfect idiot.

Tired of being addressed as "Parent," Gove took his revenge. "Dear Teacher," he wrote, "I know the name of Doris's teacher, of course, and if I were sure that you are her I would call you by name." Take that!

As for names, he said, "Doris's name is Doris." However, he went on, "it is rather uncertain what time Doris leaves the house in the morning."

There were several clocks in their house but they were not synchronized. And Doris herself was unpredictable. On her way out, she might stop in the bathroom or get distracted by a toy in the hallway or look in the kitchen for something to eat. But even if she were to check the kitchen clock as she walked out the door, more than likely she'd come back in, then leave again at a different time. Also, she was not so good at telling time to begin with. "Maybe you can get around to drilling her class on how to tell time. But first teach her to reply to notes about herself. At least, tell her what kind of answers you want, and all I would have to do is sign."

The second half of the letter was devoted to the equally bedeviling question of when Doris left school and arrived home. "She has to walk some 500 yards from the highway to our house." And, of course, the little seven-year-old was prone to distraction then as well: "If she sees a squirrel in the big oak tree, she's likely to try to communicate with it. . . . And on rainy days our dirt road fills up with puddles. They all have to be counted and stirred with a stick." Toward the end of the letter Gove happened on a bright idea for determining when Doris gets home: "If you want, we can ask her to come straight home all the way some day next week and then phone you herself. You can look at the school clock and would have the official time of her arrival for that day."

Philip Gove sent this note to his daughter's second-grade teacher, and then because the memory of it made him chuckle he recorded its contents in an essay, one of a handful of familiar unpublished memoirs he wrote over the years.

But this was several years before history's most notorious dictionary was published. Gove was still an innocent, not yet excoriated in the press as a saboteur of the English language and the dangerous proponent of the philosophy that "anything goes." In less than a decade, to quite a throng of newspapermen, schoolteachers, parents, intellectuals, mystery readers, and priests, Gove would become known as one of the most dangerous men on earth, a great relativist who was trying to sweep away all the rules of grammar and usage and doom the English-speaking West to a twentieth-century Tower of Babel. To Doris's second-grade teacher, however, he must have seemed simply a noodge, a stickler, and maybe an ass.

CHAPTER 24

AFTER MORE THAN FIFTY years with the company, Robert C. Munroe, then president and successor to Asa Baker, opened a meeting of the Editorial Board by saying, "I look upon this as one of the most important meetings this company has ever had." The date was November 20, 1951.

"We are about to develop policies for a new Merriam-Webster dictionary, a dictionary which will probably be one of the most momentous publications in all of the publishing world. Although I am not an overly religious man, I almost feel like opening this meeting with a prayer that we'll be guided in the right direction."[1]

The direction was not entirely clear and the circumstances less than auspicious. "I refer to the Black Hole of Calcutta," Munroe said, "without any daylight or fresh air, and with the mustiest old books imaginable." After that enigmatic comparison, he turned the meeting over to Philip Gove.

"It is ironic," Gove said, "that the very title of the book we are considering contains a series of words which almost defy definition. It starts out with the word *Webster*, about which there seems to be considerable doubt. The exact meaning of the word *New* is anyone's guess. The word *International* has never been clearly defined. We are not even sure of the precise definition of the word *dictionary*, and the word *English* is open to considerable discussion. The word *language* has had a multitude of interpretations, and, finally, it is almost impossible to define precisely the word *Unabridged.*"

Strange but true, the current editor of *Webster's New International Dictionary of the English Language, Unabridged*, found the meanings of these words to be so debatable that he was openly casting doubt on whether this volume was still Webster's, actually new, definitively international, really a dictionary, categorically English, or even unabridged.

Much had changed since 1934. Gone was the nineteenth-century confidence that had shaped the information and opinions of *Webster's Second*. A "universal" dictionary, a "supreme authority" was impossible if not laughable. There were now countless issues, it seemed to Gove, that could not be settled behind a closed door by a handful of men of goodwill.

"Language is infinitely complicated," he said, "and the dictionary is therefore infinitely complicated. It demands a type of understanding that defies the ability of any one individual: it demands so much understanding that no one can understand it all and only a few can move about in it comprehendingly."

These were not philosophical problems better ignored by the lexicographer, or minimized in order to sell dictionaries. Gove was far too principled for such cynicism. The layman's point of view had been shown to be primitive, superstitious, unsound. It could no longer be placated.

But now the theoretical conundrums that riddled linguists became practical challenges for the lexicographer. The basic problem was this, said Gove: "We can never know fully what any word means to another person. The nine of us could not agree on the word *girl* on any but an elementary level."

He said it was "unfortunate" that the company had billed its big dictionary as "the supreme authority," a comment that by itself represented a 180-degree turn in the zeitgeist that informed the work at Merriam-Webster. An unabridged dictionary, he added, was really only for the "intelligently literate." More than the ability to read was needed to profit from its use.

Then, finally sounding optimistic, like a man undertaking a long and difficult project, he said the new dictionary would strive for nothing less than "the widest possible coverage of standard language." So great a feat required the company to "keep step with linguistic advance." As language changed, so must the vocabulary of a dictionary, so must its sense of how words were used.

Everyone, of course, was in favor of that. Without new words and usages, new dictionaries would not be necessary; and without a need for new dictionaries, Merriam would go out of business. But this was only a short breather. Gove quickly returned to his objection to calling Webster's the supreme authority.

"Thirty years ago," he said, "one of the leading linguists in this country, Sapir, warned against identifying a language with its dictionary. Since then the studies of scientific linguists have made this warning even more significant."

This convenient fiction of the dictionary business, the unexamined idea that prompted loads of paying customers to say, *Well, is it in the dictionary?* or *What does Webster's say?*, the notion that a dictionary was the language in a bottle, or rather a book, the entire English language printed up, spelled out, and *defined*, this amounted to an intellectual error that G. & C. Merriam could no longer countenance. Philip Gove would not go around claiming his dictionary as a "register of thought" or "the indispensable basis of literature," as Professor Hart had said about *Webster's Second* in 1934.

Gove was not afraid to speak the awful truth. In fact, he seemed to like saying it. A dictionary was not the language; a dictionary, even an unabridged dictionary, was only a selective inventory of the language.

He did not essay for long on the contributions of linguistics, but he mentioned that linguists tended to belittle dictionaries because they failed to keep pace with linguistic change. He alluded to studies like

Albert Marckwardt's, which had documented how our spoken and written language were much more tolerant of deviation from the rules of classroom grammar than educated opinion and the usage notes of dictionaries suggested.

It was a rather tricky phenomenon Gove was hinting at. People thought of themselves as old-fashioned on grammar, swearing fidelity to rules they violated every day. The lexicographer who believed that practice mattered more than stated preferences could end up selling a product people said they didn't want.

A controversial reputation was already attaching to the work of these scientific linguists, so it was remarkable that their work should now become a major point of reference for a mainstream commercial dictionary. But in promoting Gove, Merriam-Webster had determined that technocratic and scholarly knowledge were more important than worldly knowledge and political instinct. In Gove they found an editor whose principles and personal habits would not allow for a cordial smoothing over of the difference between the old way and the new way.

Gove announced several policy changes, the most important being the new stand on so-called encyclopedic matter, yet another way in which the new dictionary would give up the claim to being universal. *Webster's Third* would not pretend to have answers to all possible questions; that claim now seemed a pathetic, empty boast.

Then Gove told a story about an old Merriam hand named William Wheeler who had worked under Noah Porter on the 1864 Webster's and written a three-hundred-page supplement of encyclopedic material, including character names from fictional literature, names from the Bible, information for a gazetteer, and "gleanings from history and philosophy." Wheeler expanded this material into an independent book, which was then reabsorbed almost completely in the 1890 Webster's before becoming an almost permanent feature of the unabridged dictionaries. In *Webster's Second* in 1934, about three-quarters of Wheeler's material, much of which had not been revised in seventy years, had been reprinted.

Leaving out all encyclopedic material—proper names, entries on wars and other historic events, types of ships, and so on—was not entirely possible but such material had to be massively reduced if *Webster's Third* were to remain a single-volume dictionary. Gove proposed to omit a number of antiquated learned terms, unanglicized foreign terms, proper names (*Webster's Second* had devoted thousands of lines to masculine and feminine names: *John, Mary*, and so on), epithets such as *Athlete of Christendom* and entries starting *Lady of,* the titles of literary works, and the furthest reaches of slang and dialect. "All of these recommendations could be summarized by a recommendation that, in general, we make Webster's Dictionary primarily a dictionary of the standard language as spoken throughout the English-speaking world."

After lunch he reached another important item on his agenda, getting the Editorial Board out of his way.

"Of primary importance to the successful determination and guidance of editorial policy was the formation of the Editorial Board," said the publisher's statement of *Webster's Second*. The board had been an executive committee of company president Asa Baker, editor in chief William Allan Neilson, general editor Thomas A. Knott, and managing editor Paul W. Carhart. These four had brought together business sense, worldliness, and lexicography to handle those delicate decisions that might affect the company's bottom line, reputation, or intellectual integrity.

But the board had also slowed down the works. The minutes of the Editorial Board's meetings stretched to two thousand pages, filling eleven volumes.

"To me," Gove told the current eight members of the board, "that represents a stupendous, if not stultifying, waste of time." In one instance, he said, the *Webster's Second* board had spent at least an hour discussing whether *hot dog* should be in the dictionary. (In the end *hot dog* had won admission: "a heated wienerwurst or Frankfurter, esp. one placed in a split roll;—used also interjectionally to express surprise or approval. *Slang.*")

Prior to the day's meeting Gove had circulated a particularly technical memo on how the new dictionary should handle botanical classification. Did the board members really want to read, absorb, and opine on such material? If so, he had other memos they might want to see.

"I have a memo here which consists of thirty single-space pages on the subject 'Repetition in Definitions,' referring to the use of the defined word in subsequent definitions of derivative words. Every point is itemized in clear detail, with all possible methods considered. . . . It would take anyone hours to digest and follow it. Do you want that sort of thing mimeographed and circulated before meetings? Can we afford the expense and time of it?"

Gove volunteered that all such memoranda be kept in a master book, a digest of editorial policies the board would be free to consult but not modify. "I don't want a vote," he said. "Take the botany classification memo. It's been shown to you; if anyone objects, the objection is on the record."

President Munroe readily allowed that handling such questions was really the job of Gove and the editorial staff. But, he wanted to know, if such matters were *not* brought to the attention of the board, how would the company avoid the inclusion of entries that might hurt sales?

Munroe mentioned the embarrassing entry for *journalistic*. Few things could be more dangerous than the mistake of antagonizing journalists, who not only exercised great influence over the stylistic direction of the language but among whom there appeared a number of individuals who delighted in writing about language questions and dictionaries.

Gove pointed out that the definition for *journalistic* was, essentially, a procedural mistake. The proper first sense of the word—characteristic of the work of gathering news and reporting in a periodical—was skipped, and the deprecating sense, which indeed needed defining, was given as the only meaning.

"You must grant that the editorial department consists of human beings," said Gove, "and they will make a slip once in a while. I think that the consensus seems to be that we do not need to have the detailed analyses of the Second Edition Editorial Board meetings."

Gove's appointment, like his comments, marked a major shift for Merriam. The staff expert became the company's *point man* (to use a World War II term), chosen not for his reputation among educated consumers but for his highly developed skills as an editor and lexicographer. The technical grumbling usually concealed within a company's lower ranks now surfaced at the executive level, and the happy face of a company leader was replaced by that of a truth-telling middle manager.

He took an insider's view of dictionary work, but Gove was not without broad ambitions for *Webster's Third*. Its predecessor had called itself "an interpreter of the culture and civilization of today." The same should be true of "the dictionary of 1960," Gove said, even if "the culture and civilization of 1960 is not coequal with that of 1930."

CHAPTER 25

"WHAT SHALL WE DO about grammar? What is the relationship of English to a core program? Shall we have separate courses in English and speech? How should the literature program be organized? What shall we do about radio, television, newspapers, magazines?"[1] Such questions—illustrating how *shall* in the first-person plural interrogative had come to seem hopelessly earnest—were asked of the leadership at the National Council of Teachers of English in the 1940s and '50s.

The old rules were in doubt; classroom drills were out of favor. In the optimistic glow of postwar rebuilding, students were to be treated as individuals, equals even, all worthy of an education, and education was to reflect the goals of society. *Communications* was the new byword, as teachers talked of the powers of mass media, and language skills were understood to go far beyond reading and writing. Learning was a *cooperative* activity. And listening, it was said in all seriousness, might just be the most important skill of all. (No laughing.)

In 1945, the council had established a special commission on the English curriculum and divided the field into four parts: reading, writing, speaking, and listening. The resulting four subcommittees multiplied into twenty or so sub-subcommittees, as almost two hundred concerned educators representing kindergarten to graduate school outlined a new curriculum for language development. The results would fill five portentous volumes, the first of which, an introductory overview, was published in 1952 under the title *The English Language Arts*.

NCTE had come a long way from the 1920s, when organizers had to worry whether at least fifty people would attend the annual conference, thus qualifying members for a discount on train passage.[2] Yet the spirit and person of its onetime president Charles Carpenter Fries were still influential, even if Fries himself was no longer an officeholder in the council's growing bureaucracy. Other linguists close to Fries had become active: Albert Marckwardt, Robert C. Pooley, Harold B. Allen.

The linguists formed an intimidating faction among the ranks of schoolteachers and college instructors. They were armed for intellectual battle to a degree the average English teacher or school principal was not. But the council's aims reflected not only the agenda of its linguists.

NCTE was, broadly speaking, a liberal organization, high-minded and eager to advocate for the latest ideas of its profession. H. L. Mencken would have called them improvers, do-gooders. Their purpose floated high above recommending a course of study. They wanted to release the American student from all that was holding him back.

"The problem," as described in the preface of *The English Language Arts*, was "looking at the learner and the society of which he is a part and aiding his growth both in and through the elements of reading, listening, and expression necessary to effective living today."

NCTE sought a better world through language arts—a world of freedom, democracy, and "effective living." Teachers were instructors in "democracy's schools." And "democracy," they added, "can be no more effective than the individuals of which it is composed."[3]

The rhetoric was almost Wilsonian in its support of educational self-determination. Students were equals. "Children will share with the teacher the responsibility for determining how effectively they now use language." The old hierarchical concept of a teacher judging a student's performance and, if unsatisfactory, holding him back, so-called nonpromotion, was a thing of the past.

Education was for everyone. Literature, however, was not. "For many young people, time spent in the effort to read the literary classics is largely wasted." For others, "the purpose of reading literature is clearly defined as an aid to personal growth."

Reading itself was overrated. In fact, people listened most, spoke much more than they read, and wrote very little. But the American school curriculum, NCTE said, made it seem like reading and writing, the least frequently used language skills, were the only ones worth teaching.

"Men communicate because they are concerned with ideas; and the ideas are conveyed and received both by oral and written means." The teaching of language arts needed to reflect the genuine uses of language in the world outside the classroom. And, according to NCTE, this outside world looked and sounded something like a welcome address to the recently formed United Nations.

"Problems of values, of interpersonal relations, of recreation and leisure, of life purposes, of the spirit and aspirations of the democratic society, of world unity, of the motives of human beings, of the intelligent utilization of the mass media of communications, of the meaning of life itself—these should provide the substance of the language arts program."[4]

Yet while promoting world unity and discovering the meaning of life teachers also had to teach grammar. And not grammar as it was once taught.

It was no longer "a set of fixed facts and principles, a logical structure of rules." Such a "static and authoritarian point of view" no longer obtained. "In the last half century linguists . . . have evolved five basic concepts which are, or should be, the foundation of the current attitude toward any teaching of the English language today."

1. *Language changes constantly.* The anonymous author of the chapter quoted Chaucer and referred to Shakespeare (literature, apparently, being sometimes quite useful) to note that over the course of years and centuries the language changed. Words sometimes changed meaning; styles of expression came and went. The language of older generations and found in books documented these changes.

2. *Change is normal.* More than normal, change was good, said *English Language Arts.* "The changes which take place in all languages, but especially in English, are in the direction of simplification and clarification." *Good* itself, the author noted, had once been used with various endings for case, number, and gender, in addition to two adjectival declensions for weak and strong. Was the shedding of all this complexity not improvement?

3. *Spoken language is the language.* First-rate speakers and writers set the standards for the language. Second-rate minds made these standards into rules that, often enough, one could not avoid breaking. "We have the ludicrous picture of teachers solemnly enunciating rules and creating exercises for their practice when at the same time they and their educated colleagues violate these very rules in their normal speech and writing." For example, *the reason is because* was condemned by teachers and composition books for being logically redundant, but "an actual count of the idiom will find it quite frequent in our best current publications and spoken without self-consciousness by highly educated persons."

All five principles bore the influence of Charles C. Fries, but this one practically quoted him, saying "the language of today is not to be identified with that found in books but is to be found chiefly upon the lips of people who are currently speaking it," echoing the language Fries used in 1940 to argue for the standards of "a living speech, the forms of which can be constantly verified upon the lips of actual speakers."

4. *Correctness rests upon usage.* From misbegotten rules came misbegotten notions of correctness. Under the influence of Latin and Greek,

eighteenth-century grammarians had used rules to stabilize the language and give it polish. Their doctrine brought out dissenters, who noted that correctness could not be in opposition to actual usage carefully observed. But these dissenters had little influence. In the twentieth century, however, "their position has been vindicated and the relationship of correctness to use has been made clear." Thanks to linguistics, of course.

5. *All usage is relative.* "The contemporary linguist," said *English Language Arts*, "does not employ the terms 'good English' and 'bad English' except in a purely relative sense." The passage quoted Robert C. Pooley, after Fries one of the most important linguists to lay siege to the rule of rules, saying, "Good English is that form of speech which is appropriate to the purpose of the speaker, true to the language as it is, and comfortable to speaker and listener." For differing situations, there were differing standards: "levels of usage rather than a single standard of usage." Indeed, "an educated user of English will vary his speech and writing from extreme formality to literary elegance to extreme informality, including slang and dialectal expressions. He does so knowingly and with intention."[5]

These five principles of linguistics were generalizations. They had not been inscribed on tablets by Otto Jespersen, blessed by Edward Sapir, and confirmed by Leonard Bloomfield. Instead, they were written (according to the linguist and NCTE insider Ravin I. McDavid Jr.) by Robert Pooley and bore the marked influence of Charles C. Fries.[6] They were propaganda of a kind, conceived as a way to send a message to people who did not think like linguists. Their primary intent was, of all things, corrective: to adjust the attitude of English teachers to become less rule-bound and more tolerant of linguistic variety. But the thing about propaganda, about communicating, about teaching even, is that variety needs to be simplified for the most important elements to be made noticeable amid the everyday welter of information. It was easy to see how the principles might be taken as the basis of their own

prescriptive doctrine, possibly as stiff, unforgiving, and prone to caricature as those the linguists were rebelling against. And, like that of the
eighteenth-century grammarians, the triumph of NCTE's grammatical
doctrine gave rise to dissenters.

HARRY R. Warfel, a professor of English at the University of Florida, had
long stood poised for this moment.

It was only natural that he would take an interest in the writings of
his former teacher Charles C. Fries. He and Fries were both from Reading, Pennsylvania, where they had attended the same high school ten
years apart. They pledged the same fraternity at Bucknell, and Warfel
went on to become an English professor specializing in American literature. He became a member of NCTE and contributed to *English Language Arts* by serving on the Committee on Reading and Literature. For
all that he had in common with Charles C. Fries, whom he considered
a friend, it was clear that Warfel had been stoking the coals of this disagreement for years.

He called his dissent *Who Killed Grammar?* The answer was in the
first paragraph: linguists. In the second paragraph, after mentioning the
recent NCTE report, Warfel was more specific: Professor Charles Carpenter Fries, he wrote, was the "villain" in this "murder" story.

Warfel agreed with many of the basic complaints made by Fries and
the new linguists. The author of a book on Noah Webster, he could
easily cite examples from the nineteenth and twentieth centuries of
English "as it is" parting from English as it was taught. And he could
think of many a traditional rule that was inadequate to describing good
current usage. But the addition of linguistics to the wishful thinking
of progressive education had resulted in a series of incoherent and silly
notions about language and teaching.

When linguists discussed various "levels" of English, standard and
nonstandard, formal and colloquial, educated and vulgar, they rarely

attached a clear moral to their story, Warfel complained. For instance, it was possible, he lamented, to read Fries's *American English Grammar* as showing that standard and vulgar English were essentially identical and should be treated as such. There was also an unstated political dimension to their work. Warfel quoted Fries himself, who had written in 1927, "It is indeed always a question whether a democratic society can afford to permit a class consciousness of any kind to develop, especially a class consciousness based on language differences."

It was all rather confusing. Were linguists the observers of linguistic differences or, as good liberals, the enemies of linguistic difference?

Closely related to this was the confusion regarding *colloquial* language. If some people thought *colloquial* a term of disapproval, then linguists and even lexicographers were partly to blame. Warfel cited the latest edition of *Webster's Second*, which explained that *colloquial* meant "unsuited to formal speech or writing; hence informal." The same dictionary then defined *informal* as "not in conventional or customary form." How, then, was one supposed to know that colloquial English could be good English?

Grammar itself was portrayed as intellectually bankrupt and a weapon of class snobbery. The only authentic grammar, according to linguists, was that which was observed from scratch. Such thinking led to the eminently silly suggestion, put forth in *English Language Arts*, that each student be taught to observe language for himself and draw his own conclusions.

If some people looked at all this and saw an abandonment of standards, Warfel wondered, how could it be said that they were wrong?

Warfel did not think like a linguist, and it showed in his apparently sincere assumption that science amounted to some perfectly arithmetical form of investigation, incorruptible by bad thinking and impervious to the human failings of scientists themselves. Thus anytime he found Fries drawing some conclusion that was, in Warfel's own opinion, less than perfectly supported by existing evidence, he claimed

Fries was guilty of "non-science," which Warfel then ham-handedly rechristened "nonsense." Fries invited much of this criticism, however, as his own career thoroughly blurred the lines between the academy and activism.

Warfel fastened onto one other particularly interesting dynamic. The linguist had much to say to the layman but didn't much like it when the layman spoke back. For all the enthusiasm linguists showed for democracy and the language as it is spoken, they disdained the average person's views of language and were shocked to find their own ideas roughly received by common people.

Warfel cited an exchange between Fries and the Detroit *Free Press*. Fries had been interviewed by the paper, which then published a jovial article called "Grammar? It Ain't Gotta Be Perfect. U-M Prof Defends Us as Says, 'It's Me,' 'None Are,' 'Lay Down.'" After an hour-long interview the newspaper had reported that Fries "urged us not to sneer at use of the term *ain't*" and "took an indulgent view of the interchangeable use of *shall* and *will*."

Fries responded with a long, testy letter, saying *ain't* did enjoy some currency in southern parts of the United States and he had never actually said *shall* and *will* were interchangeable. "No linguist," he exclaimed, "would suggest that because a form is used anywhere it is satisfactory to use it everywhere."

The effort to explain linguistics to the layman remained fraught with drama and misunderstanding. It was especially difficult to square its principles with the expectations of literary intellectuals such as Harry R. Warfel, who, whatever his faults, was bright and well educated and had been reading and thinking about his hometown friend's work for years.

Warfel was not unsympathetic. He thought the five basic principles of linguistics were poorly explained in *English Language Arts*, but he actually agreed with them. And yet—the word here is *ouch!*—reading that chapter of *English Language Arts* had moved him to blame the death of grammar and the disrepute of English teaching on Charles C. Fries. Instead of enlightening the layman, linguistics was antagonizing him.

Warfel hoped readers would understand that his differences with Fries were "entirely intellectual." But the next time Professor and Mrs. Fries ran into old Warfel, Mrs. Fries refused to speak to him.[7]

CHAPTER 26

WHEN WEBSTER'S GIVES TWO pronunciations, the joke went, the first pronunciation is Boston and the second is New England. Gove, now general editor of Merriam, attributed the remark to a college professor in Kentucky, which would have made sense, as Merriam-Webster dictionaries had long neglected the southern accent.[1] Yet it could have originated with Merriam's own staff, who gladly repeated the line. Because it was true.

The pronunciations in *Webster's Second* were not international or even national; they reflected a regional bias that had seemed perfectly correct when American intellectual culture was still a footnote to Boston culture, but not anymore. What made sense in Ralph Waldo Emerson's day had become outdated and provincial in the age of Faulkner and Steinbeck and the New York intellectuals, as American standards of speech and pronunciation were being influenced first by radio and then Hollywood.

Since the early 1930s, a decent variety of accents played in Hollywood movies. Many performers adopted a hoity-toity Anglophone style of pronunciation, of a kind long encouraged in American theatrical training but later used for the comic shaming of those who put on airs. Society accents could be heard from Joan Crawford of Texas and Oklahoma, Clark Gable of Ohio, William Powell of Pennsylvania, Cary

Grant of Bristol, England, and Katharine Hepburn of Connecticut, at best giving the actor a smart, Waspy edge of old-fashioned class. A competing American naturalism was heard in the place-specific accents of Humphrey Bogart (born in New York City), James Stewart (borough of Indiana, Pennsylvania), Spencer Tracy (Milwaukee), Henry Fonda (Grand Island, Nebraska), and John Wayne (Winterset, Iowa). Certain genres, detective and gangster films, worked against the old-fashioned proper way of talking. Uppity pronunciation faded gradually. In the 1940s and '50s, the newer movies used more soldiers than socialites, and more cowboys than anything else.

After the release of *Webster's Second*, Merriam had tested the market for more representative pronunciation guidance by publishing and distributing a slim pronouncing dictionary that had been developed out of house by John S. Kenyon and Thomas A. Knott. Kenyon was an esteemed phonetician and Knott, of course, was a former general editor at Merriam, the most senior editor after William Allan Neilson, but, unlike Neilson, an actual full-time lexicographer.

Kenyon and Knott's book used the International Phonetic Alphabet, breaking each word into phonemes represented by letters and symbols, some strange-looking, like the upside-down and backward *e* symbol—ə—called a schwa, which actually represented a range of vowel sounds that might commonly be spelled with an *e* or an *i* or even an *o*, but described as the second vowel in *custom*. The system took getting used to—the letter *i* stood for the long "e" sound as in *bee*, while the letter *e* stood for the long "a" sound as in *rate*—but the dictionary eased the way by including a key line on each page, referencing each symbol to the sound of a familiar short word.

The pronouncing dictionary sought to correct the stuffy New England bias of *Webster's Second*, replacing its standard of "formal platform speech" with a preference for "cultivated colloquial English." The first pronunciation of *aunt* in Kenyon-Knott made the vowel sound like the *a* in *sat*. Then came eastern pronunciations: *aunt* that sounds like *rant*, as many New Yorkers would pronounce it, and then *aunt* that sounds like *art*, as a stuffy old New Englander would pronounce it.

The introduction quoted George Kittredge: "Every educated person speaks his mother tongue in at least two ways, and the difference between the dignified and the colloquial style is considerable." The editors located the source for modern literary expression in conversational language. "Good prose," said the introduction, quoting the writer and scholar William Ellery Leonard, "is becoming more and more a skillful adaptation of the vigorous, compact, racy idiom of the best spoken speech."

Racy was often used to describe American English: H. L. Mencken more than once called it that. *Webster's Second* defined *racy* as "manifesting the quality of a thing in its native, original, genuine, most characteristic state," citing a weirdly fitting phrase from the Victorian thinker Walter Pater: "racy morsels of the vernacular."

The only problem, said Twaddell, in an Editorial Board meeting on May 14, 1953, is "the Kenyon-Knott system is still a little too much to ask of anyone to handle in a general dictionary."[2] Munroe was also skeptical. He could remember sending copies out to broadcasters. "Nearly all were sent back, with all sorts of wisecracks, some to the effect that they didn't want to stand on their heads to find out the pronunciation of a term."[3]

The IPA alphabet had a mixed history in American dictionaries. Funk & Wagnalls had once adopted it in their *Standard* dictionary, only to retreat under criticism and revert to their previous pronunciation system—a situation Merriam's salesmen had gladly exploited. Merriam's closest competitor in the college market, the *American College Dictionary*, under the influence of Charles C. Fries, had introduced the schwa as one of its pronunciation symbols, but there was negative reaction and the company now feared going any further. Twaddell, who was back at his regular job at Brown University but still consulting for Merriam, said he was glad Merriam had not adopted the IPA system, for historically it was so complex as to be unusable. Yet he acknowledged that something ought to be done to improve on the pronunciations of *Webster's Second*.

Pronunciation editor Edward Artin had developed a simplified IPA system for *Webster's Third*. Gove told the board that it had been "carefully analyzed by men in this office who represent all of the leading schools of thought in the United States today," and proudly listed the bona fides of editors whose training placed them in the mainstream of American linguistics and near some of its leading lights. Everyone agreed there was a potential competitive advantage in being the first major dictionary to really exploit the modern understanding of phonetics, but there was also danger.

Munroe and others did not want the new dictionary to seem "radical."

This kind of talk irritated Gove. Artin's system was about 80 percent the same as the old system. As he had said at the last meeting, "The radicalness is in about twenty percent. And who knows what is *radical* anyway?"

The Editorial Board, which Gove only consulted on major policy questions, considered a proposal to survey a group of influential dictionary users, mainly booksellers, publishers, and educators. But going outside the building for expertise that could be found inside the building was so *Webster's Second*. It was like writing to William Allan Neilson for advice when Thomas Knott was standing next to you.

Gove objected. "There is no group in the world better equipped to handle this matter than the people in our Editorial Department right now. Never before in the history of the company have we had better qualified men. Mr. Munroe, you would discount any reports that would include the linguists, would you?"

"You are representing the linguists," said Munroe, voicing what everyone took to be obvious, that Gove's views as a lexicographer were powerfully influenced by contemporary linguistics.

Gove insisted that he favored Artin's system because it was, in fact, simpler than the old system, which he described as chaotic and confusing despite its familiarity.

But making the pronunciations more "scientific," said Victor Weidman, the head of educational sales, would not necessarily result in a simpler dictionary.

"Apparently," said Gove, who did not mind employing the contemptuous *we* when others dared to speak to him like this, "we fell into the popular error of misusing the word *scientific*." It "doesn't mean the key is any more difficult; it only means that it is more accurate."[4]

Take that.

All the same, teams from Merriam traveled for weeks to interview dictionary users and report on their preferences. Of 120 people surveyed, 78 favored some kind of change to the present system while only 12 favored retention of the *Webster's Second* system. But Ingham C. Baker, from the business side of Merriam, considered the findings indefinite. Few respondents, he noted, had revealed strong feelings about what exactly should be done. Sadly, there was nothing to do but "battle it out right here."[5]

The heart of the problem, Baker said, was that while people did seem to feel some kind of change was in order, "it is hard to get a system that the average person will understand."

Twaddell spoke up: "Weren't you struck by the number of people who wanted the key on the page?"

Baker was. "I dislike its being removed from the bottom of the page."

This was a rearguard action, however. The pronouncing key had already been removed from the *Collegiate Dictionary* to save space. No one spoke further on its behalf, despite its obvious relevance to the problem of orienting users to a new pronunciation system.

Gove read aloud from a letter written by a college professor, saying that if Webster's adopted some version of IPA, "they will win the enduring love, affection, and vocal espousal of phoneticians, who are a growlingly powerful group in the pedagogical system."

Twaddell knew the letter-writer, Francis Lee Utley, a professor at Ohio State, and confirmed that he was a sane person whose views should be respectfully heard. "There is nothing long-haired or wild about Utley," he said.

Munroe reminded everyone of the negative reaction after Funk & Wagnalls had begun using IPA. He also mentioned that one reason Merriam had published Kenyon-Knott was that it would answer the question, To what extent does the public want such advice? Judging from sales of the pronouncing dictionary—less than five thousand per year— the answer was, Not much.

"I honestly feel we are running a big risk to throw the present system overboard and take on a new system," Munroe said. "Make some changes but don't go all the way in what Mr. Artin proposes. You must remember, while these people you are talking about—the linguists, scholars, and so forth—have a powerful following, they are nothing in comparison with the general public, and it is to the general public that we have got to sell this dictionary."

Artin had also drawn Munroe's ire by mentioning the possibility of printing the new pronunciation key on a separable page so it could be referred to while looking up words. "I should like to comment on that suggestion of yours for something in the dictionary that is separate from the dictionary. That is an extremely bad idea."

Said Artin, "I wasn't suggesting that seriously. I merely mentioned it as one of the possibilities."

Munroe was quite worked up, tired of opposing these linguistically trained lexicographers, having to speak up for company values that were commonplace in his time. It was good the new men were dedicated to improving the dictionary, but their impatience with tradition was all too zealous. He told them, "You will say that compromise is not satisfactory, but nearly all history is made up of compromises."

Twaddell, a noted linguist who did not have to apologize for his sympathy with Munroe, returned to Gove's earlier comment about what percentage of Artin's system could be described, or not described, as radical. "I think the figure of twenty or thirty percent is about what I would feel makes sense . . . about what an automobile manufacturer would do in a comparable period of time."

Gordon Gallan—Merriam's president for the last few months, who had been pretty quiet throughout the meeting—spoke up. "One thing that disturbs me is Utley's statement that Webster's can get away with the change. I don't go along with the idea that merely because we lend our name to something, success is assured."

Gallan had been talking to a lot of advertising agencies, looking to select a new one for Merriam. He described survey research showing that of all the dictionaries in use, one-third were five to ten years old, while another 25 percent were more than ten years old.

Dictionary users apparently felt little urgency about getting the newest advice. Moreover, Gallan pointed out, guidance on pronunciation ranked low in the reasons people consulted dictionaries, fourth to be exact, behind finding out the meanings of strange words, finding out secondary meanings of familiar words, and learning the correct spelling of words. A lot of money was being spent on highfalutin scholarship, he said, expenditures that could only be justified if *Webster's Third* reached a mass market.

"We are interested in why people buy dictionaries, and today we feel our greatest potential is in the home market, the masses."

Gallan wanted Weidman to weigh in. As head of educational sales he was in a position to comment on how the Artin system might affect sales. He was already on record as favoring moderate changes to the pronunciation system, but then he had been rudely corrected by Gove. He now said the Artin system would have at best a neutral effect on sales if not a wholly negative one. "I feel we would be making a much bigger mistake to use the Artin system than to leave pronunciation as it is," he said.

Dictionary buyers were, indeed, conservative. As Weidman pointed out, one out of every six Merriam-Webster dictionaries were sold to the U.S. government, not exactly the avant-garde. If the new unabridged dictionary did not end up in a great number of American living rooms, it would not make back its investment.

Charles Sleeth, the chief etymologist working on *Webster's Third*, made a run at reconciling these views. Hired by Twaddell and J. P. Bethel, Sleeth was a former Rhodes scholar who had studied under C. T. Onions, the *Oxford English Dictionary* editor, before studying at Princeton with Harold Bender, the chief etymologist of *Webster's Second*.[6] One of Gove's early confidants, he urged the Editorial Board to see that even if pronunciation was only the fourth-most-important reason why people bought dictionaries, without reform of the old Webster's pronouncing system they would be resigning Merriam-Webster to a second- or third-place finish behind the competition in this albeit fourth-most-important category.

It seemed to Sleeth that the *American College Dictionary* and the *Webster's New World* "were in the position of someone who got up the nerve to take a 15-foot diving board; later they will get up nerve enough to take the 30-foot diving board, unless we take it first." Like Gove, he was positive Merriam-Webster should be the one to go first off the thirty-foot diving board.

"Why is it," he asked rhetorically, "that those of us in the Editorial Department feel confident that we can keep the Merriam Company in first position by going along pretty substantially with Ed Artin's proposals? The reason is this: There has been considerable development in IPA."

The last twenty years had been very good for IPA. "It was in 1933 that Bloomfield's *Language* appeared," Sleeth pointed out. "Bloomfield was the first in this country to bring out the highly important difference between significant and non-significant sound varieties. There is no need to discuss phonemes and the like. The point is that these old-style IPA systems were calculated to be used in the production of any little incidental unimportant variation in sound." With Bloomfield, researchers had begun to reduce the variety to those most salient differences in pronunciation. "We are not dealing here with anything faddish or anything that is likely to be superseded, because the present tendencies are not toward dissent but toward greater unanimity, and therefore we have something more practical for general use than anything that has been available before the linguistic events of the last twenty years."

Twaddell immediately said, "I endorse that historical survey." Gove followed with more scholarly testimony, quoting an English professor from Duke University: "If Merriam leads the way in converting to IPA (or a slight modification), it should be no more than a few years before all dictionaries of any consequence follow suit."

In the end, the issue was settled the old way, in private. Munroe and Gove stepped out into the hallway to discuss. Gordon Gallan joined them. When they came back Twaddell motioned for the room to vote on a basic principle of 70 to 80 percent continuity. Former president Munroe seconded the motion, and it carried by a vote of nine to one.

CHAPTER 27

THE EDITORIAL OFFICES AT Merriam were always quiet. Production was constant, as the only machines in use whirred away silently in the heads of Merriam staff. Oral communication was reduced to a minimum. To interrupt a fellow editor, you handed him or her a note saying you needed to talk. The two of you then met in the hallway.

The making of a dictionary was quiet and uneventful. Books were marked up; citations sorted into senses; draft entries circulated to special editors; the work of definers, pronunciation editors, etymologists, and usage editors all collated by an assembling editor and then proofread. And proofread again. And again. It could take years for some batches of entries to be completed, and each step required patience, concentration, and a high tolerance for tedium.

Lexicography, as one drudge put it, "was writing for a living and not to be confused with *belles lettres*."[1] It was intellectual work that could rarely be done without a large amount of formal education, but more than a few highly educated people of vaguely literary bent found the work too boring to accept. To succeed, you had to not mind the boredom.

It always sounded more lively than it was. People would hear you're a lexicographer and say, "Oh, isn't that interesting? That would be the perfect job for me. I love to flip through the dictionary and look at all those words." When you hear this, you think, Lady, you wouldn't last the morning. But you don't say that out loud. Repressing the urge to knock people over with words is something you learned as a lexicographer if not well before becoming one.

The question was no longer how to make the best dictionary possible. It was how to make this dictionary as Philip Gove said it should be made. And Gove would know if you didn't follow his directions, for he had vowed to read every single word in the dictionary he was editing.

Procedures were codified in dense technical memoranda that had to be reviewed again and again as particular words and sentences begged for more individual treatment. These were numbered and collected in Merriam's "Black Books," which under no circumstances were to leave the building. Gove had to upbraid one definer who had taken a Black Book home to study, risking exposure of Merriam's confidential procedures to unscrupulous competitors. That the Black Books could be hard to read and understand was no excuse. All such work, however difficult, had to be done on the premises.

A long shift of silent routines and carefully remembered policies could be trying to the nerves, especially for the man in charge. He considered chitchat the enemy of productivity, and worked quietly in his office, avoiding meetings. Word around the office was that at the end of each day, when Gove got home, he poured himself a belt of whiskey.

Merriam was a serious, thrifty place. The intellectual hierarchy was determined by what college you attended and whether you obtained an advanced degree. Salaries were low for the junior staff, whose dependable habits were the necessary precondition of success but often not as appreciated as a hot shot's résumé.

Men wore jackets, of course, which they draped over their chairs while sitting at their desks in the undivided editorial office space. Bathrooms were the only places you were allowed to smoke. The men's room was the most convivial spot in the building. The day included two breaks and a long lunch. This allowed time to run home for a midday meal, take care of an errand, or for the younger staff to plan a card game after work.

The first step in making a new unabridged dictionary was to cut up the old unabridged dictionary, pasting every definition and every sense from the 1947 printing of *Webster's Second* onto 3×5-inch slips. These were then divided into 107 separate categories and 18 separate etymological lineages.[2]

The next step was to add new material. With black or red pencil in hand (never blue, purple, or yellow), Merriam editors read continuously for up to two hours a day.[3] Gove had numerous publications delivered to his home, where he kept a stack of 3×5 slips next to his chair by the fireplace.[4] Readers were expected to scan, more than any other literature, contemporary nonfiction: newspapers, magazines, learned journals, popular science titles, house organs, annual reports, mail-order catalogs, college catalogs, transportation schedules, bulletin boards, menus, food containers, and owner's manuals. Contemporary fiction also needed to be read—the works of Norman Mailer, John Updike, Bernard Malamud, Saul Bellow, and many others were all being examined— but Gove believed fictional dialogue and speech were "contrived" and therefore not good examples of the language "genuinely at work."

"We are particularly interested in getting enough cits to show the language situation in which a word commonly appears." A cit was a citation, an illustrative quotation, and it was profoundly important to Gove's "contextual method of defining." In describing this method, and laying down rules for how it should be carried out, Gove was able to articulate his philosophy of language and a few choice bits of literary criticism. Here in the Black Books, more than anywhere else, Gove seemed to be at home in his thoughts.

Words, he observed and argued, never appeared in the language as they do in the dictionary: isolated and defined, as if their meanings could be separated from other words, always with the unjustified suggestion that dictionaries have the authority to say where a word began and where it ended. In answer to the criticism that a dictionary was not the language itself, Gove sought to make *Webster's Third* especially rich in illustrative quotations, for these quotations *were* the language, or at least genuine examples of it. They were "language as it is," not as some helpful lexicographer tried to make it appear.

He asked that special attention be paid to words that *Webster's Second* had labeled prohibitively with such terms as "slang, opprobrious, derogatory, vulgar, jargon, humorous, jocose, facetious, informal, colloquial, cant, local, dialect, illiterate, low," especially when context and usage contradicted *Webster's Second* treatment of the word in question.[5] Gove preferred it when examples of such nonstandard language, as he called it, were found in a standard context where the usual norms of grammar and usage applied. The idea that a word, and any context it might appear in, were always slang, forever and irredeemably so, was a fiction of *Webster's Second* and the genteel tradition.

Such thinking rested on the artificial premise that a given word was always, very simply, either polite or not, just as a person was polite or not—and never would a polite person utter an impolite word. And never could an impolite word be uttered in a polite fashion. In reality, however, a president might use slang and a criminal, though born to the streets, might employ legalese, and formal and informal language were often mixed to heighten the comic, dramatic, ironic, frivolous, documentary, or other possible effects of their joining.

"The editor cannot . . . assume that because an elegant writer employs a term it cannot be slang," Gove wrote. "The hearty house organ, the casual *New Yorker*, and the breezy *Time* all achieve their effects by variations upon familiarity which means, among other things, the studied use of slang."[6] Characteristic features included the use of contractions, ellipses to signal a silent drum roll of anticipation, words generally labeled slang, a colloquial tone so intimate it might be expressed through use of the first and second persons: *I* and *you*.

The source of a quotation, Gove allowed, might give some hint of whether a word should be labeled slang. "Walter Winchell, *Variety, Metronome*, are good examples" of sources notorious for their slang, but Gove's philosophy indulged few such prejudices. A simple majority of citations was the only firm basis for deciding whether a word ought to be labeled slang. The memo for labeling contained a sample of colloquial terms from *browned-off* to *look-see* to *square* that might be considered slang. Ten out of eleven of these disputed terms had been labeled slang in *Webster's Second*. With the new procedure, less than half of the same list was to be labeled slang in *Webster's Third*.

Too often the slang label had been used as a cover for snobbery, as when "the social status of the activity . . . determines the status of the terminology of the group." One way of separating out slang was to ask whether there were standard equivalents. Gove gave examples with equivalents in parentheses: "*jive* (jazz), *horse* (heroin), *con* (confidence), *duck* (urinal), *hash mark* (service stripe), *platter* (phonograph record)." Such terms could be fairly labeled slang. *Bebop* and *zoot suit* "on the other hand represent phenomena peculiar to a special activity for which no other term is available."

Gove was more comfortable with the linguist's terminology of standard and nonstandard or substandard, which *Webster's Third* editors used in place of old terms such as *erroneous, illiterate, vulgar*, and so on. The label *colloquial*, an old standby of lexicographers, Gove dropped entirely, a testament to how often it had been misunderstood to mean incorrect. Yet no word better described the increasing informality of contemporary English, a phenomenon that otherwise weighed very heavily in Gove's thoughts.

Colloquial meant spoken—the tonal, and often structural, opposite of nineteenth-century literary prose from which many familiar rules of usage were drawn. It captured language that was acceptable for informal communication, but it was also a product of a time when the lines between formal and informal, educated and vulgar, literary and illiterate, seemed much brighter than they did in the 1950s. These lines were not only linguistic, they applied to actual people, who were not so easily divided into standard and vulgar anymore. The GI Bill was putting more Americans than ever through college, and higher education was increasingly scientific and technical, its lessons no longer founded on training in Latin and Greek. One might develop a highly technical vocabulary for work and speak like a regular joe at home. And the language of regular joes was current in journalism, movies, and literature. Standards for printable language and educated speech now differed profoundly from the Victorian remains that had informed *Webster's Second*. There were good intellectual reasons to rethink *colloq.*—in addition to being misunderstood, whether a word was colloquial often depended on context, a point Gove loved to make—but in dropping the label a great range of contemporary usage was going unnamed.

In the Black Books, Gove discussed *arse, bum,* and *snot,* by no means a full roster of the obscenities making their way into *Webster's Third.* Gove did not exercise unlimited freedom in this respect. When he circulated two page proofs with entries for *fuck* as both a noun and a verb, with another entry for *fuck up,* President Gallan made use of his rarely brandished veto power to keep the F-bombs out.[7] Other such terms "not commonly in use in some circles of polite society," wrote Gove, would not be labeled vulgar but would carry a note saying "usu. considered vulgar." Derogatory words were a related but separate matter. "Particular care should be taken to see that no smear word be entered without an identifying note."

Chinaman, "which must surely be used very often without derogatory intent," Gove observed, was included without a prohibitive note in the first printing of *Webster's Second,* and its page had to be subsequently plate-changed. "*Dago, hunky, papist* usually reflect conscious hostility on the part of the user," so their entries need to say "used disparagingly." Gove went on, trying to allow for the innocent usage of malicious language while drafting an approach that would make his dictionary sound less judgmental and less categorical than its predecessor. "For a number of other terms, however, such as *nigger, Negress, Jap, Jewess*, there is evidence that although they are frequently used innocently, or naively, they are usually (depending on the circumstances) offensive to those to whom they are applied."

GOVE CLEARLY saw that a dictionary scheduled to come out in 1960 needed to be built on a new foundation. "We must see to it that a mid-twentieth-century dictionary gives evidence of having been written by editors who lived in the twentieth century."[8] In the *Webster's Second* definition of *chase*, Gove had found, the editors had given as a typical usage "to *chase* the boar." Under *limp*, they had written "as in a *limp* cravat." For *meet*, they had allowed "to *meet* carriages in the street." Gove eagerly collected many such anachronisms, ranging from the merely out-of-date to the willfully archaic. Under *gall* in *Webster's Second* it was written, "the troops were *galled* by the shot of the enemy." Anybody who could have come up with that, said Gove, "must have died many centuries ago."

These were verbal illustrations. Unlike quotations, they were thought up by lexicographers as brief, typical uses of a word. In *Webster's Third* they would need to sound easy and natural. And they should appear typical. "One could illustrate *pirate* or *crochet*," wrote Gove, "by 'the *pirate* was *crocheting* a doily' which is grammatically correct, brief, and not impossible, but so untypical of the supposed activities of pirates that to use it would be to mislead the naïve and amuse the sophisticated."

Illustrations should be blameless, banal even, making no comments and telling no stories. Under the verb form of *shoe*, *Webster's Second* had the illustration "the cost of *shoeing* a family," which, said Gove, "sets up a distracting narrative situation." Forgo names—"pusillanimous John and Mary" Gove called such mealy-mouthed name-mongering—in favor of *he* and *she*, but make sure "the pronouns contain no sinister overtones." About this Gove felt very strongly. "The phantasmagoric world of antecedentless pronouns," he wrote, "is full of potential narrative distraction."

Definitions should be impartial. "Editorializing has no place in definitions," said a memo, containing numerous examples from *Webster's Second* of what to avoid.[9] *Aleut* had been defined as "a peacable, semi-civilized people." *Apache* were described as "Nomads, of warlike disposition and relatively low culture." *Holi Hinduism* was called "a licentious spring festival," and *wood duck* was defined as "a handsome American duck." To an editor who challenged Gove's rule on editorializing, arguing that it did not seem out of place to mention that a certain varietal was "the best known wine of [name of district]," Gove replied that *Webster's Third* was not a wine list.[10]

Verbal illustrations, too, had to be policed for tendentious content. The illustration for *supersede* in the fifth *Collegiate Dictionary*, published in 1937, had said, "electricity has superseded gas." Under *improvement*, the same dictionary had written, "electricity is an improvement on gas." Unfortunately, said Gove, "both definitions were picked up by gas companies, one in California and one in Springfield, who were downright unpleasant about our alleged bias."

Contextual defining relied on illustrations and quotations to illuminate a word's actual range of meaning and usage, where *Webster's Second* had relied more on generalizing definitions to convey a word's particular role in the language. Gove's method proceeded from the assumption that it was quite difficult to precisely state the limits of a given word; *Webster's Second* had confidently assumed that mission and left the worrying to others.

Gove urged his lexicographers to increase the number of quotations.[11] These had to represent the standard language of mid-twentieth-century America but also be immediately readable and clear to the average user. The job of a dictionary, thought Gove, was not to flatter readers with mighty classical allusions or other snippets of high culture. The job of a dictionary was more pedestrian: to illuminate standard meaning and usage.

Dictionary users were, according to Gove, ill-served by poetic flourishes. "It is no defense, for example, for the ordinary writer who uses an antiquated subjunctive to plead that he can quote a parallel in a good poet." Gove had collected fourteen examples of literary subjunctives that had been used in *Webster's Second*, quotations such as "The father banished virtue shall restore," from Dryden.

"The hard truth is that the literary flavor of W34 and its predecessors," wrote Gove, using the in-house shorthand for *Webster's Second*, "represents a luxury of a bygone age."

The old dictionary was "rather liberally sprinkled with hapax legomena," said Gove, referring to words that appeared but once in the history of the language. "Some of Shakespeare's surcharged figures result in senses that never but for him would have been isolated for dictionary definition." Shakespeare, the only author Gove would allow to be mentioned by last name alone, also lost standing in Gove's ban on puns, which he worried would confuse readers. "Your means are very slender and your waste is great," had to go, as did Hamlet's incomparable dying words, "The rest is silence."

In his Black Books, Gove was nullifying Asa Baker's preference for elegance and literary effect and contradicting Noah Porter's view of the dictionary as the source of literary habit and cultivation. The new turn at Merriam-Webster was especially visible in Gove's instructions on whose words should be quoted in *Webster's Third*. "Since the illustrative quotation is to be chosen primarily for its contribution to an understanding of meaning, not for its decorativeness and not for lending authority to a definition, it follows that it doesn't much matter who is quoted."

The Webster's enterprise may have hinged on the authority of a single prestigious name. And Noah Webster's successors thought very carefully about what other names should be set in smaller type beneath that first great one, choosing other prestigious names, belonging to figureheads within a figurehead culture, such as college presidents Noah Porter and William Allan Neilson. But under Gove, the non-name editor in chief, it was possible to say that "any prestige a name lends must be considered accidental."

Gove wrote to his editors: "Feel free to quote Mickey Spillane, Edgar Guest, Grace L. Hill, G. A. Henty, Elinor Glyn, Billy Graham, Bill Cunningham, Polly Adler, N. V. Peale, Fred Allen, Gypsy R. Lee, Walter Winchell, Al Capp—they all use standard English, some of them rather rewardingly." The only limitation was that no one working for Merriam-Webster could be quoted.

"Time was," Gove added, "when the cultured consultant, on being told that a locution was to be found in Pope, would gravely and docilely feel that he was getting a glimpse of choice English." Today, Gove said, a dictionary user was liable to ask why Webster's was still relying on so much old stuff. Reading *Webster's Second*, Gove often asked the same question. He had no special animus against Alexander Pope, but every line the dictionary devoted to genuflecting before the great tradition was a line that could not be devoted to elucidating contemporary American English.

"There must be no hesitation," he wrote in the Black Books, "about pulling out Milton and putting in Sinclair Lewis."

Another reason to avoid literary quotations, Gove thought, was their tendency to utter falsity. *Webster's Second* had quoted a line from Tennyson: "Whitest honey in fairy gardens culled." Gove could not object more strenuously. First, "bees do not gather honey except by an extension of meaning." Second, "white is a symbolic, nonsignificant, and false standard applied to honey." Third, and last, "there just are no fairy gardens." Gove thought Tennyson's line "perfectly illustrates why Tennyson was not a great poet," but more important, it "does not illustrate the meaning of *cull*." Sadly, "literary flavor is sometimes very wide of the mark."

FOR HIS predecessors, being editor in chief of a Webster's dictionary meant carrying on a tradition. For Gove, it meant he was personally responsible for verifying the dictionary's intellectual integrity. Not that he wasn't proud to hold his position. "To a scholar devoted to the English language and its lexicography no higher distinction could come than had already been given to me, the opportunity to be editor in chief of a major edition of Webster's New International Dictionary," wrote Gove in a letter to President Gallan.

He asked to be made a vice president of the company. This promotion, said Gove, would reassure the editorial staff that its work was recognized as essential to the company's success. If granted, the vice presidency would also certify that Gove and his brain trust were much more powerful right now than in the days when editors were only as free as the company's guardians of reputation, the Editorial Board, allowed them to be. Gallan, however, must have thought differently, for Gove did not receive this promotion.[12]

BEING AN editor requires drawing lines, and Gove never shrank from this responsibility. In one of his first acts as editor, he had even drawn a chart, full of lines, connecting and overlapping in a series of boxes.[13] One central box was labeled Standard Language, to mark off that portion of American English that Gove proposed to cover in *Webster's Third*. It overlapped with small portions of several other large boxes labeled dialectal, slang, obsolete, technical, foreign-language, and non-lexical, meaning the names of people, places, commercial products, ships, wars, laws, political parties, tribes, religious festivals, and so on. The largest thing it left out was encyclopedic or "non-lexical" information. Such an omission, though done for practical reasons, was not unprecedented. The *OED* and the earliest Webster's dictionaries also omitted general reference information.

Many of Gove's subsequent decisions were but a refinement of his chart, including his unusual policy on definition-writing. *Webster's* first (1909) and second international editions had both used a style called "systematic defining," in which basic definitions were followed by general information. The entry for *insurance* was a perfect example. Around line seven of this entry in *Webster's Second*, the lexicographer began listing the many types of insurance one might purchase: life, fire, marine, accident, health, automobile, and fifteen others. For Gove, this was yet another way in which *Webster's Second* ceased to be a dictionary and insisted on being an encyclopedia. And the essay-like writing was far from accidental. Encyclopedias were, of course, filled with articles. A dictionary, however, ought to be filled with definitions.

And definitions should not be written, thought Gove, in complete sentences and paragraphs. They ought to be phrased in single statements, as if an invisible "is" stood between the headword and the definition, with cumulatively greater detail incorporated, without interruption, until the definition was complete. Although he had been uncertain that two people could agree on the meaning of even so simple a word as *girl*, Gove was positive that there was but one way to write a definition.

In a memo for the Black Books, Gove referenced two definitions for *air*, one from *Webster's Second* and one prepared for *Webster's Third*. The one from *Webster's Second*, with nine periods and several semicolons, looked and acted like a short essay. The one prepared for *Webster's Third* contained the same identifying details but followed Gove's preferred defining pattern.[14]

Air, the *Webster's Third* definition said, is "a mixture of gases, invisible, odorless, tasteless, compressible, elastic, sound-transmitting, and liquefiable, composed chiefly of nitrogen and oxygen nearly in the ratio of four volumes to one, together with 0.9 per cent argon, about 0.03 per cent carbon dioxide, varying amounts of water vapor, minute quantities of helium, krypton, neon, and xenon, varying small amounts of such other substances as ammonia, nitrous and nitric acids, and sulfurous and sulfuric acids, and such suspended particles as dust, bacteria, and yeast spores, that surrounds the earth, extending outward for an indefinite distance, with rapidly decreasing density, half its mass being within four miles of the earth's surface, its pressure at sea level being about 14.7 pounds per square inch and its weight being 1.293 grams per liter at 0° C. and 760 mm. pressure. See *element* 1."

On his copy of these instructions, after the final cross-reference, "see *element* 1," Gove wrote, "or your psychiatrist." It was often said at Merriam, by Gove and others, that *Webster's Third* embraced the common idiom of contemporary language, but as a result of Gove's defining style its definitions sounded totally unnatural. And Gove seemed to realize this. The definition for *air*, he wrote, "may be something of a tour de force and certainly is not a model of simplicity, but it is a definition, which the W34 version is not."

Another line Gove drew concerned initial upper-case letters, which he categorically opposed in headwords. By excluding encyclopedic material, *Webster's Third* was excluding proper nouns, which represented a huge set of words that would have had to be capitalized. Beyond proper nouns, however, capitalization became much less consistent. It stood to reason, Gove thought. He quoted Otto Jespersen's opinion that "linguistically it is utterly impossible to draw a sharp line of demarcation between proper names and common names." Complicated as this sounded, it led to a simple ban on capital letters. *Russia* was no longer being defined, but the adjective *russian* was, and it was spelled with a lowercase *r* and labeled "usu. cap." All headwords were to be set in lower case, and for those words normally capitalized the editor had to add one of the following labels: *cap, usu. cap, sometimes cap*, and *often cap*.

"Such usages as *aristotelianism, johnson grass, magellanic cloud, french fried potatoes, march winds, chinawoman*," said Gove, were no longer mere exceptions to the old rules. In fact, educated usage was increasingly unpredictable on the capitalization of such words. The only ones Gove could identify that always appeared in capital letters were *God*, "in nearly all aspects of speech," and the first-person pronoun *I*.[15] Readers of *Webster's Third*, however, later found that, aside from abbreviations, *God* was the only headword given a capital letter. The headword for the first-person pronoun *I* was set in lower case (*i*) and labeled "cap."

CHAPTER 28

AS COLOR TELEVISION WAS being introduced, the language of American entertainment saw the arrival of *sitcom*. It was the early fifties, and television programming had only been around for a few years while television ownership in America went from less than ten thousand before the war to several million made and sold annually. The quality of programming was considered low by sophisticates. The comedian Fred Allen said, "Television is called a new medium, and I have discovered why they call it a medium—because it is neither rare nor well done." Yet its presence in the living room continued to redirect household activity, setting the table for *TV dinner*, dated 1954 in the Merriam-Webster files. But one year later, another phrase was making the rounds: *idiot box*.[1]

Sometimes, not long after something has been named the language records complaints about its existence. *Fast food* is dated 1951 in the Merriam-Webster files, three years before Ray Kroc went to work for McDonald's. *Junk food* followed in 1960 as Kroc took control of the chain and built the quintessential American food franchise. The midcentury lexicon was filled with new words for the construction boom, including *housing development*, *half-bath*, *exurb*, and *exurbia*, followed closely by *dullsville*.

A large cache of computer language was patented, including many words that would not become familiar until the rise of the personal computer in the 1990s: *information retrieval, online, random access memory, data processing, artificial intelligence, integrated circuit, software, virtual memory*. Technical innovation and the spread of higher education also helped give rise to new vocabulary of measurable accomplishment— *overachiever, underachiever,* and *meritocracy*—along with a string of unflattering names for the A-students: *egghead, nerd,* and *wonk* were all coined in the 1950s. *Maven* too, which William Safire later adopted as a preferred term for a language commentator like himself, comes from this period, when Safire was a young publicist angling to get his client's model home into the famous kitchen debates between Richard Nixon and Nikita Khrushchev.

Other-directed and *inner-directed*, David Reisman's well-known sociological categories from *The Lonely Crowd*, were coined in 1950. They described different character types, as different as William Allan Neilson and Philip Gove, as different as the public-spirited man and the technocrat, as different as Henry Seidel Canby's age of confidence and age of doubt. *Establishment* and *organization* came into vogue with other attempts to understand the tensions between the individual and a public seemingly dominated by large organizations, from the armed forces to higher education and modern corporations. William H. Whyte's *The Organization Man*, a work that first took shape in articles Whyte wrote for *Fortune* magazine (and was read in draft form by David Reisman), was published in 1956. *Mass man*, an older term used by Ortega y Gasset, among others, gains traction in such discussions, while *mass media*, coined in the 1920s but left out of *Webster's Second*, becomes an officially important subject for educators, social critics, and anyone else interested in what's going on.

A basket of terms come into view describing the postwar American childhood: *Little League, talent show, show-and-tell,* and *hula hoop*. *Do it yourself* and the acronym DIY have been rallying cries in recent years for everyone from punk bands to at-home cheesemakers, but they were first recorded in the Merriam files in 1952 and 1955. The decade is popularly viewed as the incubation stage for the American family stereotype consisting of a male breadwinner, a female homemaker, and 2.2 children, the so-called *nuclear family*, a term noticed in 1947. Yet it is also when these familiar categories start to bend. *Househusband* was recorded in 1955, and, with Gregory Pincus's invention of a birth control pill, *oral contraceptive* joined the language. After the Kinsey Report, *gay* is increasingly used for homosexuals.

Swing expressed the sassy blend of decadent fun that was no longer *gay*—this, of course, prior to when *swinging* came to mean spouse-swapping. The *Oxford English Dictionary* cites a Norman Mailer sentence published in *Dissent* in 1957 that captures the fifties tone of *swing*: "Still I am just one cat in a world of cool cats, and everything interesting is crazy, or at least so the Squares who do not know how to swing would say." *Swing* in its new meanings was popularized by jazz, which also gave us the whole *cat* business and did much to bring out the new flavor of *cool*. In 1957, Miles Davis released his pioneering album *Birth of the Cool*. Three years later, *Webster's Third* gave the following as the eighth sense: "showing a mastery of the latest of the approved technique and style," with verbal illustrations, as in "cool jazz" and "as an actor he's real cool."

Corny was defined in the 1950 addendum to *Webster's Second* as "tiresomely trite, outworn, and old-fashioned." The second definition referred to music, "contrasted with *hot* . . . lacking spontaneity, freedom, and enthusiasm of swing." *Hot* was now defined as "impassioned and exciting in rhythm and mood," as in "hot jazz." *Square*, meanwhile, was covering ground similar to *corny*. Eventually labeled slang in *Webster's Third*, sense 4g in 1950 reads, "having unsophisticated or conservative tastes . . . belonging to or characteristic of the respectable law-abiding tradition-bound classes of society." A *square* was the opposite of a *cat*, sometimes called a *hepcat*.

Desegregation was recorded in 1951, three years before the U.S. Supreme Court ruled in *Brown v. Board of Education* that segregated schools were "inherently unequal." The popular culture of the era, or at least that remembered in *American Graffiti*, is recalled in such new language as *ponytail*, *sweater vest*, *dragster*, and *hot rod*—the delinquent side in the abbreviation *OD*. By the middle of the twentieth century, Americans had gone abroad and fought on several continents, but *Bermuda shorts* and *Hawaiian shirt* smack of the early days of commercial air travel, as does *jet set*. But our taste for the Orient was evidenced by the appearance of *Peking duck* in our culinary vocabulary.

American art was taking its place on the world stage. The modernism celebrated in journals like *Partisan Review* led to *abstract expressionism*, a 1951 coinage actually belonging to Robert Coates in the *New Yorker*. The new art was personified by Jackson Pollock, so domineering a figure that *Life* magazine famously asked if he was the most important painter in the United States, and his drip style was parodied, though ever so gently, by Norman Rockwell. The alternative name for *abstract expressionism*, *action painting*, coined by Howard Rosenberg, was recorded in 1951. *Pop art* followed in 1957, several years before anyone had heard of Andy Warhol.

McCarthyism was recorded in 1950, and for years the growth of Cold War language accelerated like an arms race. From *launchpad* and *lift off* to *ballistic missile* and *ICBM*, our words reflected a growing investment in high-tech weaponry that, like the A-bomb, would spare nothing but American lives. The *aerospace* industry was born, delivering not only planes and *cruise missiles* but the promise of a *moon shot*, which the Russians accomplished first with *Sputnik*, inspiring not only fear, envy, and hand-wringing over the quality of American education but the use of *-nik* to form *beatnik* and *neatnik*. The American study of Russia gave us the *Kremlinologist* a decade after George Kennan penned his famous article as "X" and called on policy makers to think more seriously about the Russian threat, while popularizing *contain-ment* into a mainstay of foreign policy discussions. *Sovietologist* had more of the institutional flavor associated with American area studies, whether conducted on campus or at a *think tank*, another coinage of the 1950s.

CHAPTER 29

PREFIXES POSE A PROBLEM for the lexicographer. An *anti* or an *un* can be attached to countless words. The question becomes how many should be acknowledged. Gove erred on the side of non-recognition when it came to *anti*—the meanings of many *anti-* words being self-evident once you knew the rest of the word—but more accommodating of *un*. So while many words from *un-american* to *unworldly* received separate entries, Gove and his editors showed little interest in two defining terms of American politics: *anticommunism* and *anti-anticommunism*.

An anticommunist was anyone from Senator Joseph McCarthy to Whittaker Chambers to Sidney Hook to Dwight Macdonald who defined their politics in opposition to the Soviet Union and its doctrines. An anti-anticommunist was one who defined his or her politics in opposition to anticommunists. They were *anti* the antis—just the kind of regressive messiness a lexicographer would prefer to avoid. Nor would Gove's editors take note of two other coinages that increasingly preoccupied Dwight Macdonald: *masscult* and *midcult*.

IN 1954, Macdonald separated from his wife, Nancy, then flew to Alabama to expedite a divorce. This brought an end to his increasingly faithless commitments to her and to radical politics. Already, Geoffrey

Hellman, whom after a couple of drinks he used to call a Tory, had helped him get a job at the *New Yorker*.[1]

Such changes didn't stop Macdonald from criticizing the *New Yorker* in an essay he wrote for the Ford Foundation, not to be confused with an essay he wrote criticizing the Ford Foundation in the *New Yorker*.[2] Dwight was still Dwight. One day he was flattering his boss, William Shawn, with an almost teary fan letter, its humble words shivering with gratitude for taking him in and treating him so well. Other days Mr. Shawn, like Henry Luce before him, received from his prickly writer point-by-point denunciations of articles by other writers he had been wrong to publish.[3]

But he was productive. Now in his fifties, Macdonald transformed himself into a critic at large, a funny, smart decrier of the cultural decline he believed to be rampant in America. One could see it in Fannie Hurst novels, rock 'n' roll music, automotive design, *Life* magazine, Norman Rockwell illustrations, pulp mystery novels, Hollywood films, and television comedies. Macdonald specialized in authors and works that enjoyed some claim to being highbrow but, in his view, fell short of their own standards. The heartless mockery he'd once rained down on Henry Wallace found new targets in the overly prosaic Revised Standard Version of the King James Bible and the pompous Great Books Club, both of which the former "revolutionist" attacked in the name of tradition.[4]

Macdonald had never cared much for religion, but in reviewing the RSV he was distraught that "my cup runneth over" had been retranslated as "my cup overflows." The Elizabethan cadences of the King James Version had been rewritten, as the translators put it, in "language direct and clear and meaningful to people today." The new language, Macdonald said, was "also flat, insipid, and mediocre." Poetic Latinate verses had been toned down, while homelier, direct passages had been poeticized. "If they tone down some strings, they tone up others, adjusting them all to produce a dead monotone."

Mr. Shawn loved the article, as did many readers. Macdonald's essay on the Great Books Club was another hit. Published by Encyclopaedia Britannica Inc.—itself a symbol of decline in Macdonald's eyes, as the once-admired British institution was now owned by former U.S. senator William Benton (a true vulgarian in Macdonald's estimation) and the University of Chicago—the Great Books were to Macdonald's eye a more ponderous and commercially compromised version of the Harvard Classics. Edited by Mortimer J. Adler, author of *How to Read a Book*, whom Macdonald had previously counted as one of the greater philistines around, and Dr. Robert Hutchins, former chancellor of the University of Chicago, the series seemed utterly fatuous to Macdonald, especially as it pretended to extend the shelf lives of classic titles that were still in print.

Macdonald gleefully aired the unintentionally comic boasts of the Great Books' champions. Clifton Fadiman, an establishment literary critic who served with Henry Seidel Canby on the Book-of-the-Month Club jury, had compared the Great Books subscribers to the monks of early Christendom whose dedication had preserved great remnants of Western civilization through the Dark Ages. Hutchins had called the set "a liberal education for Americans, on which depended "the fate of our country, and hence of the world." Nothing, however, drew Macdonald's withering attention more than Adler's *Syntopicon*, which took up two volumes and came with the Great Books set. It was a dictionary of ideas that make up the Western literary tradition, each laboriously cross-indexed to allow their tracking from one great author to the next. The *Syntopicon* smacked of the gratuitously academic, needlessly classifying bureaucratic-mindedness that Macdonald hated.

The set of books was reductionist and antiliterary, according to Macdonald, showing the editors believed "the classics are not works of art but simply quarries to be worked for Ideas." The news that the Great Books sold poorly until Britannica's door-to-door salesmen began pushing them on timid housewives who paid through an installment plan confirmed Macdonald's worst suspicions about the unholy alliance between commerce and culture.

MACDONALD WAS true only to himself. He sounded ever so conservative when he found a kind word for William F. Buckley Jr., whose fearless brief against their alma mater, *God and Man at Yale*, must have brought back memories, though Macdonald had less sympathy for the new conservative magazine Buckley founded, *National Review*, and for Buckley's defense of Senator McCarthy, whom Macdonald had the boldness to call in print a "pathological liar."

Among the anticommunists, however, of the Congress for Cultural Freedom, Macdonald stood out for being insufficiently pro-American. And among the anti-anticommunists, including his new wife, Gloria, an apologetic liberal with no radical background, he seemed a cantankerous red-baiter. A protracted negotiation to work for *Encounter* magazine, the storied intellectual journal co-edited by the English critic Stephen Spender and the former *Commentary* hand Irving Kristol, which was secretly being funded by the U.S. State Department, ended without an offer of regular employment. The magazine's Cold War raison d'être was to promote American ideals in postwar Europe, a mission for which Macdonald, politically undisciplined and never so happy as when he was telling someone off, had always been an odd recruit.[5]

It nevertheless brought him to London for an extended stay, where he found much to admire. "Today," he would write, "the best English is written and spoken in London"—an appropriate sentiment for a man who had once said of Henry James, "No writer I can think of at the moment is so blandly, easily, triumphantly sure of his mastery of language."[6]

Quintessentially American writing received low marks. Mark Twain he discounted as a folk writer who relied too much on spoken idiomatic English and lacked the will to defy the "terrible American pressure to conform." Months after Ernest Hemingway's suicide, Macdonald savagely parodied the author's "primitive syntax," calling it the prose equivalent of Jackson Pollock's "drip and dribble" method, showing also Macdonald's low opinion of abstract expressionism.[7]

Now and then, Macdonald tended to his masterpiece, "Masscult and Midcult," developing ideas he had first broached with "A Theory of Popular Culture" in *Politics*. It evolved into his most ambitious essay—though never a book in its own right. Despite some flirtation with Jason Epstein at Doubleday about placing it between hard covers, Macdonald remained able to boast that he had never written a book "in cold blood."[8] It was finally published in 1960 in, appropriately enough, *Partisan Review*.

The essay was a great and varied rant against the American faith in progress, against consumerism, and finally against the elevation of the common man from his feudal preliterate state. It was both—unlikely as this sounds—Marxist and aristocratic. It saw great dialectical forces at work in the unfolding of history, and sniffed disdainfully at the results.

For two centuries, Macdonald argued, since before the Industrial Revolution, culture has been increasingly split between the high and the low. With the rise of the masses came the rise of culture for the masses, or *masscult*, which "is not just unsuccessful art. It is non-art. It is even anti-art."

Like kitsch, masscult was "easy to assimilate." Gone were the idiosyncratic feelings and thoughts of the individual artist. Gone were the standards of great older works of art. "Those who consume masscult might as well be eating ice-cream sodas, while those who fabricate it are no more expressing themselves than are the 'stylists' who design the latest atrocity from Detroit."

Masscult not only corrupted the individual artist, it corrupted the individual. Mass man had mass morality, the morality of "a crowd that will commit atrocities that very few of its members would commit as individuals." Macdonald cited David Reisman's pioneering work on the "lonely crowd" but actually reserved some of his harshest comments for sociologists, who accept "statistical majority as the great Reality." These cynics were the intellectual equivalents of those publishers and Hollywood executives whom Macdonald called the Lords of Masscult. They are "willing to take seriously any idiocy if it is held by many people."

Masscult was the cultural analog to the very worst movements of the twentieth century. "Nazism and Soviet Communism . . . show us how far things can go in politics, as Masscult does in art." But masscult was democratic, so democratic it destroyed the ability "to discriminate against or between anything or anybody." Its rise could be traced to the growth in literacy in the eighteenth century, Samuel Johnson's day, when the number of books published annually suddenly quadrupled. In the dawn of widespread literacy, the prelude to popular education, and the beginning of what historians now call the culture of print, the seeds of our cultural demise were sown.

"Midcult" was masscult with a fig leaf, covering its essential vulgarity by paying homage to high culture and sometimes trading on the discoveries of the avant-garde. Midcult was the Revised Standard Version of the Bible. "Midcult is the Book-of-the-Month Club, which since 1926 has been supplying its members with reading matter of which the best that can be said is that it could be worse." Midcult was Hemingway's *The Old Man and the Sea* and the play *Our Town* by Thornton Wilder, which compared with *Winesburg, Ohio*, by Sherwood Anderson, was, well, "kitsch," according to Macdonald.

Today social critics are more likely to talk of middlebrow culture from the 1930s, '40s, and '50s as a triumph. Short stories were published in popular magazines. Novels were regularly deemed major cultural events. Senator Benton soon voiced the objections of many, complaining that television was a vast wasteland, but in the meantime his sales force at Encyclopaedia Britannica established actual book clubs for Great Books subscribers to discuss and argue about Plato and Locke. James Parton's *American Heritage* magazine, under the editorship of Bruce Catton, popularized American history.

Not all progress was lost on Macdonald. He mentioned that since World War II a great number of classic works and scholarly books had come out in paperback. And the number of American symphony orchestras had doubled in the last decade, while art house movie theaters had grown exponentially. Postwar affluence was also underwriting new support for artists and scholars, some of which Macdonald had enjoyed: grants, prizes, lecture fees, junkets, fellowships, and teaching gigs. But the sale and institutionalization of culture was part of the problem.

"We have, in short, become skilled at consuming High Culture when it has been stamped 'prime quality' by the proper authorities, but we lack the kind of sophisticated audience that supported the achievements of the classic avant-garde, an audience that can appreciate and discriminate on its own."[9] But such an audience, familiar with the great tradition while suspicious of its resellers, and able to discriminate the good from the bad (and the great from the merely good) in the newest art and literature, could, of course, only be very small even in the best of times. One might even describe it as an audience of one, resembling no person so much as Dwight Macdonald, or perhaps not even him. While speaking solemnly of the avant-garde, he disliked Pollock and preferred his modernism several decades old, from Rimbaud to Picasso and James Joyce, all of whom he mentions in the essay along with T. S. Eliot, whose poetry, to his own later embarrassment, Dwight Macdonald had once discounted.[10]

CHAPTER 30

"WORDS ARE NOT SIMPLY the casual containers and carriers of thoughts and feeling, but their incarnation," wrote Jacques Barzun in 1959 in *The House of Intellect*, another book attacking pompous, pseudoscientific language. The Columbia University professor had recently been on the cover of *Time* magazine, in which he was quoted lamenting the decline of grammar in America's schools. In his book he named names: President Eisenhower, Igor Stravinsky, and the New Critics were all cited for one rhetorical failing or another. But his true enemy was the typical young professor with nothing new to say but all of it embedded in jargon. And there was the rub. The scholar's manner of abusing the language, more than the verbal tics of a military man or a musical composer, truly exposed the anti-intellectualism in our civilization's "house of intellect."

Beginning in the nineteenth century, according to Barzun, science began to "wage war against philosophy and theology." Science won. And the search for new facts arose as the most important of intellectual activities. Discovery became the main criterion of merit, and where no handy statistic or laboratory result could be brandished to justify one's worth, "a special language, marked by abstraction and heroic detachment," was employed.

Artists began to speak a kind of solemn nonsense, and even a square like President Eisenhower refused to use *work* when talking about a Russian colleague. Instead, he said, "Marshal Zhukov and I *operated* together very closely." Stravinsky, praising his own composition, would not call it beautiful and leave it at that. He said (in Barzun's translation), "It is extremely thoroughly worked out." And the New Critics, following the path blazed by I. A. Richards and others, taught fellow professors and students to turn reading and interpretation into *method*. Literary symbols were organized into systems, and meaning became this ridiculously complicated and convoluted thing. In the pretensions of the nonscientist, the power and the prestige of science were written.[1]

Barzun especially disliked how this affected the common language. Taxi drivers, instead of putting gas in their cars, spoke of "the filling-up process." Phrases like "as far as" and "in terms of" inflated simple utterances. Actors and actions vanished in a phrase smoke of processes, operations, programs, and so on.

Pedantry inverted standards across professions and society, creating a new order in which to speak clearly and neatly is to appear a snob and "the users of pretentious mouth-filling phrases esteem themselves the friends of democratic light and simplicity." Learned conversation became impossible, as did conversation between the pseudoscientist and those who spoke older jargons, such as the sailor and farmer.

Modern linguists bore "a grave responsibility" for this terrible state of affairs, especially the man who said, "There can never be in grammar an error that is both very bad and very common." Charles Carpenter Fries, said Barzun, had "engineered the demise of grammar in the American schools."

In some classrooms, Barzun had noted, students used what was called the General Form. This book, over a thousand pages long, had been developed during World War II by linguists to expedite the learning of foreign languages, but it was now being employed by native-English students to study their own language. It bypassed the Latinate categories of the old grammar—noun, verb, et cetera—and in their place required pupils to learn four parts of speech, fifteen function words, and nineteen classes of forms.

"And when we ask," wrote Barzun, "on what body of English speech this 'experimental' grammar was based, the answer is that it was derived from three thousand letters written to the United States War Department after 1918 and dealing with the single theme of pension money."

Fries and other linguists, said Barzun, did not think intelligently about what their carefully collected facts indicated ought to be done in the schools. And what science left blank they filled in with politics. "As scientists they maintained that the speech of any group is good speech for that group; as democrats and progressives they maintained that the child should not be made to feel inferior (or superior) by changing his speech." Their motives were philanthropic and liberal, not strictly pedagogical.

To gauge the extent of this disaster, one needed only to scan the 1952 report *English Language Arts* produced by the National Council of Teachers of English. "The volume is one long demonstration of the authors' unfitness to tell anybody anything about English." It optimistically posited that "change in language is not corruption but improvement," especially in English, where change is always "in the direction of simplification and clarification."[2] To Barzun, this last bit was instantly ridiculous. Pretentious academic jargon and the way it blighted the air and fouled the printed page clearly demonstrated this could not be true.

What this plague on our language did show, however, was the demise of nonscientific ways of thinking. The simple human capacity for passing judgment in intelligible speech, for gathering information and impressions and presenting them sensibly and in the right words, what Barzun called *esprit de finesse*, had no purchase on the modern mind.

BARZUN WAS quoted many times in the citation files for *Webster's Third* (as under the synonym paragraph at *hateful*: "'the *invidious* task of improving other people's utterance'—J. M. Barzun"), but it was prob-

ably not Philip Gove who had been reading him. In 1961, two years after
The House of Intellect was published, Gove also looked back to *English
Language Arts*, as he wrote an article for *Word Study*, a newsletter published by Merriam and circulated by the sales staff to universities, bookstores, government offices, and other important customers.[3]

Gove's subject was the arrival of *Webster's Third*. The opening paragraph of his article, "Linguistic Advances and Lexicography," made
clear where his allegiances lay. In the last three decades, "the study of
English has been deeply affected by the emergence of linguistics as a science." The relevance of linguistics was, by now, beyond debate. "Acceptance of the basic tenets of this new science is hardly any longer a matter
of opinion."

The turning point, according to Gove, came when Leonard Bloomfield published his postulates for a linguistic science, after which his
1933 book, *Language*, "became the prerequisite and indispensable text."
The key to Bloomfield's method was "observing precisely what happens
when native speakers speak." It marked a radical break from analyzing
the English language in terms of its past by relying on Latin grammar.
By now schoolteachers had shown an appreciation for the findings of linguistics, which was good, because it was in the classroom, Gove thought,
that a better understanding of "language behavior" should be developed.

Said Gove: "Five basic concepts set forth in the *English Language Arts*
supply a starting point." Then he listed them:

1. Language changes constantly
2. Change is normal
3. Spoken language is the language
4. Correctness rests upon usage
5. All usage is relative

The concepts had been endorsed by the National Council of Teachers of English, Gove noted, "but they still come up against the attitude

of several generations of American educators who have labored devotedly to teach that there is only one standard which is correct." Gove compared the belief in one correct linguistic standard to a belief in revelation, in the Ten Commandments specifically. And he quoted the structural linguist W. Nelson Francis on the old notion that "there is some other source and sanction for language." Gove, of course, had no such faith that there was someone somewhere who knows all there is to know about what's right and what's wrong, some "they" who knows the different rules for *more than* and *over* or about ending a sentence with a preposition or about using the objective case in the sentence "It is me."

For the rest of his article Gove discussed how linguistics had affected lexicography, but he had already understated one important part of his answer: Linguistics had profoundly influenced his own views, the views of America's most important lexicographer, who may have started out as a Samuel Johnson scholar but sounded like a typical prewar linguist as he criticized the old notions of correctness. Webster's new system of nonjudgmental usage labels, which Gove did not mention, obviously resulted from this influence. Gove acknowledged that linguistics had altered his understanding of syntax and grammar, but he did not come out and say, "About the only thing I have in common with William Allan Neilson is a job title."

In the area of meaning, linguistics had not actually affected lexicography, according to Gove. This was another understatement, since Gove clearly shared in linguistics' history of ambivalence toward word-defining. Like Bloomfield and Fries, Gove was convinced that even the most familiar of terms—*apple* (in Bloomfield's example), *chair* (in Fries's), *girl* (in Gove's)—proved insuperably complicated in actual use, so complicated that a roomful of people could not agree on basic definitions. Gove's position on the undefinability of words was indistinguishable from that of the linguists. But he wrote here as if little had changed since 1934, which of course was not true. There was an old-fashioned confidence and assertiveness to *Webster's Second* that he found suspect, of a piece with its casual editorializing on the loyalty or courage of certain breeds of dog. His suspicion of the Second Edition's simpler approach to language Philip Gove learned, at least in part, from linguistics, and he had not minded saying so behind closed doors.

It was fortunate that his intellectual reservations had not crippled him as a professional lexicographer. He had innumerable decisions to make in order to bring this project in on time. That Gove was less forthright now about all that he had learned from linguistics was interesting. It showed Gove, like an actor just starting to find the stage lights and move accordingly, gaining a newfound sense of audience. Now was not the time to talk about how "infinitely complicated" language was, or how only very few people could move within it "comprehendingly." That would sound scary and not be good for sales.

Nor did Gove mention that he had overhauled the style of definition-writing for *Webster's Third*, though mostly in his own manner and not according to any orthodoxy of linguistics.[4] His decision to extend the use of illustrative quotations, however, does seem to have been influenced by linguistics and its emphasis on "language as it is," but this too he avoided mentioning.

Instead, Gove discussed the area where linguistics had had its most visible effect on *Webster's Third*: pronunciations. And, he said, there was really no difference between the five concepts published in *English Language Arts* and the principles that guided pronunciation in *Webster's Second*. But, like sweat on the brow, the strain required to make this argument showed.

Kenyon and Knott themselves had found the pronunciation guidance in *Webster's Second* so inadequate to describing current practice that they had developed an entirely separate volume, *A Pronouncing Dictionary of American English*. And a glance at the five concepts gave Gove away. "All usage is relative" (number five) is obviously a far cry from the principles of "best current practice" and "formal platform speech" touted in *Webster's Second*.

Still Gove sought to mark a trail leading from *Webster's Second* to Kenyon-Knott's pronouncing dictionary and finally to *Webster's Third*. In this evolution, Merriam-Webster's pronunciation guidance had become less formal, more American, and it had ceased relying on Webster's proprietary pronunciation key. But there was another change that Gove failed to mention: the new sense of variety in the spoken language. In *Webster's Third*, the sheer number of possible pronunciations would make even the scientifically informed and up-to-date Kenyon-Knott look like Simple Simon.

IN CLOSING, Gove brought his essay back to lexicography in general, which, unlike linguistics, was not a science but "an overpowering art, requiring subjective analysis, arbitrary decisions, and intuitive reasoning. It often uses analogy, precedent, and probability." Gove then showed something of his true colors in what would become his oft-quoted statement, "But it should have no traffic with guesswork, prejudice, or bias, or with artificial notions of correctness and superiority. It must be descriptive and not prescriptive."

A dictionary must be "a faithful recorder . . . it cannot expect to be any longer appealed to as an authority." A long generation of cultural and intellectual change had reshaped the lexicographer's art. And Gove was the spokesman for the new lexicography: "When the semantic center of gravity appears to have moved far enough," he wrote, "when the drift of pronunciation is ascertainable, when a new science makes new knowledge and new methods available, then revision of the affected parts of a dictionary becomes the conscientious duty of the lexicographer. It is in the execution of this duty that Merriam-Webster dictionaries have begun a new series suitable to a new age."

CHAPTER 31

SOMETIMES LESS IS MORE, Jacques Barzun thought. In *The House of Intellect*, he wrote, "Beyond the last flutter of actual or possible significance, pedantry begins."

It was often better for a scholar to stop short of exhausting a subject (and his readers) by using less information than was available. Knowledge was not an unlimitable good. Accuracy and completeness were only relative merits. It was even possible for a scholar to make a fair number of errors yet still deserve praise for answering a few large questions correctly. James Parton, the nineteenth-century biographer who had been criticized for minor inaccuracies, came to mind. Barzun quoted Albert J. Nock's pardon of Parton: "There are qualities that outweigh occasional and trivial inaccuracy, and Parton has them, while the other biographers of Mr. Jefferson, as far as I can see, have not."[1]

JAMES PARTON surely read and appreciated Barzun's indirect defense of his grandfather, whom the president of American Heritage was said to resemble in his love of history. But it could not have occurred to him that he and Barzun would soon both accuse the quintessential American dictionary of not only pedantry but much, much worse. Parton—sometime journalist, Luce alumnus, and World War II air force veteran—was merely interested in buying G. & C. Merriam Company. In 1959, it looked like the perfect investment for American Heritage.

Parton's colleague Gerald P. Rosen (who had also run track with Parton at Harvard) went up to Springfield and learned what he could. He interviewed Samuel E. Murray, a former Merriam employee who had been shown the door several years back after trying to organize a syndicate to buy the company. Management had been utterly opposed to selling. Murray still had the list of Merriam's stockholders and gave it to Rosen. The new president, Gordon J. Gallan, would be more open, Murray thought, to selling the company.

But that was not Rosen's impression. After a few days of snooping around Springfield, he concluded that Gallan would "vigorously fight any effort to acquire this company." And so would, he thought, the Springfield Safe Deposit and Trust Company. The bank had almost a proprietary interest in Merriam, Rosen believed. It acted as executor of the estates of several of Merriam's trustees, and Gallan was a member of the bank's board.[2]

American Heritage then retained a former *Fortune* researcher named Sara Springer to gather basic facts on Merriam and the dictionary market. If Merriam was buyable, her findings showed, American Heritage should buy it. The demographic outlook was excellent, and the company was in a position to reap huge profits. What neither Springer nor anyone else could find was a reason Merriam would want to be sold to American Heritage. There were other, more likely courtiers, and even if the company did not sell, its future looked pretty bright.

More Americans were becoming more educated, and this was unqualifiably good news for the education publishing business. "In view of the upsurge in college enrollments as the large crop of war babies comes of age," the report said, "sales of dictionaries should increase to keep pace with this expectation."

Sales of dictionaries in 1958 totaled $25 million, in Springer's estimation. They were, according to some, second only to Bibles among all-time bestsellers, but they were more expensive to make. The *American College Dictionary* had reportedly cost Random House $2 million to make from scratch. The *Webster's New World* had reportedly cost $1 million in 1950.

The market worked well. Bookstores considered dictionaries stock items. Springer had visited Scribner's and Brentano's in New York and learned that dictionaries were almost never returned. Also, they presented no overstock problems since copies eventually sold. A dictionary did not lose value at the same rate as many other books, which quickly became old news or last year's sensation.

Merriam never released sales figures, so the only information Springer could gather was out of date. Between 1936 and 1949—despite the lingering Depression, paper shortages, and a major war—Merriam had sold four and a half million *Collegiate* dictionaries, which it claimed were required reading at most American colleges and universities. Its 1947 *Pocket Dictionary* was an especially big seller with six million sold. And the company was on sound financial footing with enough government securities to cover three times its current liabilities, which, however, were mounting fast with the production of the new unabridged dictionary.

Merriam was the leader of the industry, the oldest publisher in the game, with *the* great name in American dictionaries. Its citation files were thought by some to be the most complete in the world. But its management was rather conservative. Despite the increasing size of the education publishing market, in 1957 Merriam had spent less than 5 percent of its gross income on promotion.[3]

Parton was not impressed by Sara Springer. "It's obvious we made a very bad choice in Mrs. Springer, and I'm damned if I know how she managed to survive as a *Fortune* researcher if this is typical of her work. . . . About the only real value of the report is its slight further evidence that G. and C. Merriam Co. would be a really desirable acquisition if it is indeed available at anything resembling a normal purchase price."

He sensed that he still knew very little about how a dictionary was made. "Presumably if we bought a going dictionary concern, we would get reasonably competent management with it or could hire same away from competitors. But what does dictionary management consist of? What determined the difference between a good dictionary and a bad? What special production criteria are involved?"

And there were major editorial questions. "How big a staff does a dictionary have? What kind of people are they? What do they do? How long does it take? What supporting reference resources are called for? Are there special fees for various specialists?"[4]

Then, in late 1959, came confirmation that Merriam was, in fact, trying to attract a buyer. Curtis Benjamin, the president of McGraw-Hill and a friend of Parton's, said that his company had been invited to take a look at Merriam. They passed on it in order to pursue other opportunities. It looked, Parton had said, as if Merriam had very poor top management, and Benjamin commented that this was "certainly so."[5]

A month after the new year, Parton wrote a letter introducing himself to Ingham C. Baker, the largest single stockholder in Merriam. It was his practice to send along a box of American Heritage publications. He did not ask outright to buy Baker's stocks, but suggested rather vaguely that the futures of American Heritage and Merriam might become aligned, and asked for a meeting to discuss the matter. Baker passed the letter along to Gallan, who responded rather brusquely.

"Mr. Ingham C. Baker has asked me to acknowledge your letter of February 3. The Directors of G. and C. Merriam Company are not interested in a merger."[6]

Parton wrote back saying that he was ever so sorry that his letter to Baker had been misunderstood. "We are not interested in mergers either," he wrote to Gallan. "We do have some ideas of possible mutual interest to your company as well as to mine." The letter closed with Parton asking Gallan to let him know the next time he would be in New York so they could have the pleasure of lunching together.

In the meantime Parton and others at American Heritage were considering the possibility of approaching all Merriam stockholders simultaneously with a sweeping offer to buy everyone out. But Parton believed the plan had two major disadvantages. The first was the transactional cost of completing a vast number of small buys with no guarantee of gaining a majority position. The second was that it would invite "a serious Gallan counterblast."[7]

In November, Gallan was finally in New York City and available to meet with Parton, who did his best to convince Gallan that his intentions were mild. Writing to him afterward, Parton said, "You were very gracious to pay me a visit yesterday, and I found our chat both pleasant and instructive." Then he reiterated some basic information about American Heritage, whose annual sales were around $10 million. The company's products had secondary value in schools and libraries, and this naturally led Parton to think more broadly about educational publishing. Perhaps the next time Parton was in Springfield they could talk again about some kind of joint venture.[8]

Parton began working with a team of fixers to find a way to take over Merriam. In the spring, he was lunching with three of them, each one a link to the next and finally to people of influence inside Merriam. The first, Jennison or "Tunny" Newsom was an investment counselor from Hartford, Connecticut, and he knew the second, Guy Holt, the son of Lucius Holt, who had worked on the 1909 Webster's and was an assistant editor on the 1934 Webster's. Scott Stearns, a real estate developer in Springfield with contacts at Merriam, was also there.

Recalled Parton afterward, "All three struck me as very civilized and intelligent men, but not notably aggressive ones. I came away with the impression that the pursuit of the prize is being conducted in a pretty leisurely fashion."

To raise their intensity a little, Parton tried to give the impression that Merriam was only so attractive to American Heritage. He summarized the dictionary market as he understood it. "Merriam is widely regarded as an obsolete and doddering enterprise," he said. Random House and New World had both intruded on its turf and were hardly suffering as a result. And, now, what was the latest that Parton had heard? That Merriam's new editor had "embarked on a wildly radical revision of its long-standing concept of how a dictionary should be organized." Just imagine that.

"Merriam's apparent solidity," Parton concluded, "might really be nothing more than a brittle façade."[9]

But not one of Parton's lunch partners had until now heard the part about Philip Gove and the dictionary's new editorial policies. These supposed insiders were shocked that the new unabridged was going to depart radically from the design of the old unabridged. Then one thought led to the next. This business about the radicalness of the new dictionary was, they all thought, a very strong argument to use in favor of selling the company to American Heritage.

Parton—the onetime assistant to public relations pioneer Edward Bernays and former aide-de-camp to Ira Eakins, the man who sold Churchill on American airpower—had found his sales pitch.

CHAPTER 32

IN ADDITION TO A lively cast of characters—Betty Grable, Mickey Spillane, Polly Adler, Dwight D. Eisenhower—the story of the making of
Webster's Third came with enough impressive-sounding, gee-whiz facts
and figures to be picked up by many a local and national newspaper.
The dictionary weighed thirteen and a half pounds and featured 100,000
new words and senses, a massive amount of new language that Merriam called "the greatest vocabulary explosion in history." While new
words were being added, a quarter million entries were subtracted, and
all remaining entries were revised. "Every line of it is new," Gove wrote
in the preface. With 450,000 total entries the new dictionary contained
100,000 quotations from more than 14,000 authors. The foundation for
Merriam-Webster's lexicography comprised some 10 million citations,
and the new edition had cost $3.5 million to make.

Gove's preface to *Webster's Third* said it had taken 757 editor-years to
make the dictionary, while another promotional piece emphasized the
number of outside experts, 200, and advanced degrees held by members of the Merriam staff: 33 doctorates and 62 master's degrees.[1] By
the numbers, the story offered plenty of material for a nice article on a
newspaper's front page or to lead off its business section, its figures to
be ably recalled by future tour guides as they escorted visitors around
the Springfield offices of G. & C. Merriam Company. If anything, the

jolly tone of these particular numbers understated the dreary intensity of the work. In a letter to Merriam, one chemistry consultant lamented that over six long years, while also serving on a college faculty, he had reviewed 12,790 definitions, a task that had involved approximately 250,000 slips of paper.

The initial press release was also funny, and it provided conflict with its news of a dictionary embracing informal English and standing up for that quintessential ne'er-do-well *ain't*. What actually sent the story into overdrive, however, was a remarkable string of mistakes.

The press release—which had been read and approved by President Gordon J. Gallan—so abbreviated the dictionary's entry for *ain't* that it amounted to a misquotation. From the usage note written into the first sense, "used orally by many educated speakers," it left out that *ain't* was "disapproved by many and more common in less educated speech." And the press release failed to show that a substandard label was attached to the second sense. Compounding these errors, the release said that *"ain't gets official recognition at last."*

So, not only was *ain't* being defended, perhaps even recommended for the oral use of educated speakers, the press release also suggested that this was the first time *ain't* was recognized by a dictionary. But none of this was true. It was not being defended and it had been in many dictionaries before. Also, by blurring the distinction between a word's appearance in the dictionary and its status as standard English, the press release invited critics to blame *Webster's Third* for "recognizing" every last silly, awkward, dialectal, jargonish, or slang word it provided an entry for. All of these mistaken claims tended in one direction, implying that *Webster's Third* was much more permissive than it actually was, and that all other dictionaries, by comparison, were much more censorious than they actually were.

This is how the newspaper controversy over *Webster's Third* began. The first publication to accuse Merriam-Webster of being linguistically radical was its own press release. By hiring out the work of announcing its dictionary to PR professionals, President Gallan and Editor Gove had lost control of saying what the new dictionary stood for. Instead of presenting a united front of America's learned class, they had circulated a saucy and sloppy notice (with more than a couple typos) designed not to command respect but to catch a news editor's eye. In this way the dictionary launch was highly successful, but at the price of significant embarrassment to Merriam. For obvious reasons one cannot imagine Robert Munroe or Asa Baker and William Allan Neilson—all of whom took seriously the public image of Merriam—stumbling like this.

One also wonders what the father of public relations, Edward Bernays, would have said. By his lights, the first question to ask in building a PR campaign was not, What are you selling? It was, What do people actually want?

In the case of dictionaries, the answer was clear: the knowledge to improve understanding and avoid mistakes in meaning, usage, spelling, and pronunciation. Gallan and others knew this from market research they had read and discussed. The dictionary consumer was conservative. Now, what was this press release selling? An extreme, almost comic form of linguistic liberalism, a license to use *ain't* and the right to sound like a Mickey Spillane character.

It was no wonder, then, that newspaper reporters glommed on to this part of the story. "The word *ain't* ain't a grammatical mistake anymore," said a hammy United Press International wire story picked up by the *Chicago Tribune* and the *Sun-Times*. "This is certainly a far cry from the dictionary's 1934 edition," said the *Washington Sunday Star*, "which bluntly—and correctly, in our view—brands *ain't* as a 'dialectal' and 'illiterate' expression employed by people on the fringe of polite society."

Headline writers gleefully (and very predictably) seized on the word in question. "Saying Ain't Ain't Wrong," said the *Tribune*; "It Ain't Good," said the Washington *Sunday Star*; "Ain't Nothing Wrong with the Use of Ain't," said the *Louisville Times*; "Ain't Still Has Tain't," said the

Binghamton Sunday Press; "There's Them as Ain't Using Ain't," said the *Jacksonville Journal*. Accompanying articles highlighted the news that, as the *Los Angeles Herald-Express* put it, though rather positively, "The word *ain't* has at long last come into its own."[2]

Editorial writers also weighed in before the week was out. The Toronto *Globe and Mail* called *Webster's Third* to account for "the death of meaning" and complained that while the political air grew heavy with the threat of nuclear destruction, the new dictionary "will not assist men to speak truly to other men." *Webster's Third* may, however, "prepare us for that future it could help to hasten. In the caves, no doubt, a grunt will do." Three days later, the Washington *Sunday Star* was also warning that the new dictionary of *Sputnik*, *beatnik*, and many other new words would fail to fortify us against the likes of Nikita Khrushchev and worse, the likes of Allen Ginsberg, "who are developing a style of writing that may best be described as literary anarchy."

The first part of a speech act, according to Leonard Bloomfield, is the stimulus. The second part is the reaction. In this case, the stimulus was a dictionary saying it had thrown out the old rules. The reaction was swift, loud, and cackling.

Merriam-Webster sent out another press release correcting the earlier statements on *ain't*, which mainly inspired newspaper critics to look for other entries to single out for abuse. The reigning opinion on *Webster's Third* hardly changed at all.

The Sunday *New York Times* gave exasperated notice of several other usages cited in *Webster's Third*: *orientate*, *upsurge*, *hipster*, *dig* (as in, to understand), *jazz* ("Spouted all the scientific jazz at him"—Pete Martin), *beef up*, and *finalize*. The editorial swapped these terms for more natural choices in its own prose: "In orientating themselves toward the upsurge of new words, G. and C. Merriam Company . . . faced this puzzler: Were there enough hipsters to dig all the new jazz or would the old bop do for a while?"

Days later an article in *BusinessWeek* showed that Gove and Gallan were unaware of the beast they had awoken. Gallan was quoted, sounding boastful, "We might make more money selling beer, but we have a heavy responsibility to the English-speaking world." Gove, too, cooperated with the article and sounded the first of many democratic notes, saying language was "an instrument of the people." The magazine reported that the new dictionary had, in the name of science and linguistics, departed from prescriptivist tradition.

Another P-word was quickly introduced. The *Saturday Review* commented: "It would seem that permissiveness now on the wane in child-rearing has caught up with the dictionary makers."

On October 4, Dwight Macdonald wrote to Philip Gove to say he was writing a review of *Webster's Third* and had a number of questions. These included whether there were other unabridged dictionaries to which *Webster's Third* might be compared, what were the sales for *Webster's Second*, and why did the *Third* drop the gazetteer and the biographical dictionary. He wanted to know more about the principles behind *Webster's Third* and about the process of making a dictionary. Gove invited Macdonald to Springfield for a visit. They had a long, civil discussion and Gove gave Macdonald a copy of his recently published *Word Study* article containing the five principles of linguistics that NCTE had endorsed.[3]

On October 12, the *New York Times* issued a call for *Webster's Third* to be remade. In the bitter history of dictionary criticism, few passages are more well known than the opening paragraph of this editorial.

"A passel of double-domes at the G. and C. Merriam Company joint in Springfield, Mass., have been confabbing and yakking for twenty-seven years—which is not intended to infer that they have not been doing plenty of work—and now they have finalized Webster's Third New International Dictionary, Unabridged, a new edition of that swell and esteemed word book."

And then the *Times* explained itself: "Those who regard the foregoing paragraph as acceptable English prose will find that the new Webster's is just the dictionary for them. The words in the paragraph are listed in the new work with no suggestion that they are anything but standard."

Webster's, said the *Times*, had "surrendered to the permissive school," which already had been undermining the teaching of English. But the problem went far beyond mere classroom instruction. "Webster's is more than just a publishing venture: For generations it has been so widely regarded as a peerless authority on American English as to become almost a public institution."

The editorial, which was widely reprinted and commented on in other newspapers, closed by calling for a return to *Webster's Second*. "We suggest to the Webster editors that they not throw out the printing plates of the Second Edition. There is likely to be a continuing demand for it; and perhaps that edition can be made the platform for a new start—admittedly long, arduous, and costly. But a new start is needed."[4]

James Parton immediately made copies and sent one to James Bulkley, a well-connected lawyer in Springfield who was trying to purchase Merriam stock for American Heritage. "This is a terrible black eye for Merriam," Parton wrote, "and confirms the worries about the big new dictionary which I expressed to you several months ago when we first got acquainted.

"Just what the financial results of this severe condemnation will be, I cannot assess. Conceivably it might knock a major hole in Merriam's business; certainly the competition can be counted on to show this editorial to every library and every scholar in America. It is a most unfortunate development.

"On the plus side, however, it may serve to bolster your case in approaching major stockholders by providing overwhelming evidence of the incompetence of the present Merriam management."[5]

Life magazine, with a circulation in the low millions, entered the fray two weeks later, calling *Webster's Third* "a non-word deluge." *Webster's* "has now all but abandoned any effort to distinguish between good and bad usage—between the King's English, say, and the fishwife's." The popular Luce publication then faulted *Webster's Third* for including *irregardless,* the popular suffix *-wise* (memorably used not long after this by Jack Lemmon in *The Apartment*: "That's the way it crumbles, cookie-wise"), the suffix *-ize*, the dialectal variant *heighth,* and *hain't,* which *Life* called a "hayseed" variation on *ain't.* According to *Life, Webster's Third* had even approved *enormity* as a synonym for *enormousness.* The article closed with a nod to *Webster's Second,* a copy of which the editors said they would keep "around awhile for little matters of style, good English, winning at Scrabble and suchwise."

After the botched handling of *ain't, Webster's Third* was being condemned for including any and all words its critics didn't like, as if the dictionary were responsible for their existence in the first place. In *Life* magazine's complaints about *hain't* and *heighth, Webster's Third* was treated as culpable even for including words explicitly labeled dialectal. But in constantly evoking *Webster's Second* to express their revulsion for *Webster's Third,* critics tended to expose the full range of their ignorance. *Orientate, upsurge, finalize,* and the suffix *-wise* were all included in *Webster's Second,* and none were so labeled there to suggest an inferior status.

Claiming to be astonished by the *Times* parody of Merriam as a passel of double-domes who had been yakking and confabbing for twenty-seven years, Gove, in a letter to the editor, called the rhetorical maneuver a "monstrosity." Such an artificial jumble, he indignantly complained, could just as easily have been assembled using materials from *Webster's Second.* And it "obscures the fact that there are many different degrees of standard usage which cannot be distinguished by status labels." Also, said Gove, the *Times* had failed to examine the quotations in *Webster's Third,* which at least gave one "a little of the feeling that surrounds a word by quoting it in context."[6]

Some of this was true but, alas, not interesting, and some of it was neither true nor interesting. Gove had failed, in his preface to *Webster's*

Third and elsewhere, to explain that his dictionary's illustrative quotations were partly intended to describe usage. Then again, soft-pedaling this line may have been a strategic decision, for the inquiring mind who looked to see if the quotations effectively characterized usage levels would have learned that often they did not. The only quotation under *confabbing* was a Saul Bellow usage—"I would see them confabbing in the shed"—that hardly contained enough context to suggest the word's frequently humorous and dismissive flavor. The entry for *double-dome* included an even less revealing quotation: "had demonstrated his machine to scores of scientific *double-domes*." To understand that both these quotations achieved their effects by mixing standard language and slang, the reader had to be able to label the words himself.

Gove had erred on the side of minimizing use of the slang label, and having dropped the colloquial label entirely, there remained no obvious way to acknowledge, for the reader's sake, informal subtleties such as the playful use of *confabbing* and *double-domes* in these illustrative quotations. Here one could also see how Gove's instructions to his readers to look for slang words in standard contexts actually made it harder to know a word's status from the company it kept. The unexpressed lesson to be taken from the quotations for *confabbing* and *double-domes* was one much favored by Gove but not very helpful: that a word may look like slang in some contexts but not in others. This was true, but it also looked like a way for the lexicographer to throw up his hands and say, "Well, it depends," which was, finally, useless to demonstrating that *Webster's Third* took usage status seriously.

Where Gove did score points was in discovering when his critics had simply failed to examine the entries they had complained about, which happened with amusing frequency. *Irregardless*, Gove pointed out in a letter to *Life* magazine, was also included in *Webster's Second*. Both dictionaries had, in fact, given the redundantly cased dimwitticism its due: The *Second* had labeled it "erroneous" or "humorous," while the *Third* labeled it (in its always detached manner) "nonstandard." *Enor-*

mity, Gove said, was simply not given as a synonym for enormousness in *Webster's Third*. And while holding fast to their beloved *Webster's Second*, the editors at *Life* should have known that *normalcy* and the *-ize* suffix, which they were so upset to find included in *Webster's Third*, were also to be found in *Webster's Second*.

Merriam thus won back some points it had lost earlier, but it never really played to win. The strategy pursued by Gove and Merriam was to minimize direct combat, as when Gove made nice in his letter to the *Times*, saying, "We plan to continue reading and marking the *Times* as the number one exhibit of good standard contemporary cultivated English." He would not show the *New York Times* or *Life* magazine the contempt he had revealed to his daughter's schoolteacher or the Merriam salesman who dared to misuse *scientific* in his presence. After all, the *Times* and *Life* commanded huge audiences and were in a position to affect sales.

Gove came closer to showing his contrary side in presentations to such minor bodies as the English Lunch Club in Boston and the nearby Monson Rotary Club. Here in the semiprivacy of local news coverage Gove called the *New York Times*–led criticism of his dictionary "nitwitted" and complained of "critics whose linguistic notions of propriety were formed three or four decades ago." But this was not the brazen new editor who had questioned whether *Webster's Third* would be literally Webster's, actually new, in fact international, or even a dictionary as such.

Saying *Webster's Second* had dated more rapidly "than any unabridged dictionary ever produced," Gove nevertheless described *Webster's Third* as a clear successor volume. This did not, however, even gel with the preface for *Webster's Third*, where he did not waste a comma to say that "prescriptive and canonical definitions have not been taken over nor have recommendations been followed unless confirmed by independent investigation of usage borne out by genuine citations."[7]

The only alternative to downplaying the differences between his dictionary and *Webster's Second* was direct combat, in which Gove would have had to clearly and loudly label the statements of his detractors as humorous but erroneous, and this hesitation to forthrightly battle the know-it-alls seems to have been rooted in his editorial principles. In theory (though not always in practice), Philip Gove had long rejected the kind of self-assertive linguistic authority needed to teach these naughty critics a lesson. Appealing baldly to his own standing as a dictionary editor and thus some kind of all-knowing authority on language was inimical to his most basic beliefs. Instead, he wrote officious letters to critical publications, letters that always ran several pages long, listing countless citations in defense of some faintly etched point thoroughly bleached of any humor or zing.

In dropping *colloquial* and replacing the judgmental categories of *Webster's Second* with labels such as *nonstandard* and *substandard*, Gove, for all his populist gestures, had made it harder for dictionary users to know what *Webster's Third* was saying. His own hesitation to play the grammar cop on words like *ain't* had resulted in an oddly worded, ambiguous-sounding treatment for the most famous example of a vulgar, illiterate word in the English language. And now this same hesitation to speak from authority—along with his obligations to defend his company's reputation—was inhibiting his responses.

It was also emboldening his critics. From the erroneous press release to the hyperventilating doomsayers to the public spanking from the *New York Times*, the story of *ain't* was proving *rich*, as in "high in entertainment . . . strongly amusing," and even more so when it was disclosed that the now-infamous entry for *ain't* had been written by Gove himself.

CHAPTER 33

BERGEN EVANS WAS LYING in a hospital bed when he read the *Life* magazine editorial pasting Merriam-Webster for its handling of *irregardless*, *enormity*, the use of *like* where rule favors *as*, and for blurring the distinction between *imply* and *infer*. It made him angry. He continued reading, pen in hand, and counted.[1]

Evans was the co-author with his sister Cornelia of *A Dictionary of Contemporary American Usage*, which took a hard line on *irregardless* ("there is no such word") but expressed liberal scientific principle in its acceptance of the conjunction *like* in "You don't know Nellie like I do." The three chief sources for this book were the *OED*, the seven-volume grammar of Otto Jespersen, and the works of Charles C. Fries. The Evanses acknowledged the usual distinction between *imply* and *infer* ("The speaker implies; the hearer infers"), while observing that distinguished writers such as Milton and James Mill had violated the rule. Their article on *ain't*—like many "dictionaries," the Evanses' book freely used ordinary prose in its entries—discussed its nonstandard status in almost all uses, but mentioned that "a few bold spirits" had adopted the word to skip past the awkwardness of *Am I not?* and *Aren't I?*

In this and other ways, the language was becoming less stuffy. "Forty years ago it was considered courteous to use formal English in speaking to strangers, implying they were solemn and important people. Today it is considered more flattering to address strangers as if they were one's intimate friends. This is a polite lie, of course; but it is today's good manners. Modern usage encourages informality wherever possible and reserves formality for very few occasions."[2]

On this particular occasion, Bergen read the whole issue of *Life* and counted all the words and meanings not in *Webster's Second*. His tally came to forty-four. And he determined that the editors of *Life* were not his friends.

Wilson Follett was not his friend, either. The literature professor had, a year earlier, reviewed and damned the Evanses' *Dictionary of Contemporary American Usage* in the *Atlantic*, which had magnanimously allowed Bergen Evans to publish a full rejoinder one month later.[3]

Follett had begun by complaining that "linguistic scholarship, once an encouragement to the most exacting definitions and standards of workmanship, has for some time been dedicating itself to the abolition of standards." For a telling illustration of this woeful truth, said Follett, one need only examine the Evanses' *Dictionary of Contemporary American Usage*.

The heart of Follett's review was a list, filling almost an entire magazine column, of usages tolerated by the Evanses that did not deserve the name of good English. It might have been taken from Sterling Leonard's lists of disputable expressions that contemporary educated people increasingly found acceptable. The Evanses had countenanced such usages as *He is taller than me* (*me* instead of *I* in the objective case); *the reason is because* (faulted for redundancy); *neither of them had their tickets* (*neither* must be construed as singular, according to Follett); *if one loses his temper* (for consistency, instead of *if one loses one's temper*); *back of* (as an adjective to mean behind but considered vulgar); *between each house* (*between* must always describe a relation of two things); *he failed, due to carelessness* (*due*, an adjective, being misused as an adverb). It was, in other words, a list of commonplace English, much of which could even be found in professionally edited publications.

Follett scored more points in asking, as few linguists ever did, what positive lessons could be derived from more complete evidence on usage. "Is it not one of the shames of modern scholarship that it has so little to say for what is really good, what is best, and so much to say about what is merely allowable or defensible?" Even if linguistic scholarship could show that *like* was widely used as a conjunction, as in "You don't know Nellie like I do," it refused to show an interest in whether it was better to say, "You don't know Nellie as I do" or "the way I do." The argument from usage, indeed, yielded a binary distinction between usages that can be evidenced and usages that cannot, while ignoring on scientific grounds the kind of thinking that led to preferences for one form over another.

Evans fought crankiness with enthusiasm. He evoked the example of Samuel Johnson, whose idealistic plan to fix the language had given way to an understanding that (in Johnson's inimitable words) "to enchain syllables and to lash the wind are equally undertakings of pride unwilling to measure its desires by its strengths." After eight long years of "sluggishly tracking the alphabet," Johnson said he had come to understand that lexicographers and grammarians "do not form, but register the language." Johnson, commented Evans, had begun as a "medieval pedant" and emerged as a "modern scientist."

Then Evans looked to corner Follett on the singularity of *none* and *like* as a conjunction. The case that *none* should be construed as a singular had the example of Latin *nemo* and logic in its favor, so "the prescriptive grammarians are emphatic that it should be singular." The historical record did show that from 1450 to 1650, *none* was three times as often treated as singular, but then in the last three hundred years, *none* was treated as a plural almost twice as often. The imbalance had since increased to the point where Evans could happily say that today *none are* was the preferred form.

If the literary critic was at his best in taking science to task for ignoring taste, the scientist was at his best in amassing evidence for these discrete pitched battles over single instances of disputed usage.

"Anyone who tells a child—or anyone else—that *like* is used in English only as a preposition has grossly misinformed him." Then Evans touched on the example of "Winston tastes good, like a cigarette should," the famous ad line that was always mentioned in this context. "Anyone who complains," said Evans, "that its use as a conjunction is a corruption introduced by Winston cigarettes ought, in all fairness, to explain how Shakespeare, Keats, and the translators of the Authorized Version of the Bible came to be in the employ of the R.J. Reynolds Tobacco Company."

As reviews of *Webster's Third* came out in the fall of 1961, Evans and Follett again sharpened their sticks and headed into the fray. Evans wrote Philip Gove praising the new dictionary. But Follett thought it a terrible, terrible book, much worse than even the *Dictionary of Contemporary American Usage*.

CHAPTER 34

THE *NEW YORK TIMES* pursued *Webster's Third* like a blood vendetta—well, maybe I overstate, but that's what writers and journalists do—while the dictionary was denounced in one newspaper, magazine, and trade publication after another, and the condemnation grew ever more dark, thunderous, and weird.

After running a pair of editorials piling up examples of questionable terms that appeared in *Webster's Third* without usage labels, the *Times* fired two more salvos in late November. The first called President Kennedy to account for publicly using one of the *Webster's Third* stinkers. "In the course of his highly articulate news conference today, President Kennedy struck one grating note for lovers of the English language. He used that bureaucratic favorite 'finalize.'"

Under *finalize, Webster's Third* had cited words of President Eisenhower: "soon my conclusions will be finalized."

One day later, yet another editorial ran in the *Times*. "Mr. President," it said, "are you sure you gave the old place a housecleaning after you moved in? . . . When you said yesterday, 'We have not finalized any plans,' it sounded for all the world like a previous occupant who once said, as quoted in Webster's Third (or Bolshevik) International . . ."[1]

Take that.

It would be near impossible for any dictionary, even *Webster's Third*, to be like Ike and Bolshevik at the same time. And perhaps the newspaper of Stalin apologist Walter Duranty, who had denied all reports of famine in Russia, should have been a little more reluctant to red-bait a dictionary with an innocent Cold War record. But newspapers not only report news, they generate news, and they do so by picking causes and pursuing them with all the bluster of a wisecracking politician. Subtlety goes out the window. To do something well is to overdo it. To state well is to overstate. Sketching pencils and watercolors are put away; only the strongest pigments will suffice. If red, after a decade of McCarthyism and several months after the Bay of Pigs incident, seems particularly eye-catching, well, then get the red.

Mario Pei had reviewed the dictionary for the *New York Times Book Review*. He repeated the story of *ain't* as told in the press release, but pointed out that *ain't* had "consistently appeared in dictionaries" before this. He emphasized the dictionary's embrace of informal language, saying, "it leaves me wondering just how far the process of informality can go before it incurs the charge of outright vulgarism." Fair enough. Pei listed some commendable features and some less commendable. *Don* in the British sense of professor was included in *Webster's Third*, along with the Spanish meaning señor, but why not the Italian-American slang for mafia boss? The Columbia professor missed the encyclopedic matter but was impressed by the Polly Adler–assisted entry for *shake*, a word whose expansion of meanings he found startling. It was a qualified though positive review. But Pei came around. Months later, he was saying that *Webster's Third* "blurs to the point of obliteration the older distinction between standard, substandard, colloquial, vulgar, and slang." By the lights of its editors, Pei wrote, "good and bad, right and wrong, correct and incorrect no longer exist."[2]

In the meantime, Theodore M. Bernstein, the *Times*' well-known assistant managing editor, took to the *Bulletin of the American Society of Newspaper Editors* to expand the paper's case against "permissiveness gone mad." *Webster's Third*, he wrote, "has methodically removed all guideposts to usage except for an infinitesimal number labeling the most obvious pieces of slang and vulgarity and has turned the dictionary into a bewildering wilderness of words."[3]

In January, Bernstein issued a directive to the staff of the *Times*, addressing whether the arrival of *Webster's Third* would affect the paper's style. "The answer is no. Editors representing the news, Sunday and editorial departments have decided without a dissent to continue using *Webster's Second Edition* for spelling and usage." (Oh, to have seen the editors voting on this! "A motion to reject *Webster's Third* and all its works and pledge allegiance to *Webster's Second* until a suitable alternative is put forth: All in favor say aye." "Aye." "All against, say nay." Silence.)

This same month Wilson Follett published his review in the *Atlantic*. It raised the serial denunciation of *Webster's Third* to a new intensity. Ever so briefly, the article faked a tone of scholarly detachment. Follett granted that it was impossible to know all the merits of such a book except after years of use but then said, "On the other hand, it costs only minutes to find out that what will rank as the great event of American linguistic history in this decade, and perhaps in this quarter century, is in many crucial particulars a very great calamity."

Indeed, a very great calamity.

Follett pounced on the loss of encyclopedic material. "Think—if you can—of an unabridged dictionary from which you cannot learn who Mark Twain was . . . or what were the names of the apostles or that the Virgin was Mary the mother of Jesus of Nazareth, or what and where the District of Columbia is!"[4] But "unabridged" was always a term of art, and one had only to think of the well-known *Oxford English Dictionary* to think of a scholarly dictionary that did not provide encyclopedic information. But the underlying point was solid: This was not the Webster's dictionary you grew up with.

Follett looked back to *Webster's Second*. He might have been raising his water glass at the Hotel Kimball as he spoke of William Allan Neilson and "the most important reference book in the world to American writers, editors, teachers, students, and general readers—everyone to whom American English was a matter of serious interest."

Where the Second Edition had "provided accurate, impartial accounts of the endless guerilla war between grammarian and anti-grammarian," the Third Edition set out to "destroy . . . every obstinate vestige of linguistic punctilio, every surviving influence that makes for the upholding of standards, every criterion for distinguishing between better usages and worse." It had "gone over bodily to the school that construes traditions as enslaving, the rudimentary principles of syntax as crippling, and taste as irrelevant."

Good grammar had become bad, and bad usages were good. The dubious notion—introduced by Merriam's own press release—that a word's mere inclusion in the dictionary equaled endorsement by the dictionary was linked to the use of fewer and less judgmental usage labels. A perfectly logical connection, its meaning was however exaggerated to say that the descriptivist *Webster's Third* was positively prescriptivist when it served the critic's point.

The most frivolous words and phrases, according to Follett, enjoyed all the status once belonging to only the most polished and public of utterances. Follett, in high dudgeon, listed *wise up, get hep, ants in one's pants, one for the book, hugeous, nixie, hep cat, anyplace,* and *someplace,* all of which appeared unlabeled in *Webster's Third.* "These and a swarm of their kind it admits to full canonical standing by the suppression of such qualifying status labels as *colloquial, slang, cant, facetious,* and *substandard.*" Thus did *ants in one's pants* (entered under *ant* with an uncharacteristically formal *one*) become "officially applauded English."

On a host of issues, *Webster's Third* (like the *Dictionary of Contemporary American Usage*) had ignored traditional classroom rules: on singular-plural agreement in *everybody had made up their minds,* on *different than* (instead of *different from*), and the use of *like* as a conjunction, which Follett described wonderfully though nuttily as "that darling of advanced libertarians." The "saboteurs of Springfield," as Follett called Gove and his co-conspirators, had knocked down one after another of the "traditionary controls." But, like the obsolescent *traditionary*, much of Follett's indictment revealed him to be an absolute mossback. The commonplace use of *due to* in *the event was canceled due to inclement weather* was, Follett thought, an "abomination."

But Follett's traditionary argument also recognized the extent to which *Webster's Third* was, by design, an especially present-minded dictionary. According to Merriam, most of the 14,000 authors represented in the dictionary's illustrative quotations, as Follett noted, came from the mid-twentieth century. Which is exactly how Gove wanted it. Also, Follett's case did not rest exclusively on the long list he had assembled of the Third Edition's criminal handling of *like*, *due to*, and so on, for there was plenty of other evidence to show that *Webster's Third* was possessed by tendentious thinking.

The new defining style, Follett wrote, produced "a great unmanageable and unpunctuated bloc of words strung out beyond the retentive powers of most minds that would need the definition at all." It is hard to know whether Follett knew he was practically demonstrating this breathless declarative style in his own sentence, but he gave an excellent example with the dictionary's entry for *rabbit punch*: "a short chopping blow delivered to the back of the neck or the base of the skull with the edge of the hand opposite the thumb that is illegal in boxing." So weird-sounding, it was a definite mark against Gove's dictionary. The new defining style and its aversion to commas helped give *Webster's Third* the slightly robotic air of an intellectual who lacks basic social skills.

In February, J. Donald Adams penned an article for the *New York Times Book Review* that quoted Follett at length and questioned why *Webster's Third* relied so heavily on quotations collected in the last few decades. These, Adams assumed (not unreasonably), were for the sake of reinforcing definitions, not for describing usage as a label might (as Gove intended). Bemoaning the reduction of usage labels and the dictionary's "atrocious" prose, Adams said with the wounded air of a jilted lover, "I shall never turn again to the new Merriam-Webster."

The *Times* was tracking the circulation of its own pronouncements, admiring the shadow it cast across this debate. The paper reported that two other journals had joined the protest: the *American Bar Association Journal* and the *Library Journal*. The ABA journal accused *Webster's Third* of devaluing the verbal currency of the English language, as a nation's currency might be devalued by corrupt monetary policy—a rather bizarre analogy with not a few preposterous legal implications, which would suggest that Merriam, a private company with not even a monopoly on American lexicography or even the Webster name, was a kind of U.S. Treasury or Federal Reserve for American English. The ABA journal had cited *Life* magazine's error-ridden editorial, repeating its mistaken claim that *Webster's Third* offered *enormity* as a synonym for *enormousness*, and, whaddaya know, it also referenced the *New York Times'* own editorials. If President Kennedy was to be faulted for not reading or learning from the *New York Times* editorials, then the ABA journal had certainly earned a favorable mention.[5]

The ABA journal did light upon one of the most notorious pairs of entries to be found in *Webster's Third*, those for *imply* and *infer*, which the *Times* and *Life* had also mentioned, though too briefly for its subversive style to be fully appreciated. *Imply* was defined in *Webster's Third* as "to indicate . . . by logical inference," while *infer* was defined as "to derive . . . by implication." For those who insist that *imply* and *infer* are forever as separate as oil and water, what could be more annoying than to define each word using the other?

The case against *Webster's Third* spread to the *Richmond News Leader* and the *Washington Post*, both of which cited Follett's damning review, while the latter accused the new dictionary of "pretentious and obscure verbosity." The *Post* added substantially to the communal argument by simply quoting the dictionary's circuitous and giggle-inducing definition for *door*: "a movable piece of firm material or a structure supported usually along one side and swinging on pivots or hinges, sliding along a groove, rolling up and down, revolving as one of four leaves, or folding like an accordion by means of which an opening may be closed or kept open for passage into or out of a building, room, or other covered enclosure or a car, airplane, elevator, or other vehicle."[6] Mixing the essential and nonessential in one long, barely readable, determinative phrase, it was a definition of *door* written by someone who seemed to doubt that *door* can be defined.

The case against *Webster's Third* was most persuasive when focused on individual absurdities like the definition for *door* or the entries for *imply* and *infer*. These demonstrated how the whole Philip Gove approach seemed to rob language of its surety. Instead of making the language simpler, it became more complex, harder to grasp, to use, and to trust. In such odd and complicated entries as *door* (see also *hotel*), *Webster's Third* seemed nervous and uncertain, puffing itself up with great shows of specificity and literalness as it groped with the slippery edges of meaning.

But if *Webster's Third* was at times more than a little awkward, much of the criticism of its principles was bizarre. *Webster's Third* "makes no pretense of being a guardian of the language, and does not pass judgment on what is correct," wrote the Right Reverend Richard S. Emrich in the *Detroit News*. "It is not a dictionary as Samuel Johnson or Noah Webster conceived of one; it is a catalog. It is a kind of Kinsey Report in linguistics."[7]

This line of argument quickly gave way to more hysterical, *Timesian* suggestions that this new dictionary was the lexicographical embodiment of Soviet Russia. The Reverend Emrich borrowed words from William Ralph Inge, a British newspaper columnist who was a fierce anticommunist and skeptical of philosophies, like Marxism, that trafficked in pseudoscientific certainty.

Wrote the Reverend Emrich: "The Bolshevik spirit . . . is to be found everywhere, not just in Russia. Wherever our standards are discarded in family life, the care of the soul, art, literature, or education, there is the Bolshevik spirit. Wherever men believe that what is, is right, there is bolshevism. It is a spirit that corrupts everything it touches." Including dictionaries.

One wishes Emrich had understood all the changes that had been wrought in *Webster's Third*. Then he might have fully translated Inge's parallelism to fit his analogy. He could have written, "Wherever disputed rules of grammar are discarded and simple words are complicated, there is the bolshevik spirit. Wherever overconfident labels have been jettisoned in favor of less judgmental and less helpful ones, there again is bolshevism. Wherever good prose has been replaced by bad, and wherever typographic peculiarity lowers the upper-case, there is still more bolshevism. And wherever encyclopedic matter has been dropped so an unabridged dictionary might fit between two covers, there is—did you see this one coming?—even more bolshevism. Oh, there is so much bolshevism! It is a spirit that corrupts everything it touches, threatening the whole English language as spoken by tens of millions of people. If those bolsheviks Lenin and Stalin had been lexicographers, *Webster's Third* would have been the result."

Amusing, perhaps, but insane.

CHAPTER 35

IN DECEMBER 1961, JAMES Parton said to his own board of directors that American Heritage's chances of taking over G. & C. Merriam Company were less than 50 percent.[1] By Massachusetts law, they would need support of two-thirds of the company's stockholders—which, even if things went according to plan, would be a stretch. Merriam was reassuring its stockholders with extra dividends, and it had just announced a special stockholders' meeting. Also, the release of *Webster's Third*—for all the Sturm und Drang surrounding it, or rather because of it—was going well. Sales were way up.

An interesting piece of cocktail party gossip had reached Parton: that Merriam had seriously underestimated sales of the new dictionary and that their printer, Riverside Press, was getting ready for another printing just three months after publication.[2] Also complicating matters, word of Parton's approaches to major stockholders was getting back to Merriam.

President Gallan wrote Parton to say that he was wrong that the company's sales were poor. They had, in fact, doubled since he became president, Gallan said. Parton had claimed the company was underperforming in a letter offering to buy Robert Merriam's stock, a letter that Merriam, a loyalist to the firm that bore his family's name, had forwarded to Gallan. But, according to Parton's numbers, the growth in sales from 1956 to 1960 only came to 9 percent while the industry as a whole was up about 56 percent.[3]

Gallan also insisted that scholarly reaction to *Webster's Third* was positive. Parton returned shot by mentioning Follett. "May I invite your attention to the January 1962 *Atlantic Monthly*, published today, with a six-page article entitled 'Sabotage in Springfield—*Webster's Third Edition*' and describing the book as 'a dismaying assortment of the questionable, the perverse, the unworthy and the downright outrageous.'"[4]

Still, it was an uphill battle for American Heritage. Robert Merriam, the largest stockholder, who lived in California, repeatedly turned down Parton's offer to buy him out. Parton was betting on the usefulness of intermediaries such as James Bulkley, but so far it only meant that communications were circuitous. Merriam's "no" came from his wife, Helen, who told Earla Rowley Carson, a Springfield family friend, to tell Parton's agent James Bulkley that Bob was definitely not interested.[5]

Parton then tried a more direct approach, asking to visit Mr. Merriam on his next trip to California. Said Robert Merriam: "It is not in the cards for me to sell any Merriam Company stock. This is a firm decision. I hope you will not come out here with ideas of changing my mind. Call me stubborn, if you will, but I must stick with a negative decision, come hell or high water."[6]

On December 26, Gerald Rosen at American Heritage summed up the early action in a memo: "Opposition is hardening to the gentlemanly assault this company has directed at G. and C. Merriam."

American Heritage's initial strategy was to win over the major stockholders, all of whom they called "oldsters" (a nineteenth-century coinage left out of *Webster's Second* but included in the *Third*). Their last names echoed the names of the firm's founders and later presidents: Merriam, Baker, Rowley. But this strategy had not worked, said Rosen: "Persuasion failed on old Merriam. It has not yet moved Rowley. It is unlikely that it will be successful with Baker. These people require a shove a good deal harder than that coming from a negotiated proposal."

James Bulkley said it would be easy to pick up about 25 percent of the total share from small holders. There was also the matter of price. As one of Parton's confederates put it, "Is Merriam still a good buy at $300, or has the New International laid such an egg that the company is worth a lot less?"[7]

On January 30, 1962, American Heritage sent a letter to all Merriam stockholders offering only $150 per share. Parton was prepared to pay much more for sizable lots, and at least one of his delegates was talking of a purchase price starting at $300.

Two weeks later, Merriam responded. President Gallan sent out a letter to make certain that Parton would not be able to pick up a lot of stock on the cheap. He stated that American Heritage had actually been pursuing a merger for years now, so the attempted takeover was really in no way related to the controversy over *Webster's Third*. Also, the purchase offer was far too low, he thought. A conservative pricing, Gallan argued, would equal twenty times earnings, and 1961 was the most profitable year in Merriam's history. A conservative price for Merriam shares, then, would be around $330 per share.[8]

Parton needed to respond, and he knew from a complete list of the stockholders he had only just obtained that Gallan's letter was, in fact, the first time some stockholders had even heard of the American Heritage offer. Scrambling, he adjusted the deadline for his company's purchase offer and began making a very blunt case. The January offer was largely a formal, procedural letter. Now Parton looked to exploit the material that had been served up by the controversy, wrapping his entire sales pitch around the idea that *Webster's Third* was a radical dictionary, an offense to the English language, and an embarrassment to Merriam. It was an appeal to respectability, based on the not-irrational fear that this prestigious name in American dictionaries was in danger of no longer being considered an authority on the English language.

Merriam-Webster dictionaries, Parton wrote, were the "lineal descendants of America's first dictionary, the *American Dictionary of the English Language* by Noah Webster. . . . Its latest distinguished successor, Merriam's New International Dictionary, Second Edition, first published in 1934 . . . has for many years been universally regarded as the leading authority on our language. For reasons baffling and unknown to us, the Merriam Company has decided to break with this illustrious tradition."

Webster's Third "radically departed from the distinguished Second Edition." It eliminated capital letters from headwords, it used an "unintelligible pronunciation guide," and all the general encyclopedic information was deleted. "What distressed us and many others the most, however, was the abdication of all standards, so that, for example, words like *ain't* are given status and recognition." Parton quoted the dictionary's critics, the *Washington Star* calling it "literary anarchy"; the *Library Journal* calling it "deplorable"; the *New York Times* saying, "a new start is needed"; the American Bar Association complaining that *Webster's Third* was "of no use to us"; Wilson Follett, in the *Atlantic*, calling it "sabotage," a "scandal," a "calamity," a "disaster"; a recent *Times* article calling it a "gigantic flop."

"As I write this," added Parton, "the *New Yorker* (March 10th issue) this week carries still another devastating condemnation extending over 24 pages in the Books section beginning on page 130."

The flip comment of early reviews, telling readers to hold on to their old Webster's, had matured into the *New York Times*' call to start anew, which now became the rallying cry of Parton and American Heritage. "If we are given the opportunity," said Parton, "we intend to take the Third Edition off the market immediately. It is a shameful book and we want no part of it. Instead, we would set about producing a Fourth Edition, based on the scholarly principles of the Second, as fast as possible. This would certainly take several years."[9]

CHAPTER 36

WHILE NEWSPAPERS AND MAGAZINES from Toronto to Chicago to New York to Washington, D.C., shrieked with alarm over *Webster's Third*, smaller newspapers in Pennsylvania, Indiana, and California remained neutral while reporting on the controversy. And a quiet defense of *Webster's Third* began to mount as several positive reviews were published. The *Wall Street Journal* applauded the new dictionary and, instead of saying it would hasten the decline of Western civilization, observed that it might fortify us against Orwellian distortions of the language. The *St. Louis Post-Dispatch*, whose shrewd reviewer, the Appalachian-born onetime schoolteacher and all-around character Ethel Strainchamps, knew more about dictionaries than any other journalist writing about *Webster's Third*, called the new dictionary a "staggering accomplishment."

Life's sister publication *Time* gave it a very friendly write-up, happily noting that "the results may pain purists." As the *New York Times* had used unlabeled words from *Webster's Third* to embarrass Merriam, *Time*, always voracious for neologisms, demonstrated what the hip new words made possible, such as *"cool cats* who make *stacked chicks flip."* Such words of youthful delinquency (many of which *Webster's Third*, indeed, labeled slang) exercised a special charm for the *Time* writer, who suggested they were at the very heart of the new vernacular and thus essential for a new unabridged dictionary. "Without *drips* and *pads* and *junkies*, who *bug* victims for *bread* to buy *horse* for a *fix*, the dictionary of 1961 would not be *finalized*."

The Catholic weekly *America* took a bemused look at the dictionary's critics: "To the barricades! Man the breastworks! The dignity of the noble English language, at least as she is spoke by us Amuricans, is being assaulted." Roy Copperud, language columnist for *Editor & Publisher*, calmly dismissed the "flurry of nitwitted commentary" that wrongly assumed it was the function of a dictionary "to lay down the law." Copperud had spoken with Gove and knew why the encyclopedic material had been dropped, and he understood the rationale for leaving the colloquial label behind. But, he insisted, there was a need for usage discriminations, perhaps beyond what a dictionary is capable of. At the same time Copperud wondered why all the four-letter words had been included except the one found in *Lady Chatterley's Lover* and meaning "copulate with."

Ethel Strainchamps returned to the subject of *Webster's Third* to note the absurdity of journalists who introduced so much novelty to the language suddenly pretending to be so old-fashioned. The critics' own prose betrayed their pretensions. "A foreigner, or even a native speaker of English, who has been taught formal English and has held his reading to the classical works in the tongue, would have a hard time understanding all of almost any article in any issue of the *Saturday Review*, the *New York Times*, or *Life*, and his 1934 Webster's would be of little help to him on the very words that would puzzle him most."[1]

The *New Republic* ran a short and bitter notice bragging that it had been quoted twice in the new dictionary and then complaining that "the dictionary's compilers have abandoned a function indispensable in any advanced society, that of maintaining the quality of its language." This was no laughing matter. "If that language is primitive, vague, and illogical, so will the thought be." As an example, the magazine insisted that *bimonthly* means once every two months, and yet ignorant people went around using *bimonthly* to mean twice in one month.

This kind of condescending lecture on other people's usage really irritated James Sledd. His thoughts forever racing with irony and humor and not a little dram of anger, the Samuel Johnson scholar had faulted Gove for his naïve assessment of eighteenth-century plagiarism and, on another occasion, had faulted Charles C. Fries for forever beating the dead horse of classroom grammar.[2] He didn't love *Webster's Third*. The dropping of the colloquial label, despite its inadequacies, seemed to him no solution at all to the problem of describing usage levels. And the phrasing of definitions in *Webster's Third* he considered downright awful. But to him Gove's dictionary was a serious work of scholarship, and it deserved better than these mincing sermons from media bullies who flattered themselves that they knew so much about language when, in fact, every sentence they wrote revealed their pathetic ignorance.

"In your attack on Webster's Third New International Dictionary," Sledd wrote to the *New Republic*, "you start off by saying that if a language is 'primitive, vague, and illogical,' the thought of its speakers will be that way too. Maybe you'll say more about all this. Linguists swear they've never found a 'primitive, vague, and illogical' language, but everybody knows he can't trust a bunch of sneaking professionals. You may have stumbled on something big. Why don't you just up and name a primitive language and say what makes it primitive? If you do, you'll make a reputation for yourself; and *until* you do, the dirty linguists are likely to say you're another amateur, talking through your hat."[3]

Take that.

In May, Bergen Evans had his rematch with Wilson Follett, again in the pages of the *Atlantic*, this time discussing *Webster's Third*. The former host of a TV show devoted to current events, Evans had the pleasantly energetic persona of a man enjoying his time on earth. The contrast with Follett could not have been more stark. Follett had known tragedy in his personal life: financial struggles, a broken marriage, and many years earlier, his daughter, a noted young novelist, had walked out of her apartment one day and was never seen again.[4]

The condition of American English Follett saw in tragic terms. But for the efforts of trusted guardians such as those who had labored on *Webster's Second*, the language would be defenseless against the forces of ignorance, duplicity, and ugliness.

Evans was the opposite. He frankly admired the contributions of linguistics, having learned a great deal from the work of Bloomfield and others. And he had been humbled more than once, when a language opinion of his was undermined by someone else's more careful parsing of the evidence. In a note to Philip Gove, he mentioned that he had been reviewing the galleys of his forthcoming book, in which he had collected several words that were so new that they had not yet been recorded in a dictionary. Checking his brand-new *Webster's Third* to make sure this was still true, he learned it was not. Every last one was there.[5]

Later defenders would insist that *Webster's Third*, in its basic methods, was really no different from *Webster's Second*. And to whatever extent *Webster's Third was* different, it had little to do with linguistics. This was not what Philip Gove thought, and it was not what Evans thought.

"There has been even more progress," Evans wrote in the *Atlantic*, "in the making of dictionaries in the past thirty years than there has been in the making of automobiles."[6] And the difference was modern linguistics, which, he added, found its charter in Leonard Bloomfield's *Language*. Bloomfield, Evans noted, did not study language by reading Strunk's *Elements of Style*, but by studying dialects of Cree Indian. Evans seemed to overlook how strange this must have sounded: Our new understanding of English comes from studying Cree?

The answer was, in a way, yes. By examining American English only through observation, as linguists did when studying foreign languages, modern linguistics, as practiced by scholars like Bloomfield and Fries and many others, had come to a radically different view of the language than had hitherto reigned in schools, dictionaries, and usage guides. By 1962, the findings of Bloomfieldian linguistics were, in fact, so well established that they were old hat and were fast being superseded by the work of Noam Chomsky and generative linguistics.

Nevertheless, Evans ventured to give his own version of the principal findings of linguistics, after having read Gove's use of the five concepts found in the 1952 NCTE study, *English Language Arts*. Thus did he continue a publicity effort that dated back to Charles C. Fries's first efforts in the 1920s: explaining linguistics to laymen raised on traditional classroom grammar.

First off, Evans said, language was not properly studied by looking up rules and using them, but by "observing and setting down precisely what happens when native speakers speak." Logic and the grammar of other languages (Latin, obviously) were irrelevant. The only evidence of correctness that counted was evidence from actual use. Even a rule that aptly described actual practice was liable to become inapt over time, so remember, "change is constant—and normal." And last: "all usage is relative."

Evans toured the errors committed by the naysayers. Not only had *Life* magazine misquoted *Webster's Third* on *enormity* and *irregardless*; like the *New York Times*, it had failed to acknowledge that the language it used was not that of *Webster's Second*. *Life* had also asked whether Lincoln could have written the Gettysburg Address using *Webster's Third*. Evans easily cut this argument down. Gove had been overwrought and indignant when the *Times* editorialist employed unlabeled words from *Webster's Third* as no native or even foreign speaker would have used them. Much more calmly and directly, Evans pointed out the obvious. "Nothing worth writing is written *from* a dictionary."

Numerous points made by Evans were clearly shaped by communicating with Gove: that *Webster's Third* had jettisoned encyclopedic material to save space; that telling the truth about contemporary English required admitting that "there are many areas in which certainty is impossible and simplification is misleading"; that meaning is "complex, subtle, and forever changing." Evans went so far as to defend the new dictionary's laughable definition for *door*, as Gove had tried in an interview with a *New York Times* reporter.

Evans—like Gove—interpreted some criticisms too literally. "The *New York Times* and the *Saturday Review* both regarded as contemptibly 'permissive' the fact that one meaning of one word was illustrated by a quotation from Polly Adler." Perhaps their objections addressed only one Adler quotation, but Polly Adler had, in fact, been quoted scores of times in *Webster's Third*. Also, Gove made the point elsewhere (a point that Evans echoed) that quoting Adler was as legitimate as quoting anyone, and if it was legitimate to quote her book once, it was legitimate (and more efficient) to do so forty times. In fact, Gove had instructed his readers to dump any book that did not readily yield usable material.

Evans's broadest point was his most persuasive: that the language itself had changed profoundly since 1934. "It has had to adapt to extraordinary cultural and technological changes, two world wars, unparalleled changes in transportation and communication, and unprecedented movements of populations." And, he continued, "more subtly, but pervasively, it has changed under the influence of mass education and the growth of democracy." Whatever its faults might be, Evans argued, *Webster's Third* was an enormous effort to capture and describe, in sufficient detail and without undue prejudice, this great shifting thing called contemporary standard American English.

After receiving an advance copy of Evans's article, Gove heartily thanked him for it, saying, "It shines like polished silver."[7]

ONE OF THE MOST memorable criticisms of *Webster's Third* appeared in a *New Yorker* cartoon. It showed a visitor to G. & C. Merriam Company being told by the receptionist, "Sorry. Dr. Gove ain't in." It says a lot about him that Gove didn't find this at all funny.[1] The field was unevenly split between entertaining critics who hated *Webster's Third* unreservedly and a smaller band of defenders, who knew more about dictionaries but sometimes sounded like they were working from a common script as they heaped unqualified praise on Gove's dictionary. Bergen Evans and Ethel Strainchamps, who published her third and longest defense of *Webster's Third* in *Harper's* both made solid observations but found almost nothing to complain about in *Webster's Third*—which, as reactions go, seems incredible, given the dictionary's many idiosyncrasies. Like Gove's complaining letters to the *Times* and other critical publications, such writing could and did blunt some of the effects of earlier attacks, but it was not so good that it would have lingered in the mind.

Dwight Macdonald spent many hours and probably several days looking over *Webster's Third*, checking on its treatment of important contemporary terms and its handling of classic usage disputes. Such intensive reading could not substitute for years of routine use, of course, but it yielded a lot of material and convincingly demonstrated a sincere engagement with the book. After visiting Springfield and talking with Gove, whom he found pleasant but unexceptional, Macdonald also read Gove's *Word Study* article about the contributions of linguistics to lexicography.

Before writing any drafts, he habitually gathered a formidable pile of notes and clippings. Once, as a younger writer trying to figure out how to organize an essay, he'd been told to divide his notes into aspects of the subject, putting like with like, and then write his essay by going from one aspect to the next. It sounded way too simple at the time, but this seems to have been the method he followed thirty-six years after quitting *Fortune*.[2]

The basic Luce approach of turning simple, telling facts into a little narrative, all tending to a single idea of the story, worked extremely well for him. This nonanalytic, classically journalistic approach was dressed up and made provocative by Macdonald's man-of-the-world pose and his caustic, condescending humor. His long-maturing style of the journalist cum man of letters proved to be profoundly adaptive as he took on *Webster's Third* and used the dictionary to continue his siege on middlebrow culture. But what also made this essay memorable was the breathtaking extremity of its final judgment.

Webster's Third, Macdonald started, told us a great deal about changes in American culture since the publication of *Webster's Second*. The main difference between the two dictionaries was that most of the words that were labeled *slang, colloquial, erroneous, incorrect,* or *illiterate* in *Webster's Second* "are accepted in the 1961 edition as perfectly normal, honest, respectable citizens."[3] It was not true that a word's mere inclusion in the dictionary without a label made it respectable in all contexts, but by the standards of the *New York Times, Life,* and the *Atlantic,* Macdonald's characterization sounded altogether measured.

Since 1934, he then stated, "a revolution has taken place in the study of English grammar and usage, a revolution that probably represents an advance in scientific method but that has certainly had an unfortunate effect on such nonscientific activities as the teaching of English and the making of dictionaries. . . . This scientific revolution has meshed gears with a trend toward permissiveness, in the name of democracy, that is debasing our language."

Others—*BusinessWeek*, Bergen Evans, et al.—had noted that linguistics had influenced *Webster's Third*, but Macdonald fused this insight with the main complaint against Gove's dictionary, that it ignored the question of usage and failed to make "discriminations." "The very word has acquired a Jim Crow flavor," said Macdonald, before arriving at the underlying politics: "It is assumed that true democracy means a majority is right."

There was little of the bulging forehead vein or the clenched fist to Macdonald's personality on the page: It always appeared interested in officially serious, intellectual matters but was happy to show its own well-founded snobbery about, well, stupid things, such as the anti-intellectual premise of majority rule. It was *Fortune* magazine meets H. L. Mencken— but with only a smidgen of Mencken's linguistic learning.

No one better described the making of *Webster's Third* than Macdonald in the most reportorial portions of his review, and, after appearing to give it a more or less fair hearing, no one damned it more completely. The essay was lively and fun even, a great accomplishment given that it took up more than twenty pages of magazine. The piece was also intriguing and high-minded, but never academic. Not deeply informed about key principles, it was, in a word, middlebrow.

An admirer of Samuel Johnson, Macdonald freely opined on standard lexicographical practice, which "assumed there was such a thing as correct English" and that it was the lexicographer's job to decide what it was. This was a great simplification and wrong in many well-known particulars, but Macdonald cited the telling example of William Allan Neilson, who had, he noted, included many homely words to which he attached warning labels. Gove took a different approach, which Macdonald described by quoting the *Word Study* article, where Gove said that a dictionary "should have no traffic . . . with artificial notions of correctness and superiority." Gove, Macdonald explained, was "sympathetic to the school of language study that has become dominant since

1934. It is sometimes called structural linguistics and, sometimes, rather magnificently, Modern Linguistic Science."

Not a few treatments of this controversy describe the main drama as that of a scholarly but politically tone-deaf dictionary set upon by a pack of growling media wolves—for which there is much evidence. But in two main instances the words that inspired the most heated disputation—the *stimulus* that preceded the *reaction*—came from Merriam itself. First, the press release, which had been seen and approved at Merriam, misquoted the dictionary's entry for *ain't* and broadcast the notion that a word's appearance in the dictionary equaled its endorsement by the dictionary. And now, the idea that *Webster's Third* embodied the principles of structural linguistics was circulating and being used against *Webster's Third*, with the help of Philip Gove's *Word Study* article.

Said Macdonald about structural linguistics: "Dr. Gove gives its basic concepts as: 1. Language changes constantly. 2. Change is normal. 3. Spoken language is the language. 4. Correctness rests upon usage. 5. All usage is relative."

Of course, Gove was quoting *English Language Arts*, but Macdonald had collected some good string on the linguistics angle. He drew connections between structural linguistics and the National Council of Teachers of English and even Charles C. Fries. Gove himself had opened this door, but it was still far from clear how much of the weirdness of *Webster's Third* was really attributable to structural linguistics.

Macdonald himself volunteered that he shared the new dictionary's impatience with the old rules on *shall* and *will* and *who* versus *whom*. And Gove may have been using the same language as Bloomfield and Fries when he chose the labels *nonstandard* and *substandard*, but he was acting as his own man when he rewrote the defining style for *Webster's Third*. The absence of capital letters certainly derived from some over-interpreted notion about words not being identical to their appearance in print—a lesson Gove definitely could have picked up from reading linguistics—but the frustrating policy of excluding capital letters from a dictionary and then adding each and every time the laborious usage label *usu. cap* must surely be blamed on Gove and not his reading habits. Also, it was simply not the case, as the linguist Raven McDavid later pointed out, that Gove himself was a structural linguist—a question Macdonald might have thought to ask after reading the *Word Study* article. Gove was, however, a rather advanced example of the educated layman that Bloomfield and Fries had been trying to bring around to the scientific view of language. And with Gove they had succeeded.

"The new school of linguistics," Macdonald said, "is non-historical if not anti-historical." This was simply false. Bloomfield credited historical linguistics as one of two major streams of language study that had formed contemporary linguistics, and Fries was nothing if not painstaking with the history of usage. Furthermore, one of the tools that helped make modern linguistics so impressive was its use of the *Oxford English Dictionary*, which was, of course, organized on historical principles. Last, and most important, *Webster's Third* itself was not ahistorical. Its definitions, Macdonald did not seem to realize, were historically ordered, with the oldest coming first.

Macdonald wasn't all wrong about linguistics making *Webster's Third* into an especially present-minded dictionary. When Philip Gove had explained to the Editorial Board that *Webster's Third* would be more up-to-date than *Webster's Second*, he cited the criticism of linguists who pointed out that new dictionaries were too conservative to describe the usage of their own times. But, again, the fact that linguistics was in the air doesn't explain all that was done with it. In the late 1940s, Frederic Cassidy and Albert Marckwardt—both candidates for Gove's job, and both students of Charles C. Fries—had published a completely inoffensive grammar, complete with the usual linguistic categories and a prohibition on the use of *ain't*, even while citing Fries's *American English Grammar* as the main piece of research underlying their work. But Gove was too proud and impolitic to camouflage his principles in the policies of *Webster's Third*, the greatest accomplishment of his life.

Macdonald accused the editors of lacking common sense in their treatment of pronunciations: "The editors of 2 found it necessary to give only two pronunciations for *berserk* and two for *lingerie*, but 3 seems to give twenty-five for the first and twenty-six for the second." This Macdonald connected to the second *English Language Arts* principle—spoken language is the language—and asked, "Does anybody except a Structural Linguist need to know that much?"

The pronunciation editors had listened to speech samples from Helen Hayes, Adlai Stevenson, Lionel Trilling, Allen Dulles, Jonas Salk, and many others. And they had adapted the International Phonetic Alphabet, but the result was not the 20 percent change once agreed upon at Merriam. At that meeting with Robert Munroe, among others, playing the skeptic, Gove and Artin had not mentioned any ambition to present a vast array of pronunciations, in the cases of some words many times more than *Webster's Second* had presented. Tallying all the variations listed for each discrete sound that makes up *a fortiori*, one scholar claimed to have counted 132 possible pronunciations in *Webster's Third*. The sheer numbers were laughable and made finding a suitable pronunciation maddening, while the absence of a pronunciation key at the bottom of the page also made the pronunciations more difficult to decipher.

"Things get quite lively when you trip over a schwa," said Macdonald about the upside-down *e*. "Bird is given straight as bûrd in 2, but in 3" there were three possible pronunciations, all using a schwa. "This last may be *boid*, but I'm not sure." Macdonald must have recognized this classic New York City pronunciation when he tripped over it, but that didn't stop him from playing the point for laughs.

Much more so than Follett, Macdonald achieved a cheerful eloquence when listing the little things he liked and disliked. "No great harm is done if a word is labeled slang until its pretensions to being standard have been thoroughly tested. . . . Both 2 and 3 list such women's-magazine locutions as *galore*, *scads*, *scrumptious*, and *too-too*, but only 2 labels them slang."

Macdonald had read Gove's letter to the *Times*, so he should have realized the illustrative quotations were intended to describe usage. In the cases of *galore*, *scads*, *scrumptious*, and *too-too*, Gove's method of using quotations to indicate usage status was, actually, rather effective. *Galore*, for instance (which, pace Macdonald, was labeled colloquial, not slang in *Webster's Second*), had two quotations, one describing the word just as Macdonald had ("bargains galore") and one with a rather different feel ("Philadelphia, which boasts history galore") from Lewis Mumford, the well-known writer who certainly rated as an educated user of standard English. For someone wondering whether *galore* was too informal for one occasion or another, the range of evidence was instructive.

Reading Macdonald's essay, one might think there was a contest afoot between him and *Webster's Third* over who knew more about Freudian psychology or *Stalinism* or *abstract expressionism*. Macdonald cited Fichte and Kant to argue that the definition for *ego* was wanting, while noting that *action painting* had not been entered though *abstract expressionism* had, which was not really a criticism. *Action painting* had fallen out of usage, as Macdonald surely knew, and *abstract expressionism* had persevered as the preferred term for the art of Pollock and company. Mentioning the matter only showed that Macdonald was *hip* to the language of modern art.

The entry for *McCarthyism* was smug, Macdonald thought, and perhaps it was, but it captured how the term was used to describe "indiscriminate allegations esp. on the basis of unsubstantiated charges." That the definer didn't realize he would have to come up with a definition to satisfy Dwight Macdonald's tormented anticommunism was really not the definer's fault. Such jabs were among Macdonald's most enjoyable, and most unfair, passages. Good journalism (like *kitsch*) predigested what might otherwise seem complicated; the downside was that such facility turns difficult judgments into simple matters of prejudice.

But while Macdonald played the snob, he also demonstrated that he didn't always read the dictionary carefully. "There is no *mass culture*," he wrote, "and the full entry for the noun *masses* is 'pl. of *mass.*'" Actually, under the third sense of the second entry, Gove's dictionary very ably gave the Marxist-flavored usage of *masses*, complete with quotations from Harry Warfel and Henry Seidel Canby and a cross-reference to *proletariat.* Under the adjectival entry for *mass,* it was true, *mass culture* was not listed, but the sense was defined and given in *mass psychology* and *mass hysteria* and approximated in separate entries such as *mass man.*

Knowed, Macdonald complained, was given as the past tense for *know,* which truly would have been absurd. *Knowed,* however, was listed as dialectal variant under *know* and presented in its own alphabetical position at *knowed.* But in the separate stub entry Macdonald had read past the cross-reference, printed in small capitals, and so thought he was reading the full definition.

The third edition "gives *disinterested* as a synonym of *uninterested,*" said Macdonald. But, again, he had misread a cross-reference as a definition. The word *uninterested* did appear in the definition for *disinterested,* in small caps, to instruct the reader to compare one term with the other—to help the reader avoid confusing the two.

Macdonald did present a convincing case that *Webster's Third* was guilty of what he called *gnostomania* or scholar's knee. In addition to giving twenty-six pronunciations for *lingerie,* the dictionary expended thirty-four pages listing words starting with *un-* and gave definitions for every number up to a hundred, each one reading as if it had been written by Leonard Bloomfield, who had used the example of *two* as a word that could be defined so long as you knew what *one* was. In *Webster's Third, sixty* was "one more than fifty-nine," and *sixty-one* was "one more than *sixty,*" and so on. Macdonald did not seem to notice, however, that *Webster's Second* had given identical definitions for numbers up to twenty, though its editors had the good sense to stop there. Gove apparently liked the principle so much he extended it for another eighty entries. "*Pedantry,*" wrote Macdonald, "is not a synonym for *scholarship.*"

Errors aside, Macdonald's review was compelling, and it helpfully illuminated the dictionary's production with neat reportorial findings, such as that Gove claimed to have saved eighty pages by minimizing the use of commas and that staff reading had failed to produce a sufficient number of citations for the most common words in English, leading Gove to convene a set of backup readers for all the most obvious words.

With the help of research, Macdonald sailed past many earlier misunderstandings, such as the story of *ain't* and the basic reason behind the deletion of encyclopedic material, but as he entered less charted waters, he was, indeed, a bit lost. If the piece had ended three or four pages short of the end, the reader might have thought that Macdonald liked a few things about *Webster's Third* but that his complaints far outnumbered his compliments. In short, an entertainingly negative review, but not a wholesale rejection. And because of Macdonald's sometimes lighthearted style the negativity might have seemed attributable to the reviewer's personal biases.

But Macdonald did not stop there. He returned to his thesis: that structural linguistics was bad for language instruction and bad for dictionaries. It was superior, perhaps, to the scholarship of old, but "as a scientific discipline structural linguistics can have no truck with values or standards." Its only concern was "the Facts." If popular usage paved over older distinctions, structural linguistics was of no help. And "if the language is allowed to shift too rapidly, without challenge from teachers and lexicographers, then the special character of the American people is blurred, since it tends to lose its past."

Just then a hush came over the page, as Macdonald reminded the reader of what *Webster's Third* had done with *knowed* (or, rather, what Macdonald thought it had done with *knowed*). A dictionary that described the language on the basis of citation slips and other evidence, he said, was powerless to stop people from mispronouncing *invidious* once the mispronunciation became popular. Linguistic decline became inexorable unless people insisted on standards—such as those enumerated by the "magisterial Fowler," whom he had cited earlier. Teachers, lexicographers, and writers needed to insist that old niceties be observed. "They might look up Ulysses' famous defense of conservatism in Shakespeare's Troilus and Cressida." This moving but profoundly pessimistic speech Macdonald—the onetime Marxist, on-and-off anti-American, and longtime Anglophile—quoted at length.

> *"The Heavens themselves, the planets, and this centre*
> *Observe degree, priority and place*
> *Insisture, course, proportion, season, form*
> *Office and custom in all line of order . . .*
> *Take but degree away, untune that string,*
> *And, hark, what discord follows! Each thing meets*
> *In mere oppugnancy. The bounded waters*
> *Should lift their bosoms higher than the shores*
> *And make a sop of all this solid globe*
> *Strength should be lord of imbecility*
> *And the rude son should strike his father dead.*
> *Force should be right, or rather right and wrong. . . .*
> *should lose their names, and so should justice too.*
> *Then every thing includes itself in power,*
> *power into will, will into appetite*
> *And appetite, a universal wolf,*
> *So doubly seconded with will and power,*
> *Must make perforce a universal prey*
> *and, last, eat up himself. . . ."*

This was what Philip Gove had wrought, said Dwight Macdonald. In *Webster's Third*, he and his fellow lexicographers had "untuned the string, made a sop of the solid structure of English, and encouraged the language to eat up himself."

JAMES SLEDD WAS IN full combat mode. He wrote a sixty-five-page rebuttal of the reviews of *Webster's Third* and was co-editing a collection of critical and defensive writing from the controversy, to be published by Scott, Foresman. A southerner and, in his own words, a conservative, Sledd was in a lather after reading Dwight Macdonald's review.

"In my view," he told Macdonald, "you've led a mob in an intellectual lynching. You haven't just attacked the Third International. You've attacked history itself, and you didn't even get your facts straight."[1]

Macdonald answered that he'd never been accused of "attacking history itself," but that it was "rather flattering." Sledd's suggestion that he'd committed errors was more troubling. "Heads will roll" in the magazine's fact-checking department, said Macdonald, if that was the case—a statement that rather bothered Sledd, who was more than a little sensitive about how underlings should be treated. But in all modesty, asked Macdonald, wasn't it really the case that he had only followed the mob? So many others came first.[2]

"It's not much of a defense, is it," answered Sledd, "to say you didn't catch the victim and tie his hands—you just shot him?" His point was that Macdonald had given credibility to the anti-intellectual hysteria swirling around *Webster's Third*. "Friends of mine in four major universities have cited your essay to me. They think it's brilliant. Of course, they haven't studied the dictionaries, either; but they won't bother to now. You've told them what to think, so they're happily thinking it and repeating it to their students." He did not want to get any fact-checkers fired, but Sledd mentioned that Macdonald had missed some cross-references and that he needed to reread the definition of *ego*—a suggestion he meant literally.

Sledd had spent serious time in the guts of both *Webster's Third* and *Webster's Second*. He cited page numbers and prefaces, pulling out of the "downstairs" footer of page 111 in *Webster's Second* a stub entry for *an't*, a variant of *ain't* that it called a "colloquial contraction of *are not, am not*"—which amounted to a much more liberal treatment of *ain't* than found in the main entry.

Macdonald didn't know the first thing about structural linguistics, said Sledd, as he put the phrase in quotes, so absurd did he find Macdonald's use of it. Then returning to his academic friends, he told Macdonald that he owed it to them to admit that he was against English linguistics and dictionaries in general. "They ought to know, for instance, that poor old Gove's five little precepts (from a ten-year-old book for middle-aged schoolmarms) can all be matched quite nicely in W2."[3]

This became the classic defense of *Webster's Third*: the argument that it was really not so different from *Webster's Second*. Gove's five truisms were such banal propaganda that approximate versions of the same ideas could be found even in William Allan Neilson's dictionary. Ergo, there was no proof that *Webster's Third* had been created under the spell of structural linguistics.

Macdonald told Sledd he should reread his own letter. "What you seem to be saying is that I should be ashamed of myself because my article has been influential in academic-intellectual circles. . . . Now honestly. The alternatives you present are to write an ineffective article, or to accept guilt as a leader of a lynch mob—really, as a leader. But I wrote my piece, after much thinking and research, because I was, and still am, convinced that Webster 3 is one more example of the debasement of standards in our cultural life (others are RSV Bible and the Adler-Hutchins Great Books, both of which I've dealt with)."

He had no bias against Gove, said Macdonald. "I liked Gove when I spent most of a day with him in Springfield early in the course of my research, and I am convinced he is a sincere and even idealistic lexicographer. Which still doesn't prevent him from being, alas, more than a bit of a dope."

Macdonald conceded to Sledd that he had been wrong about *ego* and *masses*, but if *Webster's Second* had called *an't* colloquial, then it had attached "a warning label," warning people that the word was inappropriate for formal use, in keeping with everything else Macdonald had said about *Webster's Second*. And Gove's truisms, Macdonald had said in his article, were reasonable in themselves. As for their connection to structural linguistics, this was something he had gotten from Gove.

"I'm not, of course, 'against English dictionaries and English linguistics generally' and therefore see no reason I should confess to 'innocent friends' that I am. (They must be not only innocent, but also stupid, in your terms, to have been taken in by my spiel. In fact you sound paranoiac—conspiracies everywhere, people who should Know Better being seduced by glib arguments, which you assume, as paranoiacs do, are not sincerely meant by the author—otherwise why should I feel guilty because my arguments have convinced people?)"

Macdonald then must have taken a deep breath. "Sorry," he wrote in the next sentence, "got sore. But you do put a strain on one's reasonableness." Then he asked Sledd if he had read another essay he'd just written, this one for *Life*, about the scientific view of language. (Sledd, of course, hated the piece.) Then Macdonald referred back to some business relating to the volume Sledd was assembling, in which Macdonald's *New Yorker* essay would be published along with a feisty back-and-forth with Sledd.

Then Macdonald said, in the closing of his letter, "Sorry to sound irritable—but you do irritate me."[4]

CHAPTER 39

JAMES PARTON'S EFFORTS WERE being thwarted not just by Gordon Gallan, but by the family names of Merriam-Webster tradition. Descendants of onetime presidents Orlando M. Baker, H. Curtis Rowley, Asa Baker, and founders George and Charles Merriam one after another refused Parton's offers to buy them out.

In March, Jim Bulkley called up Arthur Rowley, who owned close to two thousand shares in Merriam, to say that Parton would like to meet with him. Rowley, who'd long known Bulkley's family, flew into a rage. Rowley did not want to see Parton or anyone else from American Heritage because, he said, they had badly misrepresented Merriam and were now much resented by the major stockholders.

Said Bulkley, "Well, I do know they are resented by Mr. Gallan."

No, said the old man, "they are resented by all the stockholders, and I refuse to have anything to do with American Heritage."[1]

Resentment continued to run high. A week later, Rowley sent Bulkley a personal note, saying, "your participation in the attempted merger of the American Heritage with the G. and C. Merriam Co. does not meet with my approval. You certainly overstepped the bounds of friendship and good will by your actions."[2]

Bulkley drew two lessons. The first was that these families were deeply appreciative of the financial support that came from their Merriam stock, so much so that they looked upon the company as an almost maternal figure who could do no wrong.

The second lesson he took away was that "Gordon Gallan is one of the greatest salesmen I have encountered in many a year and has proven to be a much more formidable opponent than I had believed possible."

Parton saw the matter differently. "Gallan is making an ogre out of us and is undoubtedly blaming us for a lot of the critical reviews."[3] As it happened, Parton was trying to arrange negative reviews but could not figure out how to pull it off.

While reading a *Times* story mentioning an academic defense of *Webster's Third* by the Syracuse University professor Sumner Ives, Parton noticed that Ives was identified as one of fifteen members of NCTE's Commission on the English Language. To him this sounded like an august body of experts whose opinion might carry a lot of weight. "The question I now raise," he said in a memo, "is how we might adroitly get this authoritative group to express a collective judgment on Merriam's Third International." He wondered if he could get the *New York Times* to poll its members. Or maybe, he thought, the *Saturday Review* would be willing to do it.[4]

Nancy Longley, one of his colleagues at American Heritage, was skeptical. "I wonder whether their ideas of the Third International would coincide with ours? If they didn't, maybe we wouldn't be so anxious to give them a platform."[5]

Parton had someone look up the names of everyone on the commission. In addition to Sumner Ives, it included Albert Marckwardt, James Sledd, Harold B. Allen, and W. Nelson Francis. It was stacked with people friendly to linguistics and the scientific view of language.

Parton wrote to Edward Weeks, editor of the *Atlantic*, begging to know why they had felt it necessary to let Bergen Evans answer the criticisms of Wilson Follett. Because it was a divisive subject, Weeks replied, but he assured Parton that "in our *Atlantic* usage our sympathies are on the side of Follett."[6]

By June, Parton and company were focusing on some of the midrange stockholders. "I suspect that our biggest ally may turn out to be the Grim Reaper. In other words, if [Harry] Caswell, [Edward] Kronvall, or [James Brewer] Corcoran should go where the woodbine twineth (and their extreme age suggests this may be reasonably soon), it might tip the scales somewhat in our favor."[7]

Bulkley estimated that Corcoran was in his midseventies and the other two were over eighty years old. Together the three old men held about 2,500 shares, but even if they all expired at once and their heirs immediately sold American Heritage their stock, the combined pickup would only marginally improve American Heritage's position.[8]

And Parton's sales pitch continued to fail with the larger owners. The families most closely associated with Merriam history refused to budge. James Merriam Howard wrote to Parton in September. His financial adviser had reviewed the performances of Merriam and American Heritage and had concluded that "Merriam did not have much to learn about management from American Heritage."

Howard then discussed Parton's accusation that *Webster's Third* was a radical dictionary that had abandoned all standards of usage. Actually, wrote Howard, with a professorial air, "the criticisms leveled against it are very similar to those aimed at Noah Webster's *American Dictionary of the English Language* (1828) and its first revision (1840). As you know, Webster's younger contemporary, Joseph E. Worcester, issued a dictionary along more conservative lines, following Dr. Johnson's pattern of setting a standard of literary usage. Worcester's *A Dictionary of the English Language* (1860) was hailed by Webster's critics, and for several decades rivaled its popularity. But gradually Worcester faded out and Webster became the acknowledged authority by the end of the nineteenth century."[9]

As the months dragged on, Parton seemed to lose his stamina for taking over Merriam. He made little progress in amassing Merriam stock, and in the fall his wife, only forty-five years old, died from cancer.

"There is little to report on Merriam," he wrote to a friend. "We have added little to our holdings and now have a substantial minority position. But it is clear there can be no breakthrough unless one of several very old men . . . dies or the company's next annual statement indicates some significant change in its financial position. Accordingly, I have reverted to my thought of creating a new dictionary from scratch."[10]

CHAPTER 40

ONE OF THE PROBLEMS facing the willing contributor to a controversy is finding fresh logs for the fire. The stakes must somehow be raised, which becomes more difficult the longer a controversy runs. Dwight Macdonald had swept up material from many earlier reviews, but he made sure to fill in many basic details, otherwise unknown, from the story of the dictionary's creation. And he sought to produce additional evidence of the dictionary's perfidy.

He also, in his article, evoked Fowler to argue for a higher standard than popular usage to determine correctness, basically an aristocratic standard of the best users, insisting that we need to be selective about whose usage we follow. This was not an unreasonable response, but alone it would have failed to affect the general perception, already widespread, that *Webster's Third* was insufficiently discriminating. Macdonald added something new with his Shakespearean lament, the suggestion that anything short of this preferred standard would result in a savage new order, as right and wrong lost their names and the universal wolf feasted on the universal prey. It was, arguably, a return to the Toronto *Globe and Mail* doomsday scenario in which *Webster's Third* failed to save us from nuclear destruction, but the fact that a well-known intellectual was saying this in the pages of the *New Yorker* helped make it news.

That this whole wolf-eating-wolf conclusion was hardly supported by Macdonald's evidence, which wasn't half as strong as he thought, seems almost beside the point. Like the definition for *door*, the controversy over *Webster's Third* had become unhinged. Macdonald had moved the controversy into an imaginary, almost mystical realm, where minor details looked like world-destroying monsters.

Yet Macdonald's argument somehow did not appear absurd. In fact, it helped goad others to take similar action. In the spring 1963 issue of *American Scholar*, Jacques Barzun, who did know something of the intellectual roots of *Webster's Third*, took the unusual position that actual knowledge of this dictionary was unnecessary to condemn it. Writing as a member of the magazine's editorial board, he said that at a recent meeting the subject of *Webster's Third* had come up and every last member of the board wanted the *American Scholar* to take notice, expressing their common disapproval.

"Never in my experience has the Editorial Board desired to reach a position," wrote Barzun, who was appointed their spokesman. "What is even more remarkable, none of those present had given the new dictionary more than a casual glance, yet each one felt that he knew how he stood on the issue that the work presented to the public."[1]

James Sledd was right. With the help of Dwight Macdonald—Wilson Follett and the *New York Times* also deserve mention—the vilification of *Webster's Third* had reached the point where even the prestigious Phi Beta Kappa Society felt no compunction about denouncing a dictionary its officers freely acknowledged not having read.

Barzun himself weighed in, calling *Webster's Third* "the longest political pamphlet ever put together by a party." Its "scientism" allowed for no compromise. "No one who thinks at all can keep from being a partisan."

Barzun pointed to the dictionary's use of the swung dash symbol—a simple space-saving device that allows the lexicographer to avoid repeating the headword in illustrations and quotations—as typical of the dictionary's approach. The discriminating, worldly Jacques Barzun, critic of cant and champion of good sense, then argued that the piddling, totally unremarkable swung dash symbolized *Webster's Third* and its "attack on The Word."

Which, it must be said, was just plain *nutty*, a term *Webster's Third* characteristically did not label slang, despite its intensely flip, dismissive mood. Then again, when a smart guy like Jacques Barzun, on behalf of a host of committed ignoramuses, is calling a dictionary—really, a dictionary—an attack on The Word, capitalized in biblical fashion to suggest the beginning of all Creation, well, then *nutty* appears to be the new standard.

Barzun's essay may have contained the makings of the smartest critical piece to be written about *Webster's Third*. But its immoderation placed too great a strain on what little evidence it had mustered. This was a pity, for Barzun understood enough about linguistic controversies to see how Gove's ambivalence about correctness had thoroughly colored the editorial policies of his dictionary. From its muddled policies on ethnic and racial slurs—*nigger* and *kike* were "usu. taken to be offensive," as if, on some occasions, they were also considered polite—to its lack of capital letters and nonjudgmental labels, *Webster's Third* was often baffling to the well-meaning reader in search of forthright advice.

And yet Barzun was onto something when he wrote that "*Webster's Third New International Dictionary of the English Language* is thus the representation between covers of a cultural revolution." And he seemed to be reading Gove's mind as he continued: "From its tendentious title—the work being neither Webster's nor international, and only now and then a dictionary—to its silly systems and petty pedantries, the book is a faithful record of our emotional weaknesses and intellectual disarray."

Philip Gove would not have put it negatively, but in his words and his dictionary he had said almost as much. Not only had it been a practical and commercial necessity to depart from the traditions of *Webster's*

Second; it had been, for Philip Gove, an intellectual necessity. And, in his mind, the difference between *Webster's Third* and *Webster's Second* was enormous.

SCHOLARLY AND international reviews of *Webster's Third* began to appear in 1962 and 1963. The international reviews were quite positive, and the American scholarly reviews helped refute a number of charges against *Webster's Third*. Language scholars expressed great puzzlement and not a little impatience with the characterization of *Webster's Third* as a poster child for structural linguistics, while groaning over the countless simple errors of fact and the great prejudice of its critics in the press.

Albert Marckwardt said that "the presumed role of structural linguistics in *Webster's Third* reflects a most unfortunate confusion, and ironically it is the editor of the dictionary who is in part responsible for it." The notion that correctness rests upon usage (principle number 5) had been around well before Leonard Bloomfield, Marckwardt said, and it was common among such scholars as Thomas Lounsbury, Louise Pound, Charles C. Fries, and Sterling Leonard. "The structural linguists accepted this as a matter of course, but they did not invent it." Where structural linguistics specifically could be detected in *Webster's Third*, Marckwardt believed, its influence was limited to pronunciations.[2]

This, however, ducked the messier and larger question of how linguistics in general and the scientific view of language had indeed shaped many policies of *Webster's Third*. And it suggested that the writings of Fries and other linguists less exclusively associated with structural linguistics were totally uncontroversial, which was not true.

Academic commentators felt a compensatory urge to stand up for *Webster's Third* and deny any legitimacy to the controversy it had birthed. This led to new absurdities. In *College English*, James Sledd found numerous faults in *Webster's Third* but then, at the risk of giving his readers whiplash, praised it exuberantly. The dictionary's typography he found hard to read, and he thought its use of slang labels for semi-obscenities such as *pissed off* and *pisspoor* was inadequate. He criticized Gove's defining style, his system of usage labels, and the dropping of *colloquial*. Finally, he questioned the dictionary's practice of using quotations to convey usage information, especially when the lexicographer himself felt unprepared to pass judgment. The language was perhaps in an unusual state of flux, Sledd conceded, but this did not mean that distinctions between formal and informal no longer existed. And then, with little warning, he made an about-face, insisting the merits of *Webster's Third* were "infinitely greater than those of the reviews," such as his own, "which have lightly questioned them."[3] Sledd was too honest to leave out what he did not like about *Webster's Third* but, it seemed, also too angry at its critics to conclude with anything short of generous praise.

IN 1964, James Parton announced plans for the *American Heritage Dictionary*, which linguists took to calling the Goldwater Dictionary, a play on the adrenaline-charged campaign of Barry Goldwater, the Arizona senator who became the Republican nominee for president that year.[4] The original small-government conservative, Goldwater (channeling Cicero) famously declared that "extremism in the defense of liberty is no vice. And moderation in pursuit of justice is no virtue."

Parton's dictionary became known for two innovations. One, it was the first dictionary to include an entry for *fuck*, and, two, it established a usage panel of distinguished writers and scholars whose opinions on disputed usages were discussed in stand-alone articles. Its members included several critics of *Webster's Third*: Mario Pei, Wilson Follett, Dwight Macdonald, and Jacques Barzun.

Patrick E. Kilburn, a language scholar who defended *Webster's Third* against Dwight Macdonald in the anthology James Sledd co-edited, claimed to have discovered the ages of ninety-five members of the usage panel, only six of whom were under fifty, and twenty-eight of whom had been born in the nineteenth century. The advertising campaign for Parton's dictionary touted its generational bearings, with print ads showing a long-haired youth while the tagline addressed someone who was not at all a hippie: "He doesn't like your politics. Why should he like your dictionary?" All the same, the *American Heritage Dictionary* developed into a worthy rival of *Merriam-Webster's Collegiate Dictionary*.

After a couple of years, the controversy over *Webster's Third* lost its purchase on the public mind, but it remained a touchstone for disputes over usage and linguistics. Smaller controversies broke out along the way, including a quantitative dispute over exactly how much Gove had reduced the use of the slang label and whether, in fact, Merriam had sufficient evidence for its more tolerant handling of *ain't*. Rather improbably, given the continued drift toward ever more informal usage in American English, Gove remained on the defensive about *ain't* for years.[5]

The defense of *Webster's Third*, that its underlying principles were basically indistinguishable from those of *Webster's Second*—an argument developed in reaction to the controversy within a controversy surrounding the five precepts of modern linguistics cited by Gove—never squared with how utterly different the two dictionaries seemed and how they appealed to very different sensibilities and reflected very different moments in lexicographical history. In their positions on obscenities, their usage labels, their approaches to pronunciation, their views on quotable authors, their use of citations, and also their defining styles, the two dictionaries are as different as, well, 1934 and 1961.

ONE LESSON inadequately learned from the controversy was the need to respect, no, not opposing viewpoints (don't worry, I'm not going soft), but basic rules of evidence. Pride as well as something about language—its familiarity, its apparent simplicity and hidden mysteries—makes us want to claim expertise far beyond what we individually know. Those with intellectual gifts of a literary nature seem especially prone.

In April 2001, David Foster Wallace published in *Harper's* magazine a long and scathing essay on usage and linguistics, a portion of which was devoted to reaming Philip Gove and *Webster's Third*. Wallace, the most celebrated novelist of his generation and a much-ballyhooed essayist, had made use of dictionaries in his fiction as a convenient symbol of great mental power. "I'm an OED man, Doctor," says a character in *Infinite Jest*. "And *Webster's Seventh* isn't even up-to-date. *Webster's Eighth* amends to. . . ."

In his *Harper's* essay, Wallace made it known that he was definitely no *Webster's Third* man. But even as he bragged about being the type of incorrigible nerd who actually reads the introductions to dictionaries and takes language disputes very, very seriously, the great literary mind of his generation failed to open *Webster's Third* before trying to quote from it.

Citing "Gove's now-classic introduction to *Webster's Third*," Wallace listed the five precepts from Gove's *Word Study* article, which came, of course, from *English Language Arts*. So, not only was Wallace not quoting any portion of *Webster's Third*, he was quoting Gove quoting an NCTE study. Wallace also stated that *Webster's Third* had included *heighth* and *irregardless* "without any monitory labels on them"—which was simply not true, as *heighth* was called a "chiefly dialectal variant of *height*" and *irregardless* was labeled nonstandard, Gove's most prohibitive label. Wallace may as well have been a member of the *American Scholar* editorial board for all the due diligence he performed before pouncing on *Webster's Third*. And he failed to consult the recent literature on the subject, in particular Herbert C. Morton's defense of Philip Gove, *The Story of Webster's Third*, published seven years earlier, in which all of these items were discussed.

Despite its continued usefulness and good reputation among scholars, *Webster's Third* remains known as not merely a flawed dictionary, but one that some intellectuals feel free to attack with impunity. And at least two essays that misrepresent its contents—Macdonald's and Wallace's—remain celebrated and in print. The volume reprinting Wallace's essay, *Consider the Lobster*, was a *New York Times* notable book of the year in 2005 (which, from this angle, seems weirdly appropriate), while Macdonald's essay, reprinted after some slight editing for his own volume *Against the American Grain*, was republished in the 1980s and again in 2011. Macdonald slightly edited his essay but left it mostly unchanged, while none of Wallace's errors were ever corrected. In fact, the mistake about "Gove's now-classic introduction" went unnoticed except by the blogger Stephen Dodson, who writes under the name Language Hat, and, some years later, by myself, as I was doing research for an article on Morton's book.

But to get a copy of James Sledd's impressive sixty-five-page response to the controversy, his review of the reviews, in which he pulls no punches, it helps to have access to a major research library. This treatise was published in *Symposium on Language and Culture*, the Proceedings of the 1962 Annual Spring Meeting of the American Ethnological Society, not exactly *Reader's Digest*. And Raven McDavid's masterful examination of the controversy can be found in Philip Gove's papers at the University of Wyoming's American Heritage Center, in Laramie.

MERRIAM CONTINUED to sell a lot of dictionaries. Revenues were $6 million in 1963 and, in September 1964, the company sold for $14 million to Encyclopaedia Britannica Inc., the encyclopedia and Great Books publisher then owned by former senator William Benton.

Not long afterward, Dwight Macdonald cut out of *Time* magazine an article announcing the news. Then he wrote in the margin: "William Benton, chairman and chief owner of two scandalously bad reference works, the EB and the 50-volume set of Great Books . . . in the fall of 1964 completed the trilogy by paying $14 million for the third: W's

Third." Obviously, this was bad news to Macdonald: "He, Benton, is to American culture as Attila was to Rome—or Robert Moses is to New York City. Or Dean Rusk is to Vietnam."[6]

Also in 1963, Macdonald cut out from *Newsweek* a column about Lyndon B. Johnson's telephone and table manners. It contained a choice bit of evidence concerning the increasing informality of American English. At lunch with some congressmen, LBJ told an old story about House Speaker Sam Rayburn and another newly installed president, Harry Truman. Rayburn goes to see Truman and tells him that in the White House he's going to lose touch with reality. He will be surrounded by yes-men, and all of them will act like the president of the United States is just about the smartest man in the whole wide world. Then LBJ said, "And you all know he ain't."

DRAMATIS PERSONAE

Asa Baker, president of G. & C. Merriam Company and member of the Editorial Board that set genteel policies for *Webster's Second*, published in 1934. Very much knew how to present a Webster's dictionary to the public.

Jacques Barzun, Columbia professor of history and distinguished spokesman for the humanities. He abhorred jargon, criticized the influence of linguistics in American schools, and became a major critic of *Webster's Third*.

J. P. Bethel, forward-looking general editor at Merriam-Webster who argued that *Webster's Third* could not follow the basic formula for *Webster's Second* without becoming a two-volume dictionary, which everyone believed would be commercially disastrous.

Leonard Bloomfield, socially challenged language scholar who wrote a unifying treatise of linguistics in 1933. He is the classic example of what is called a structural linguist.

Henry Seidel Canby, editor of the *Saturday Review of Literature* and selector for the Book-of-the-Month Club, he was an establishment figure of middlebrow culture and loathed by Dwight Macdonald, but a worthwhile observer of the changing literary scene.

Charles William Eliot, longtime president of Harvard University, editor of the Harvard Classics, and mentor to William Allan Neilson, editor of *Webster's Second*. A remote and somewhat forbidding historical figure, but interesting.

Bergen Evans, television host and co-author of a significant dictionary of usage, he crossed swords with Wilson Follett in a major debate over *Webster's Third*.

Wilson Follett, professor of English and author of a guide to modern usage. Possibly the most furious critic of *Webster's Third*. Thought *due to* in "the event was canceled due to bad weather" was, like, really, really bad.

Charles Carpenter Fries, scourge of old-fashioned grammar and evangelistic scholar who sought to bring American English teachers around to the scientific view of language. A swimming enthusiast.

Gordon Gallan, former advertising director at Merriam and president of the company when *Webster's Third* was published. Formidable businessman but not exactly a dyed-in-the-wool lexicographer.

Grace Gove, wife to Philip, organic gardener, and co-author of a light satire used to commemorate the publication of *Webster's Third*.

Philip Gove, editor of *Webster's Third* and, by far, the person most responsible for setting its editorial policies, as revealed in his personal papers, which include a copy of Merriam's Black Books and minutes of key Editorial Board meetings.

Sterling Andrus Leonard, along with Charles Carpenter Fries, one of the more memorable critics of classroom grammar in the 1920s and '30s. Drowning victim.

Dwight Macdonald, capitalist-turned-socialist-turned-anticommunist and author of the most memorable attack on *Webster's Third*. His life as an intellectual and journalist serves as the closest thing to a cultural timeline in this book.

H. L. Mencken, famed newspaper columnist and magazine editor who authored a well-known pioneering study of American English in 1919.

Robert Munroe, successor to Asa Baker as president of Merriam, he was a traditionalist and very uncomfortable with Philip Gove's plans for *Webster's Third*.

William Allan Neilson, assistant editor of the Harvard Classics and editor in chief of *Webster's Second*. Scottish by birth, he brought a Victorian sensibility to his scholarship and his years as president of Smith College.

James Parton, journalist and president of American Heritage publishing company who sought to use the controversy over *Webster's Third* to take control of G. & C. Merriam Company.

Noah Porter, editor of 1864 and 1890 editions of Webster's dictionaries and president of Yale University.

James Sledd, co-author of a book on Samuel Johnson and the most determined defender of *Webster's Third*, which he didn't even like that much.

Ethel Strainchamps, newspaper columnist and author of *Don't Never Say Cain't*, a colorful memoir of growing up hillbilly in the Missouri Ozarks. It was too bad her defense of *Webster's Third* wasn't more arresting.

W. Freeman Twaddell, professor of German at Brown University, he worked at Merriam-Webster in 1950 and said the time had come when their dictionary series could go without a famous "name" editor to lend prestige to its lexicography.

Harry R. Warfel, longtime acquaintance and "friend" of Charles C. Fries, he wrote a book called *Who Killed Grammar?* Warfel's answer: Charles C. Fries.

Noah Webster, America's founding lexicographer, he dreamed that a people united in its language would be politically and culturally inseparable. If the Civil War had not proven him wrong, the controversy over *Webster's Third* certainly would have given him second thoughts.

ACKNOWLEDGMENTS

A NUMBER OF BOOKS appear and reappear in my notes but neverthe-less deserve further mention. Prominent among them are Herbert C. Morton's *The Story of Webster's Third: Philip Gove's Controversial Diction-ary and Its Critics* and Michael Wreszin's biography of Dwight Macdon-ald, *A Rebel in Defense of Tradition*, as well as his edition of Macdonald's letters, *A Moral Temper*. That I disagree with Morton and Wreszin on several major points does not lessen my dependence on them or dimin-ish my respect for their books. Another major resource for this book has been early issues of *American Speech*, which, along with Raven McDa-vid's one-volume edition of H. L. Mencken's *American Language*, gave me a number of ideas, large and small, about how to use the changing language and the contributions of linguistics to describe what I always saw as essentially a literary-intellectual drama.

I am especially indebted to Norwood Gove for sharing some of his family papers with me. Peter H. Fries helped me understand some of the basic thrusts of his father's research. E. Ward Gilman met with me and regaled me with stories about life at Merriam. Peter Sokolowski was always generous with his knowledge of dictionaries and *Webster's Third*. They were all generous and collegial even as I aired thoughts that did not gel with their own feelings and opinions. Geoff Nunberg made a number of important observations and suggestions that shaped my thoughts on this story, while his e-mail correspondence over several years has helped me better understand how linguists approach language.

Before writing this book, I wrote and published an article about Herbert Morton's book about *Webster's Third* in *Humanities* magazine, which is put out by the National Endowment for the Humanities, where I work. Maria Biernik, Meredith Hindley, Amy Lifson, Steve Moyer, and James Williford were, as always, good friends and good colleagues. Dona Bagley made us a lovely magazine cover. Thanks especially to managing editor Anna Gillis, who edited my article. Acting deputy chairman Michael McDonald was very helpful, and acting chairman Carole Watson was very gracious during this period. The views stated in this book are, of course, my own and not those of the National Endowment for the Humanities.

The late Dennis Dutton of *Arts & Letters Daily* helped to circulate my essay far and wide. His curatorial selections did so much to promote fine writing on the arts and humanities in recent years. Adam Keiper, editor of the *New Atlantis*, and Robert Messenger, then of the *Weekly Standard*, both read and commented on my *Humanities* essay. I appreciated the friendly criticism. I was also thankful to Mike Vuolo, then a producer for *On the Media*, who interviewed me for a program on dictionaries and whose questions along the way helped me think about how to tell this story to a broader audience. Mark Liberman linked to and wrote about my essay on Language Log, a rather incredible resource on linguistics and, for me, an important resource for understanding how linguists think.

After much additional research, including a visit to Laramie, Wyoming, to look over the Papers of Philip Gove, I developed a proposal for this book. Gove's papers changed my view of the story of *Webster's Third* and set me on a path to accumulating a new list of debts.

I am grateful to NEH chairman Jim Leach and the Office of Human Resources for awarding me time off, or what is called an Independent

Study Research Development grant, to work on this project. Mrs. McClish of the NEH library has been very helpful and kind. Judy Havemann, the agency's director of communications, has been extremely considerate during a very busy couple of years. Meredith Hindley has been especially helpful with tips on dealing with archival materials.

The current president of Merriam-Webster, John Morse, made one of the single most helpful suggestions about how to use the Merriam-Webster website to collate words by year.

I am grateful for access to collections and for the assistance I received at Yale University's Sterling Library, Harvard University's Houghton Library, the Smith College Archives, and the University of Wyoming's American Heritage Center. The wealth of materials waiting in all these libraries deepened my appreciation for the important archival resources of our country's research libraries. At the Library of Congress I found many a helpful volume and among the open shelves of the Georgetown University Library I was able to finally put my hands on a copy of Barzun's elusive *American Scholar* essay. I am also indebted to the online marketplace for enabling so many used and out-of-print books to become available at weirdly cheap prices, and to Google Scholar. I am also grateful to a number of scholars and writers who answered queries and recommended books and research relevant to this history.

Thanks to all of my *Weekly Standard* friends, from Bill Kristol and Fred Barnes on down the line, but especially Vic Matus, Andrew Ferguson, and Matt Continetti, all of whom listened and commented thoughtfully while I rattled on about this subject. I should also thank Richard Starr and Claudia Anderson, under whose tutelage I learned a lot of what I know about grammar, editing, and style. I owe a shout-out to the unforgettable Matt Labash. And my regards to Philip Terzian and Kelly Jane Torrance, who have taken a kind interest in this effort and worked with me on other writings during this period.

My JMAP friends—Jeff Capizzano and Arrow Augerot, Michelle and Peter High, and Barry and Mary Becton—were unerringly supportive.

My old friends Ben Rosen and Andrea Heiss were just lovely about this project from the moment they heard me talking about *Webster's Third* on WNYC.

My Rosemont neighbors and the Meryl Street Gang (David and Jen, Toby and Amy, Jim and Alma, Jess and Bill) for all their encouragement. Also thanks to the Maury Eagles and their wonderful parents.

Rafe Sagalyn and Shannon O'Neill at the Sagalyn Agency were very supportive and critical to helping me think about how to make a feud into a larger story.

Julia Cheiffetz bought my proposal and provided several fine insights into how the book might work. When Julia left HarperCollins, I lucked out as my manuscript migrated to the desk of Michael Signorelli. Michael has been an especially kind and generous editor, careful, thoughtful, and reliable. And thanks to Douglas Johnson for his fine proofreading and copyediting.

I have many people to thank for their hospitality and friendship when I was on the road for this book. Matt, Rosie, Ruby, and Fionna Brennan made me at home in Boston. Heather Peske and Charlie Toulmin put me up in Cambridge. Chris Skinner opened his apartment in Queens to me. Diana Paulin and Michael Lynch welcomed me in Connecticut and loaned me one of the family cars.

The Skinners—my parents and all my brothers and sisters—and the Brennans—my parents-in-law and sisters-in-law—have been especially thoughtful and supportive during this project. Additional thanks to Kerry Brennan for reading a portion of the manuscript and chatting with me about her experiences in ESL education.

The greatest of thanks to my wife, Cynthia.

I am lastly but eternally grateful to my three children, Maddy, Ben, and Tommy, for their love and also for steering clear of the cave of books and papers that has been growing in our basement these last two and a half years.

NOTES

CHAPTER 1

1. The description of Neilson's gavel and his compliments to President Baker come from the *Springfield Republican*, June 26, 1934, as do most of the speeches. Also used in this chapter was material, including the menu and décor, from a commemorative booklet found in the Papers of William Allan Neilson, Smith College Archives.

2. William Allan Neilson mentioned Baker's opinion (saying Baker had always "strongly emphasized the 'literary flavor' which our dictionaries had built up") in Minutes for a meeting of the Editorial Board, October 11, 1944, Papers of William Allan Neilson.

3. See Howard C. Morton, *The Story of Webster's Third: Philip Gove's Controversial Dictionary and Its Critics* (New York: Cambridge University Press, 1994), for a summary of the "War of the Dictionaries." See also Joseph H. Friend, *The Development of American Lexicography: 1798–1864* (The Hague: Mouton, 1967).

4. Noah Porter, *Books and Reading, Or What Books Shall I Read and How Shall I Read Them?* (New York: Charles Scribner & Sons, 1881), 302.

5. Article labeled "Springfield News" in Papers of William Allan Neilson.

6. See Carl F. Kaestle and Janice A. Radway, eds., *A History of the Book in America*, vol. 4 (Chapel Hill: University of North Carolina Press, 2009), chapter 1.

7. See Marcel Chotkowski LaFollette, "Crafting Communications Infrastructure: Scientific and Technical Publishing in the United States," in

Kaestle and Radway, eds., *A History of the Book in America*, vol. 4, chapter 12, 248, 253.

8. Neilson letter to Baker dated February 3, 1934, Papers of William Allan Neilson.

CHAPTER 2

1. "The company is passing out leggy photos of Betty Grable, who is quoted in the book," reported *BusinessWeek* on September 6, 1961. The article was collected in James Sledd and Wilma R. Ebbitt, eds., *Dictionaries and That Dictionary* (Chicago: Scott, Foresman, 1962).

2. See Morton, *The Story of Webster's Third*, chapter "Usage and Final Tasks," 150.

3. Quoted in the *Chicago Sun-Times*, September 7, 1961. No verbatim copy of the press release exists in the Papers of Philip Gove, but the quotes from this chapter appear in several press accounts collected in *Dictionaries and That Dictionary*. See also chapter 9 of Morton, *The Story of Webster's Third*, and "A Review of the Reviews of Webster's Third New International Dictionary of the English Language," a report written for Merriam-Webster by Raven I. McDavid, October 1966, Papers of Philip Gove, American Heritage Center, University of Wyoming.

4. *New York Times*, September 7, 1961.

5. Quoted from Morton's prologue to *The Story of Webster's Third*, 5.

6. Interview with E. Ward Gilman, who worked on *Webster's Third*, training definers. Gilman was later the editor and lead author of *Merriam-Webster's Dictionary of English Usage*.

7. "The Big Book" and a separate poem that was also part of the entertainment come from Philip Gove's son, Norwood Gove, whom I also interviewed and corresponded with.

CHAPTER 3

1. William Allan Neilson provides a brief description of Eliot at the podium in the preface of *Charles W. Eliot: The Man and His Beliefs*, vol. 1 (New York: Harper & Brothers, 1926).

2. All quotations from this ceremony come from *The Inauguration of William Allan Neilson as President of Smith College*, Northampton, MA, 1917.

3. See James H. Hanford, "Harvard Philology Forty Years Ago," *Antioch Review*, Autumn 1948.

4. Quoted in Edwin L. Battistella, *Do You Make These Mistakes in English? The Story of Sherwin Cody's Famous Language School* (New York: Oxford University Press, 2009).

5. For these few details on Eliot and Neilson's work on the Harvard Classics I rely on the account given in Margaret Farand Thorp, *Neilson of Smith* (New York: Oxford University Press, 1956).

6. Letters from Eliot to Neilson, August 29 and 30 and September 7, 1909, William Allan Neilson Personal Papers, Smith College Archive.

7. Paul S. Boyer, "Gilded-Age Consensus, Repressive Campaigns, and Gradual Liberalization: The Shifting Rhythms of Book Censorship," in Kaestle and Radway, eds., *A History of the Book in America*, vol. 4, 286. The editing of *Chief British Poets of the Fourteenth and Fifteenth Centuries* is discussed in Noel Perrin, *Dr. Bowdler's Legacy: A History of Expurgated Books in England and America* (New York: Atheneum, 1969), 183–184.

CHAPTER 4

1. See chapter 13 of Marion Elizabeth Rodgers, *Mencken: The American Iconoclast: The Life and Times of the Bad Boy of Baltimore* (New York: Oxford University Press, 2005). I relied on this thoroughgoing biography for basic details of Mencken's life.

2. H. L. Mencken, *The American Language*, 1 vol., abridged ed., edited by Raven I. McDavid Jr. with the assistance of David W. Maurer (New York: Knopf, 1977), 58. See also Betty Gawthorp's chapter (1911–29) in Raven I. McDavid Jr., ed., *An Examination of the Attitudes of the NCTE Toward English* (Champaign, IL: National Council of Teachers of English, 1965).

3. Quoted by Gawthorp in *An Examination of the Attitudes of the NCTE Toward Language*, 9–10.

4. See Allen Walker Read, "The Membership in Proposed American Academies," *American Literature* (May 1935) and "American Projects for an American Academy to Regulate Speech," *PMLA* (December 1936).

5. Kenneth Cmiel, in *Democratic Eloquence: The Fight over Popular Speech in Nineteenth-Century America* (Berkeley: University of California Press, 1990), and Mencken both discuss Lincoln's reception in New York City in light of rhetorical norms.

6. Quoted from the version published in 1863 by Dana Barker Gage, who rewrote what Sojourner Truth said at the 1851 Women's Convention in Akron, Ohio, adding the recurring line "Ain't I a Woman."

7. Quoted in Cmiel, *Democratic Eloquence*, 89.

8. This number is drawn from Battistella, *Do You Make These Mistakes in English?*, 122.

9. Kitty Burns Florey, *Script and Scribble: The Rise and Fall of Handwriting* (Brooklyn, NY: Melville House, 2009), neatly chronicles the rise of Spencer's schools and their eventual replacement by the Palmer method. Arthur M. Schlesinger, in *Learning How to Behave* (New York: Cooper Square, 1968), 42, notes the controversy over spoons.

10. Polly Adler, *A House Is Not a Home* (1953; reprint, Amherst: University of Massachusetts Press, 2006), 5.

11. See Schlesinger, *Learning How to Behave*, 57, 60.

12. This story is told in Morton, *The Story of Webster's Third*, 16.

13. From the preface of *Not Under Forty*, first published in 1936.

14. Quoted in Rodgers's biography of Mencken. It comes from "Talking the United States," *New Republic*, July 1936.

CHAPTER 5

1. The photo appears in *A Moral Temper: The Letters of Dwight Macdonald*, edited by Michael Wreszin (Chicago: Ivan R. Dee, 2001), a wildly readable collection of letters that I rely on in several chapters of this book. My account of The Hedonists Club is derived from Wreszin's impressively documented biography of Macdonald, *A Rebel in Defense of Tradition: The Life and Politics of Dwight Macdonald* (New York: Basic Books, 1994). All the quotations from this chapter come from the first chapter of letters in *A Moral Temper*.

CHAPTER 6

1. Quoted in Charles C. Fries, "Periphrastic Future with *Shall* and *Will* in Modern English," PMLA (December 1925), 978.

2. Robert C. Pooley, *Grammar and Usage in Textbooks on English* (Madison: University of Wisconsin Press, 1933), chapter 4, applies and explicates much of Fries's findings and also shows the state of contemporary textbook rules on the future tense in English.

3. Biographical details were found in Richard W. Bailey, "Charles C. Fries. The Life of a Linguist," in *Toward an Understanding of Language: Charles Carpenter Fries in Perspective*, edited by Peter Howard Fries in collaboration with Nancy M. Fries (Amsterdam and Philadelphia: John Benjamins, 1985). The son of Charles Fries, Professor Fries also assisted me by directing my attention to certain pieces of writing in which his father discussed the shape of his career.

4. Charles C. Fries, "Implications of Modern Linguistic Science," *College English* (March 1947).

5. See William G. Mouton's introduction to *Studies in Honor of Albert Marckwardt*, edited by James E. Alatis (Washington, DC: Teachers of English to Speakers of Other Languages, 1972).

6. Quoted from the preface of Charles C. Fries, *The Teaching of the English Language* (New York: Thomas Nelson, 1927).

7. See Fries, *The Teaching of the English Language*, chapters 3 and 4 (on pronunciation and vocabulary).

8. Peter Fries told me about the chair routine, a fond family memory, and that the discussion may have first taken place in the 1940s, was probably reprised in the 1950s, and was revisited with C. C. Fries's grandchildren.

9. The following discussion of *will* and *shall* and all quotes concerning that study come entirely from "The Periphrastic Future with *Shall* and *Will* in Modern English." General observations on usage come from *The Teaching of the English Language*.

10. See Norman R. French, *The Words and Sounds of Telephone Conversations* (N.p.: Bell Telephone System, 1930). This study is cited and discussed in the context of Fries's study in Pooley, *Grammar and Usage in Textbooks on English*.

CHAPTER 7

1. Macdonald in 1924 had written to Smith what, from his response—found in Dwight Macdonald's papers at Yale—sounds like a fan letter, asking about Smith's writings, how he got his start, etc. There is another letter from Smith in Macdonald's papers, dated 1930.

2. Quoted from Linda Mugglestone, *Lost for Words: The Hidden History of the Oxford English Dictionary* (New Haven, CT: Yale University Press, 2005).

The examples of words that Bradley disliked and the quotation from his
letters also are drawn from Mugglestone, 176–177.

3. All other quotations for this chapter come from Henry Seidel Canby,
   American Memoir (Boston: Houghton Mifflin, 1947). See part 3, chapter 2
   and chapter 15.
4. See the "Growth" chapter in Charles Lee, *The Hidden Public* (Garden City,
   NY: Doubleday, 1958).
5. See *New York Times* profile of James Laughlin by Paul Wilner, June 15, 1979.

CHAPTER 8

1. See Thorp, *Neilson of Smith*, 323. I drew several details about Neilson's
   life on campus from this book, including the priceless quotations about
   smoking (250–251). The chapter "Harvard Again" was very helpful, as
   were "The President and the Undergraduates," "The President as Scholar,"
   and "The President and the Alumnae."
2. *Nation*, May 13, 1925, quoted in Thorp, *Neilson of Smith*, 253.
3. Quoted in Thorp, *Neilson of Smith*, 326.
4. Quoted in Thorp, *Neilson of Smith*, 254.
5. Minutes of the November 20, 1951, Meeting of the Editorial Board of
   G. and C. Merriam Company. I learned this from a comment by Philip
   Gove, who had reviewed the transcripts of the Editorial Board meetings
   for *Webster's Second*, Papers of Philip Gove, American Heritage Center,
   University of Wyoming.
6. Quoted in Thorp, *Neilson of Smith*, 260.
7. William Allan Neilson, "The Theory of Censorship," *Atlantic*, January
   1930.

CHAPTER 9

1. From Macdonald's profile of Richard Weil Jr., *New Yorker*, February 9, 1952.
2. Quotation from letter to Dinsmore Wheeler, January 8, 1929, in Wreszin,
   ed., *A Moral Temper*, 30.
3. This tidbit about Luce's feelings on *Babbitt* I found in W. A. Swanberg, *Luce
   and His Empire* (New York: Dell, 1974), 61.
4. A nice journalistic account of the magazine launch was written by Daniel
   Okrent for CNNMoney.com, September 19, 2005.

5. Letters to Dinsmore Wheeler, March 13, 1929; December 12, 1929; and June 13, 1930, in Wreszin, ed., *A Moral Temper*, 33–34, 38–39, 42–43.

6. There's a nicely rounded account of Macdonald's time at *Fortune* in Daniel Bell, ed., *Writing for Fortune* (New York: Time, 1980), from which these details come.

7. Quote comes from "*Fortune* Magazine," part 2 of a two-part article Macdonald published in the *Nation*, May 8, 1937.

8. I found this recording of FDR's first inaugural at americanrhetoric.com.

9. The lines about Henry Ford and Nancy Rodman both come from letters to Dinsmore Wheeler, February 2, 1930, and January 8, 1934, in Wreszin, ed., *A Moral Temper*.

CHAPTER 10

1. L. H. Robbins, "'It Is Me' Is Now 'Pretty Good' English," *New York Times*, December 3, 1932.

2. Some of the panelists are mentioned by name in Edward Finegan, *Attitudes Toward English Usage: The History of a War of Words* (New York: Teachers College Press, 1980), 91.

3. "Exclamation of 'Oh Yeah' Traced Back to Saxons; English Teachers Told It Is Not Modern Slang," *New York Times*, October 27, 1931.

4. *Current English Usage* was reprinted in 1938 by the National Council of Teachers of English with a discussion and further research by Albert H. Marckwardt and Fred G. Wolcott as *Facts About Current English Usage*. Quotations and survey findings are taken from this book.

5. Ibid., *one*: 76; *very amused*: 102–103; *an historical*: 98; *You was*: 91; *different than*: 121–122.

6. Ibid., *busted*: 96; *Martha don't sew*: 90; *ain't*: 95; *It is me*: 77; *all right*: 130; *reason why*: 111–112; *from whence*: 110; *I wish I was wonderful*: 73; *shall vs. will*: 83–84; *on grammar in grammar schools*: 136–137.

CHAPTER 11

1. From letter to Nancy Rodman, July 1, 1934, in Wreszin, ed., *A Moral Temper*, 48–49; most of Macdonald's words in this chapter also come from this source.

2. From letter to Nancy Rodman, July 20, 1934, 49; and undated 1936 letter to Henry Luce, 67–71, in Wreszin, ed., *A Moral Temper*.

3. Letter to Dinsmore Wheeler, October 7, 1929, in Wreszin, ed., *A Moral Temper.*

4. Quoted in Wreszin, *A Rebel in Defense of Tradition*, 52, which gives a full account of this episode.

5. From a letter to Dinsmore Wheeler, June 10, 1936, in Wreszin, ed., *A Moral Temper.*

CHAPTER 12

1. Leonard Bloomfield, *Language* (1933; reprint, Chicago: University of Chicago Press, 1984), 504.

2. See Robert A. Hall Jr., *A Life for Language: A Biographical Memoir of Leonard Bloomfield*, Studies in the History of the Language Sciences (Amsterdam and Philadelphia: John Benjamins, 1990), 63. I rely on this biography, along with Robert A. Hall, ed., *Leonard Bloomfield: Essays on His Life and Work* (Amsterdam and Philadelphia: John Benjamins, 1987), for the biographical sketch in this chapter.

3. Quoted in Alex Beam, *A Great Idea at the Time* (New York: PublicAffairs, 2008), 43.

4. Items found in Robert A. Hall Jr.'s biography *A Life for Language* include the *note about r sounds*: 3; *Bloomfield's wartime experience*: 19; *his comment about a Hitler coming to power in the United States*: 56; *the Menominee Indians*: 26; *black Americans*: 56; *his use of fake bedbugs*: 31.

5. Statements from Leonard Bloomfield, *Language*, include the *discussion of correctness*: 3; *mention of lexicography and upper-class forms of speech*: 7.

6. Ibid., *on normative grammars*: 7; *Sanskrit*: 10–11; *Grimm's law*: 18; *ain't*: 22; *linguistic lack of prejudice*: 38.

7. Ibid., *substandard vs. nonstandard*: 48, 52.

8. Ibid., *"personal deviations"*: 152; *writing versus speech*: 21; *phoneticians*: 84; *slang*: 154; *meaning*: 140, 146.

CHAPTER 13

1. Letter to Leon Scott, June 2, 1936, and letter to James Pilcher, December 20, 1934. Both of these were found in the Papers of William Allan Neilson, Smith College Archives.

2. See Terry Ramsaye, "Movie Jargon," *American Speech* (April 1926), and Albert Parry, "Movie Talk," *American Speech* (June 1928).

3. November 11, 1944, Minutes of the Editorial Board for the Biographical Dictionary, Papers of William Allan Neilson, Smith College Archives.

4. The wages for Smith girls were mentioned in a letter from Merriam to Neilson dated June 3, 1925, in the Papers of William Allan Neilson. The omission of any titles or characters from the works of O'Neill, Maugham, and Wilde is mentioned in the October 29, 1954, memo on Nonlexical Matter in the Merriam-Webster Black Books, found in the Papers of Philip Gove, American Heritage Center, University of Wyoming.

5. December 23, 1954, memo on Subject Orientation in the Merriam-Webster Black Books, found in the Papers of Philip Gove, American Heritage Center, University of Wyoming.

6. Fireside Chat 2: "On Progress During the First Two Months," May 7, 1933, Miller Center's Presidential Speech Archive, www.millercenter.org/ president/speeches/detail/3299.

CHAPTER 14

1. Letter to George L. K. Morris, October 16, 1959, in Wreszin, ed., *A Moral Temper*. Also described in Wreszin's biography of Macdonald, *A Rebel in Defense of Tradition*.

2. I take this comment of Thompson's from Robert Polito, *Savage Art* (New York: Vintage, 1996), 250.

3. Macdonald moved a few times in the 1930s, actually, before and after he left *Fortune*. See *A Rebel in Defense of Tradition*, 42, 51, where I also found this excellent use of Lionel Abel's line, 46; and Mary McCarthy, *Intellectual Memoirs: New York 1936–1938* (New York: Harcourt Brace Jovanovich, 1992), 18–19.

4. Details taken from the afterword to James Agee, *Let Us Now Praise Famous Men*, edited by Michael Sragow, in *Let Us Now Praise Famous Men, A Death in the Family, and Short Fiction* (New York: Library of America, 2005).

5. From Dwight Macdonald, "Memoirs of a Revolutionist," *Encounter*, March and April 1957.

6. These appeared in the May 1, May 8, and May 22, 1937, issues of the *Nation*.

7. The Hellman material comes from McCarthy's *Intellectual Memoirs*, 19. Macdonald's reading of the Stalin trials transcripts is discussed in *A Rebel in Defense of Tradition*, 63.

8. Letter to the editor, *The New Republic*, May 19, 1937, in Wreszin, ed., *A Moral Temper*, 90–93.

9. Letter to Freda Kirchway, December 10, 1937, from Wreszin, ed., *A Moral Temper*, 94–96.

10. *New International*, August 1938.

11. "Dear Comrades" letter, July 1, 1941, in Wreszin, ed., *A Moral Temper*, 104–106.

12. *New International*, April 1938.

13. Quoted from Sidney Hook, *Out of Step: An Unquiet Life in the Twentieth Century* (New York: Carroll & Graf, 1987), 517.

14. "Avant-Garde and Kitsch," first published in *Partisan Review* in 1939, is collected in Clement Greenberg, *Art and Culture: Critical Essays* (Boston: Beacon Press, 1961).

15. "10 Propositions on the War," *Partisan Review*, July–August 1941.

16. Letter to Delmore Schwartz, December 22, 1942, in Wreszin, ed., *A Moral Temper*, 107–109.

17. The material about Rahv and McCarthy comes from McCarthy, *Intellectual Memoirs*, 68–69, 104.

18. Letter to the editors of *Partisan Review*, July 3, 1943, reprinted in Wreszin, ed., *A Moral Temper*, 111–112.

CHAPTER 15

1. *Time*, August 3, 1936.

2. *Time*, August 24, 1936.

3. This comment was made by George Sherburne, chairman of English at Harvard, in a letter of recommendation that is quoted at length in Morton, *The Story of Webster's Third*, 35.

4. I rely here on Morton's account in *The Story of Webster's Third*, 20–23.

5. Quoted in Morton, *The Story of Webster's Third*, 24.

6. Philip Gove, "The First Week," *Antioch Review* (Autumn 1965).

7. Philip Babcock Gove, *Notes on Serialization and Competitive Publishing: Johnson's and Bailey's Dictionaries, 1755*, Oxford Bibliographical Society, Proceedings and Papers (Oxford: Oxford University Press, 1940). See chapter 5 in James Sledd and Gwin J. Kolb, *Dr. Johnson's Dictionary* (Chicago: University of Chicago Press, 1957). Morton also discusses Gove's view on Bailey.

CHAPTER 16

1. H. L. Mencken, *The American Language: An Inquiry into the Development of English in the United States* (New York: Knopf, 1923). See also the 1936 edition.

2. All quotations (including this one: 27) from this point forward in this chapter come from *American English Grammar*, English Monograph No. 10, National Council of Teachers of English, 1940.

3. Ibid., *"to whom they were directed"*: 29; *"standard English"*: 30–31; *"semi-illiterate"*: 31.

4. Ibid., *"colloquial"*: 9; *standard English*: 13; *"the great mass"*: 31; *"Seldom have"*: 14.

5. Ibid., *"Six little orphans"*: 244; *"in hell all the time"*: 219; *s-less and plus-s*: 45; *"agreement in number"*: 47, 56.

6. Ibid., *doesn't*: 53; *"Times is so hard"*: 52; *"Father . . . don't"*: 53; *violations of formal concord*: 59; *"The people ain't"*: 69; *genitives*: 76.

7. Ibid., *more and most*: 200; *adjective–plus–function word*: 239.

8. Ibid., *"more nouns in the subject and object"*: 270; *get, so, and "poverty" of vulgar*: 288; *"last two hundred years"* and *"living speech"*: 290.

9. This detail comes to me from correspondence with Peter Fries, July 21, 2011.

CHAPTER 17

1. "Diamond of Death," *Time*, March 7, 1927.

2. Quoted in James Parton, *"Air Force Spoken Here"—General Ira Eaker and the Command of the Air* (Bethesda, MD: Adler & Adler, 1980), 110. Except where noted, all following quotations—and airplane numbers and other details about Eaker's command—in this chapter come from this book.

3. Ibid., *speech to city council*: 154; *Churchill quote*: 138; *Harris quote*: 140; *description of bombers coordinating*: 156; *ER visit*: 194; *Parton's diary*: 218; *account of Eaker's meeting with Churchill*: 220–221.

4. Mencken and Maverick material taken from H. L. Mencken, *The American Language*, chapter "Jargon and Counter Words." *American Speech* also published several essays on the subject of military language, some written by returning veterans, during the 1940s.

5. James Parton, *"Air Force Spoken Here," Vegesack and Churchill's congratulations*: 244; *bombing doctrine*: 250.

6. Beirne Lay Jr. and Sy Bartlett, *Twelve O'Clock High* (New York: Harper & Brothers, 1948), 251.

7. Quoted in Parton, *"Air Force Spoken Here,"* 309.

CHAPTER 18

1. J. P. Bethel memo on Biographical Dictionary—undated—gives background on *Webster's Second* policies. Decision making comes out in the Minutes of Editorial Meetings, May 24, 1938, and June 2, 1938, William Allan Neilson Papers, Smith College.

2. Letter, September 18, 1944, from General Editor J. P. Bethel to William Allan Neilson containing G. & C. Merriam Company memo of July 24, 1944, and supplement.

3. Minutes of a Meeting of the Editorial Board of G. & C. Merriam Company, October 11, 1944, William Allan Neilson Papers.

4. See "Excerpt, relevant to New International Dictionary Third Edition, from Mr. L. H. Holt's Minutes of a special meeting convened by Mr. Munroe," April 18, 1945, William Allan Neilson Papers.

5. "William Allan Neilson," *New York Times*, February 15, 1946. The "skirts" comment was learned in an informal phone conversation with Professor Daniel Aaron of Harvard University, former longtime member of the Smith College faculty.

6. Gove's employment inquiry to Merriam-Webster is quoted at length in Morton, *The Story of Webster's Third* (34–36), from which this summary and quotations of Gove's military career are also taken.

7. Robert C. Munroe letter to Gove, August 27, 1946, Papers of Philip Gove, American Heritage Center, University of Wyoming.

8. "Memorandum to Mr. Munroe," November 27, 1946, Papers of Philip Gove, American Heritage Center, University of Wyoming.

CHAPTER 19

1. Bethel memo to Robert Munroe, February 5, 1947. It contains a summary of and quotations from the views of other people, including Percy Long and Harold Bender, Papers of Philip Gove, American Heritage Center, University of Wyoming.

2. This capsule history of scientific publishing and practically all of its details are derived from Kaestle and Radway, eds., *A History of the Book in America,*

vol. 4. See Marcel Chotkowski LaFollette, "Crafting a Communications Infrastructure: Scientific and Technical Publishing in the United States."

3. Memo dated February 27, 1948, summarizing recommendations from Max Herzberg, signed "I.E. McL.," Papers of Philip Gove, American Heritage Center, University of Wyoming.

4. See Kenneth B. Clark, "The Impact of a Personality," in *From Parnassus: Essays in Honor of Jacques Barzun*, edited by Dora B. Weiner and William R. Keylor (New York: Harper & Row, 1976).

5. Jacques Barzun, *Teacher in America* (Garden City, NY: Doubleday/Anchor, 1945). All quotations in this section come from chapters 4 and 5.

6. Merriam letter to Frederic G. Cassidy, August 16, 1949, Papers of Philip Gove, American Heritage Center, University of Wyoming.

7. The comment about how to spell his name comes from Archibald Hill's memoir in the September 1976 issue of *Language*. Marckwardt's extension and commentary on Leonard's study was called *Facts About Current English Usage*, a publication of NCTE cowritten with Fred G. Walcott (New York: Appleton-Century, 1938).

8. Albert H. Marckwardt in collaboration with Frederic G. Cassidy, *Scribner Handbook of English*, 2nd ed. (New York: Scribner, 1948).

CHAPTER 20

1. Norman Podhoretz makes this point in his memoir, *Making It* (New York: Random House, 1967), where he describes Macdonald as one of the more delightful and generous members of "the family."

2. Dwight Macdonald, *Henry Wallace: The Man and the Myth* (New York: Vanguard Press, 1948), 24.

3. This essay was reprinted in Lionel Trilling, *The Liberal Imagination: Essays on Literature and Society* (1950). I quote from the 1978 edition published by Harcourt Brace Jovanovich.

4. Dwight Macdonald, "A Theory of 'Popular Culture,'" *Politics*, February 1944.

5. Letter to George Orwell, April 23, 1948, in Wreszin, ed., *A Moral Temper*, 149.

6. Mary McCarthy, *The Oasis* (New York: Random House, 1949), 5.

7. Letter to Nick Chiaromonte, April 7, 1949, in Wreszin, ed., *A Moral Temper*, 161–162.

CHAPTER 22

1. April 20, 1951, memo to J. P. Bethel from F. W. Twaddell, Papers of Philip Gove, American Heritage Center, University of Wyoming.
2. Letter from Acting President Robert C. Munroe to Philip Gove, June 17, 1951, Papers of Philip Gove, American Heritage Center, University of Wyoming.

CHAPTER 23

1. All quotations from "A Parent's Signature," an unpublished essay in the Papers of Philip Gove, American Heritage Center, University of Wyoming.

CHAPTER 24

1. All quotations from this chapter were taken from Minutes of a Meeting of the Editorial Board of G. & C. Merriam Company, November 20, 1951, Papers of Philip Gove, American Heritage Center, University of Wyoming. Since elsewhere I note my reliance on Herbert Morton's book on Gove and *Webster's Third*, it seems appropriate to mention that here I am departing, on a major question, from Morton, who totally ignored all the drama and perspective offered by this particular document, which he cited but made little use of. The words of Gove, recorded in this meeting, simply wreak havoc with the view uttered by Morton and many defenders of *Webster's Third* that the new dictionary was really not so different from *Webster's Second*. Here Gove himself is declaring that his dictionary will, in fact, be very different from *Webster's Second*.

CHAPTER 25

1. *The English Language Arts*, prepared by the Commission on the English Curriculum of the National Council of Teachers of English (New York: Appleton-Century-Crofts, 1952), viii.
2. Comment by Peter Fries, April 19, 2011, recalling stories his father told about NCTE in the 1920s.
3. *The English Language Arts*, v–vi.
4. Ibid., *nonpromotion*: 190; *reading*: 194; *"Men communicate because"*: 196.
5. Ibid., *discussion of grammar and five principles*: 274–279.
6. McDavid, who was certainly in a position to know, said that Pooley wrote the five principles in his report "A Review of the Reviews of Webster's

Third," a 69-page account and analysis of the release of *Webster's Third* written for Merriam. A copy with the notation "sent . . . October 1966" can be found in the Papers of Philip Gove. In section 4, the "Journalistic Assault," McDavid described the principles as "written by Robert Pooley, a rather conservative but objective student of the English language." McDavid's description of Pooley is curious: Perhaps by the mid-1960s Pooley qualified as a conservative but in the years leading up to 1952 he was as much an enemy of the status quo in English teaching and classroom grammar as Charles C. Fries was.

7. Mrs. Fries's reaction I know about from Peter Fries, April 19, 2011.

CHAPTER 26

1. Minutes of the Editorial Board Meeting, February 18, 1953, Papers of Philip Gove, American Heritage Center, University of Wyoming.

2. Minutes of the Editorial Board, May 14, 1953, Papers of Philip Gove, American Heritage Center, University of Wyoming.

3. Minutes of the Editorial Board, February 18, 1953, Papers of Philip Gove, American Heritage Center, University of Wyoming.

4. The exchanges between Weidman and Gove and Munroe and Gove are found in the Minutes of a Meeting of the Editorial Board, February 18, 1953, Papers of Philip Gove, American Heritage Center, University of Wyoming.

5. Minutes of a Meeting of the Editorial Board, May 14, 1953, Papers of Philip Gove, American Heritage Center, University of Wyoming.

6. Morton gives Sleeth's résumé in his third chapter.

CHAPTER 27

1. This comment comes from Sidney I. Landau's *Dictionaries: The Art and Craft of Lexicography* (Cambridge: Cambridge University Press, 1984). Details about the feel at Merriam in the 1950s come from conversations with E. Ward Gilman.

2. Memo from Gove to Gallan, June 19, 1952, Papers of Philip Gove, American Heritage Center, University of Wyoming.

3. "Marking Instructions," August 28, 1952, Black Book, Papers of Philip Gove, American Heritage Center, University of Wyoming.

4. Herbert Morton, *The Story of Webster's Third*, 98.

5. "Marking Instructions," Black Book, July 15, 1953, Papers of Philip Gove, American Heritage Center, University of Wyoming.

6. "Usage Orientation," Black Book, December 20, 1954, Papers of Philip Gove, American Heritage Center, University of Wyoming.

7. See letter to the editor by Herbert C. Morton, *New York Review of Books*, December 12, 1995, where Morton discusses the circumstances of this entry.

8. "Subject Orientation—Orientation by Verbal Illustration," Black Book, November 30, 1954, Papers of Philip Gove, American Heritage Center, University of Wyoming.

9. "Defining—Editorializing," Black Book, April 2, 1953, Papers of Philip Gove, American Heritage Center, University of Wyoming.

10. Miscellany Department, *American Speech* (February 1967).

11. "Subject Orientation—Verbal Quotation," Black Book, December 23, 1954, Papers of Philip Gove, American Heritage Center, University of Wyoming.

12. Herbert Morton quotes the letter at length in *The Story of Webster's Third*, 71–72.

13. Minutes of a Meeting of the Editorial Board, November 20, 1951, Papers of Philip Gove, American Heritage Center, University of Wyoming. Gove distributed and discussed this chart at this meeting.

14. "Nonlexical," Black Book, October 29, 1954, Papers of Philip Gove, American Heritage Center, University of Wyoming.

15. "Capitalization," Black Book, March 29, 1955, Papers of Philip Gove, American Heritage Center, University of Wyoming.

CHAPTER 28

1. In this chapter and elsewhere in this book I used the search-by-date function on the Merriam-Webster website to sort words by year of earliest citation. Of course, the year of earliest citation is different from when a word is entered into the dictionary: One reflects a word or phrase's appearance in the language, the other when lexicographers thought the word or phrase had passed beyond some invisible threshold of ephemerality and thus needed to be included in the dictionary.

CHAPTER 29

1. Michael Wreszin, *A Rebel in Defense of Tradition*, New Yorker, *job*: 275; *divorce*: 295–297.

2. Dwight Macdonald's essay "A Theory of Mass Culture" was published in the Summer 1953 issue of *Diogenes*, funded by the Ford Foundation. Macdonald's four-part series on the Ford Foundation was published in the *New Yorker* between November 26 and December 17, 1955.

3. Letter to William Shawn, November 1955, in Wreszin, ed., *A Moral Temper*. See also letter to William Shawn, April 17, 1958, saying, "I've just read West's Baudelaire review and, while I suppose it's bad taste for one staff writer to complain to the editor about another, I feel this review is such a scandal that I must do so." Dwight Macdonald Papers, Sterling Library, Yale University.

4. The essays discussed in this chapter are collected in Dwight Macdonald, *Against the American Grain* (New York: Random House, 1962).

5. I am quoting Macdonald on McCarthy from *A Rebel in Defense of Tradition*, 298. In chapter 23, Wreszin also discusses the possible job at *Encounter*, introducing material that I have summarized.

6. The line about London English comes from "The Decline and Fall of English," in Macdonald, *Against the American Grain*. The Henry James line comes from a letter to Esther Hamil, July 20, 1935, in Wreszin, ed., *A Moral Temper, 61*

7. Dwight Macdonald, *Against the American Grain*. "Mark Twain" originally appeared in the *New Yorker*, April 2, 1960. "Ernest Hemingway" originally appeared in *Encounter*, January 1962.

8. Macdonald outline for a project titled "Mass Culture in America" and labeled "This is my outline for Doubleday book," October 28, 1955, Dwight Macdonald Papers, Sterling Library, Yale University.

9. Dwight Macdonald, *Against the American Grain*, *"not just unsuccessful art"*: 4; *"easy to assimilate"* and *"ice-cream sodas"*: 5; *"a crowd"*: 8–9; *Lords of Masscult*: 10; *"Nazism and Soviet Communism"*: 11; *how masscult is democratic*: 12; *Johnson*: 17; *Book-of-the-Month Club*: 39; *"We have . . . become skilled"*: 61.

10. Macdonald compared Eliot unfavorably to Robinson Jeffers in one of his first pieces of published criticism, in *Miscellany*, which Wreszin discusses in *A Rebel in Defense of Tradition*, 23.

CHAPTER 30

1. Jacques Barzun, *The House of Intellect* (New York: Harper Brothers, 1959). See chapter on "Language of Learning and of Pedantry," from which all quotes in this chapter come. *"Words are"*: 232; *science and abstract language*: 220; *Zhukov and Stravinsky lines*: 222.

2. Ibid., *taxi drivers and "as far as"*: 232–233; *"the users of pretentious mouth-filling phrases"*: 236; *modern linguists and Fries*: 240–242; English Language Arts: 243.

3. Gove's October 1961 *Word Study* article, "Linguistic Advances and Lexicography," can be found in Sledd and Ebbitt, eds., *Dictionaries and That Dictionary*.

4. It seems to me that there was a connection between Gove's struggle with meaning and his fierce literal-mindedness about definition-writing, but it had to be indirect: Perhaps Gove's wariness about meaning helped make him fanatical about the form of definitions, as a person uncertain about the existence of God might seek refuge in strict observance of the Mass.

CHAPTER 31

1. Jacques Barzun, *The House of Intellect*, *"pedantry"*: 218; *Parton*: 249.

2. Gerald Rosen memo to James Parton, June 1, 1959, Papers of James Parton, Houghton Library, Harvard University. All quotations and evidence for this chapter come from this collection.

3. Springer's research and findings were summarized in Gerald Rosen's memo to James Parton, September 10, 1959. The number for the cost of Random House's investment in the *American College Dictionary* comes from another internal American Heritage memo, written by Fritz Hehmeyer, saying, "The editorial costs in preparing a dictionary are prodigious. Bennett Cerf told me that Random House spent $2,000,000 on its dictionary which he claims is now a big money maker."

4. Parton memo to Rosen, September 11, 1959.

5. Parton memo to Gerald Rosen, November 18, 1959.

6. Gordon Gallan to James Parton, February 10, 1960.

7. Parton to Rosen, March 22, 1960.

8. Parton to Gallan, November 4, 1960.

9. Memo from Parton, April 27, 1961.

CHAPTER 32

1. I checked these figures against "Announcing the Publication of Webster's Third New International Dictionary," first published in the October 1961 issue of *Word Study*, but collected in Sledd and Ebbitt, eds., *Dictionaries and That Dictionary*. The chemist's complaint on the following page is quoted in Gove's progress report to the board of directors, June 10, 1960, Papers of Philip Gove, American Heritage Center, University of Wyoming.

2. Morton gives a careful account of the press release. Raven McDavid also discusses the press release and press reception in his "Review of the Reviews," tracing some of the original language of the press release to a wire story in the Mason City, Iowa, *Globe Gazette*, September 6, 1961, which he assessed as a close reproduction of the press release. Sledd and Ebbitt's *Dictionaries and That Dictionary* collects the *Tribune*, 51; *Sun-Times*, 52; Washington *Sunday Star*, 55; and other key examples of the popular and critical coverage of the dictionary quoted in this chapter. The summary of newspaper headlines and the *Los Angeles Herald-Express* quotation I found in Morton, *The Story of Webster's Third*, 155.

3. The Papers of Dwight Macdonald at Yale's Sterling Library contain a draft of Macdonald's letter to Gove, dated October 4, 1961, and three letters from Gove, dated October 5, 10, and 25, 1961.

4. Quotes from newspaper articles collected in Sledd and Ebbitt, eds., *Dictionaries and That Dictionary*, Toronto *Globe and Mail*: 53; *New York Times*, September 10, 1961: 56; *Business Week*: 57; *Saturday Review*: 58; *New York Times*, October 12, 1961: 78.

5. James Parton letter to James Bulkley, October 13, 1961, Papers of James Parton.

6. *Life* magazine article and Gove's letter to the *Times* are both collected in Sledd and Ebbitt, eds., *Dictionaries and That Dictionary*, 85, 88.

7. "Excerpts from a speech at the English Lunch Club, Boston, February 10, 1962," and Thomas R. Harney, "An Editor Defends His Tome," *Evening Gazette*, March 28, 1962, both found in the Papers of Philip Gove, American Heritage Center, University of Wyoming.

CHAPTER 33

1. Morton quotes from Evans's letter to Gove about the article in *The Story of Webster's Third*, 179.

2. Bergen Evans and Cornelia Evans, *A Dictionary of Contemporary American Usage* (New York: Random House, 1957), vii.

3. Wilson Follett's review, "Grammar Is Obsolete," ran in the February 1960 issue of the *Atlantic*. Evans's rejoinder, "Grammar for Today," ran in the March 1960 issue of the *Atlantic*.

CHAPTER 34

1. The *Times*' November editorials are collected in Sledd and Ebbitt, eds., *Dictionaries and That Dictionary*, 102.

2. Pei's first review in the October 22, 1961, *New York Times*, " 'Ain't' Is In, 'Raviolis' Ain't,' " is collected in Sledd and Ebbitt, eds., *Dictionaries and That Dictionary*, 82. See also Mario Pei, "The Dictionary as a Battlefront: English Teachers' Dilemma," *Saturday Review of Literature*, July 21, 1962.

3. Bernstein's diatribe in the *Bulletin of the American Society of Newspaper Editors* is quoted in Morton, *The Story of Webster's Third*, 179. Theodore Bernstein, "A Directive Issued to the Staff of the *New York Times*," is collected in Sledd and Ebbitt, eds, *Dictionaries and That Dictionary*, 122.

4. Wilson Follett, "Sabotage in Springfield," from the January 1962 issue of the *Atlantic*, is collected in Sledd and Ebitt, eds., *Dictionaries and That Dictionary*, 111–119.

5 "Logomachy—Debased Verbal Currency," from the *American Bar Association Journal*; Foster Hailey, "2 Journals Score New Dictionary," *New York Times*, February 8, 1962; and J. Donald Adams, "Speaking of Books," *New York Times*, February 11, 1962, are all collected in Sledd and Ebbitt, eds., *Dictionaries and That Dictionary*, 105, 126, 128.

6. "Keep Your Old Webster's," *Washington Post*, January 17, 1962; "Webster's Lays an Egg," Richmond *News Leader*, January 3, 1962; and Rt. Rev. Richard S. Emrich, "New Dictionary Cheap and Corrupt," *Detroit News*, February 10, 1962, in Sledd and Ebbitt, eds., *Dictionaries and That Dictionary*, 121, 125, 129.

7. Not a few critics end up comparing *Webster's Third* to the Kinsey Report, but to my knowledge none made use of *Webster's Third*'s striking entry for *homosexuality*, which it called, in the third definition, a "stage in normal psychosexual development occurring during prepuberty in the male and during early adolescence in the female during which libidinal gratification is sought with members of one's own sex." Typically, *Webster's Second* had defined it very simply as "erotism for one of the same sex."

CHAPTER 35

1. Letter of James Parton to American Heritage Board of Directors, dated December 12, 1961, James Parton Papers, Houghton Library, Harvard University, where all the source documents for this chapter were found.

2. Nancy Longley memo to James Parton, December 22, 1961.

3. Gallan letter to Parton, December 19, 1961. Sales numbers for 1956–1960 are from Parton's subsequent letter to James Bulkley, December 21, 1961.

4. Parton letter to Gallan, December 26, 1961.

5. Helen Merriam letter to Earla Rowley Carson, October 25, 1961.

6. Robert C. Merriam letter to James Parton, December 1, 1961.

7. Alexander Hehmeyer to James Parton, December 15, 1961; Gerald Rosen memos to James Parton, December 12 and 26, 1961.

8. Gallan letter to Merriam stockholders, February 16, 1962.

9. James Parton letter to Merriam stockholders, March 8, 1962.

CHAPTER 36

1. The *Wall Street Journal* review by John Chamberlain is quoted in Morton, *The Story of Webster's Third*, 176. "Vox Populi, Vox Webster," *Time*, October 6, 1961; Ethel Strainchamps, "Words, Watchers, and Lexicographers," *St. Louis Post-Dispatch*, October 29, 1961; "Dictionary Dithers," *America*, November 18, 1961; Roy H. Copperud, "English as It's Used Belongs in Dictionary," *Editor & Publisher*, November 25, 1961; and Ethel Strainchamps, "On New Words and New Meanings, *St. Louis Post-Dispatch*, December 17, 1961, are all collected in Sledd and Ebbitt, eds., *Dictionaries and That Dictionary*, 76, 86 92, 96, 103.

2. See Sledd's review of Fries's *The Structure of English* in the November 1952 issue of *Modern Philology*.

3. The *New Republic*'s April 23, 1962, editorial, "It Ain't Right," is collected in Sledd and Ebbitt, eds., *Dictionaries and That Dictionary*, 204. A copy of Parton's letter to the editor, published May 14, 1962, I found in the Papers of Philip Gove, American Heritage Center, University of Wyoming.

4. See Paul Collins, "Vanishing Act," *Lapham's Quarterly*, December 18, 2010.

5. Morton quotes this letter to Gove about Evans's book in *The Story of Webster's Third*, 175.

6. Bergen Evans, "But What's a Dictionary For?," *Atlantic*, May 1962, is collected in Sledd and Ebbitt, eds., *Dictionaries and That Dictionary*, 238–248.

7. Gove's letter to Evans is quoted in Morton, 194.

CHAPTER 37

1. The cartoon was by Alan Dunn, and it appeared in the May 24, 1962, issue of the *New Yorker*. See Morton, *The Story of Webster's Third*, 156.
2. The advice came from Ralph McAllister Ingersoll at *Fortune*. See Macdonald's essay in Bell, ed., *Writing for Fortune*.
3. Macdonald reedited "The String Untuned" just slightly but in a key paragraph before publishing it in *Against the American Grain*. I am quoting always from the version printed in Sledd and Ebbitt, eds., *Dictionaries and That Dictionary*, 166–188, a reprint of the *New Yorker* essay which, however, contains at least one postpublication amendment, a parenthetical paragraph addressing Macdonald's mistake on *knowed*.

CHAPTER 38

1. Dwight Macdonald Papers, Manuscripts and Archives, Yale University Library; Sledd letter to Macdonald, May 1, 1962.
2. Macdonald letter to Sledd, May 14, 1962.
3. Sledd letter to Macdonald, May 18, 1962.
4. Macdonald letter to Sledd, May 29, 1962. This excellent letter is also reprinted in Wreszin, ed., *A Moral Temper*.

CHAPTER 39

1. James Bulkley letter to James Parton, March 8, 1962. All source documents for this chapter were found in the James Parton Papers, Houghton Library, Harvard University.
2. James Bulkley letter to James Parton, March 17, 1962.
3. James Parton memo to Fritz Hehmeyer, March 9, 1962.
4. James Parton memo to J. J. Thorndike, Fritz Hehmeyer, Gerald Rosen, and Nancy Longley, March 20, 1962.
5. Nancy Longley memo to James Parton, March 21, 1962.
6. Edward Weeks letter to Parton, May 10, 1962.
7. James Parton letter to James Bulkley, June 25, 1962.
8. James Bulkley letter to James Parton, June 21, 1962.
9. James Merriam Howard letter to James Parton, September 22, 1962.
10. James Parton letter to Norman Taylor, November 23, 1962.

CHAPTER 40

1. Jacques Barzun, "The Scholar Cornered: What Is a Dictionary," *American Scholar*, Spring 1963.

2. Albert H. Marckwardt, "Dictionaries and the English Language," *English Journal* (May 1963), reprinted in Philip Gove, ed., *The Role of the Dictionary* (Indianapolis: Bobbs-Merrill, 1967).

3. Sledd's "The Lexicographer's Uneasy Chair" is collected in Sledd and Ebbitt, eds., *Dictionaries and That Dictionary*, 228–236.

4. See Raven I. McDavid's introduction to *Linguistics in North America*, vol. 10 of *Current Trends in Linguistics* (The Hague: Mouton, 1973). Edward Finegan discussed the Usage Panel and quoted Kilburn (from *The Gentleman's Guide to Linguistic Etiquette*) in *Attitudes Toward English Usage*.

5. See Edward Barber, "The Treatment of Slang in Webster's Third New International Dictionary," *American Speech* (May 1963). For more on the grudge match with Sheridan Baker, one of the few academic critics of *Webster's Third*, over citation evidence for *ain't*, see Morton, *The Story of Webster's Third*. While working on this book I have collected recent numerous citations for *ain't* in printed material, finding it used in, of all places, both the *New York Times* and the *New Yorker*.

6. "Publishing: A Meeting of the Minds," *Time*, September 18, 1964; "This Is Lyndon—And It Is," *Newsweek*, January 6, 1963. Both clippings, with commentary, were found in the Papers of Dwight Macdonald, Sterling Library, Yale University.

Index

ABOUT THE AUTHOR

David Skinner is a writer and editor living in Alexandria, Virginia. He writes about language, culture, and his life as a husband, father, and suburbanite. He has been a staff editor at the *Weekly Standard*, for which he still writes, and an editor of *Doublethink* magazine. He has written for the *Wall Street Journal*, the *New Atlantis*, *Slate*, the *Washington Times*, the *American Spectator*, and many other publications. Skinner is the editor of *Humanities* magazine, which is published by the National Endowment for the Humanities, and is on the usage panel for the *American Heritage Dictionary*.